MOTHERS
Their Power and Influence

MOTHERS
Their Power and Influence

Ann Dally

The hand that rocks the cradle
Is the hand that rules the world.
William Ross Wallace

Weidenfeld and Nicolson
London

ISBN 0 297 77046 2
Printed in Great Britain by
Cox & Wyman Ltd,
London, Fakenham and Reading

And Adam called his wife's name Eve;
because she was the mother of all living.
Genesis 3 : 20

Before I got married, I had six theories
about bringing up children; now I have six
children and no theories.
John Wilmot, Earl of Rochester, d. 1680

To my Mother
and
my Children

Contents

Acknowledgements

The origins of the ideas developed in this book are too numerous
to name. Many of them are by now unconscious in my mind. But
two writers in particular have influenced me. Reading and evaluat-
ing the works of John Bowlby and D. W. Winnicott and trying to
apply them to clinical situations enabled me to formulate ideas
hitherto pre-verbal.

The book may owe its existence to my friends Elly Miller and
Beatrice Musgrave. In 1970, during a memorable drive from
London to Canterbury Cathedral, their interest and enthusiasm
concerning my observations on mothers first gave me the idea of
writing down my thoughts on this subject. The following year
The Friends of the Hebrew University of Jerusalem invited me to
lecture and the substance of that lecture became the framework of
the book. I should like to thank all those friends, relatives and
colleagues on whom I have tried out my ideas and those who have
read the manuscript and made helpful suggestions.

I should also like to thank Rosemary Legge and Andrew Wheat-
croft of Weidenfeld and Nicolson for invaluable help, and also Anne
Lingham, who has typed and retyped the manuscript. Thanks, too, to
my family. All patients who have ever told me about their mothers
or about their children have contributed to this book, and this
means nearly all my patients. Some of them may recognize themselves. Most of them will not. I have changed details in order to
avoid recognition.

I should like to acknowledge here my debt to literature in general;
and, in particular, for kind permission to quote extracts from the
books mentioned, to: Faber and Faber Ltd, for 'In Praise of Limestone' (from *Collected Shorter Poems*) and *Forewords and Afterwords* by
W. H. Auden; Macmillan, London and Basingstoke, for *Jude the
Obscure* by Thomas Hardy; Laurence Pollinger Ltd and the Estate of

the late Mrs Frieda Lawrence for The Complete Poems and Sons and Lovers by D. H. Lawrence (published by Heinemann); Jonathan Cape Ltd for Portnoy's Complaint by Philip Roth; David Higham Associates Ltd for Taken Care Of by Edith Sitwell (published by Hutchinson); and the Estate of H. G. Wells for Experiment in Autobiography; Alfred A. Knopf Inc. for The Prophet by Kahlil Gibran; and Jules Feiffer for the jacket cartoon.

Preface

Woman, behold thy son! Son, behold thy mother.
John 19:26

This book presents a new and original theory about mothers. It provides a classification and a framework for discussion that is badly needed in psychiatry and psychology, in education, in social work and in general parlance. It will also be useful to those interrested in women's rights and problems. At present we lack a framework in which to discuss women's maternal role. I have written for the general reader because at present there is no point in wrapping up so simple a theory in technical jargon for an exclusive professional readership.

Because the theory is new it is at present based solely on personal observation rather than on measurement. Before one measures one needs first to formulate a hypothesis, then to decide what one needs to measure in order to test the hypothesis. I believe that the hypotheses contained in this book can be tested by predictive studies. It will soon be possible to test a young woman according to this classification, to give a rating on each of three scales and from this to predict what kind of mother she is likely to become and what kind of difficulties she will be likely to encounter with her children, and, in some cases, to take preventive measures. It could therefore become important from a practical point of view.

I wrote the first draft of the book without consulting any authority or reading or rereading anything relevant to the subject. My theory and the case histories, both clinical and literary, which seemed to illustrate it best were clear in my head and I didn't want to blur them. Only later did I go through it and check references, quotations, etc.

I do not intend to review the literature on mothers and children, the mother–child bond, etc. Such reviews will be found in the books listed in the bibliography and it is not necessary to repeat them in order to present my theory. Those who know the literature do not need it summarized, and I would rather that those who do not know it judge my theory by direct exposure to it rather than through the haze that inevitably would be created by summary and review of other works. Like Wordsworth I have one request to make of the reader, which is that in judging this work

he would decide by his own feelings genuinely, and not by reflection upon what will probably be the judgment of others. How common is it to hear a person say, 'I myself do not object to this style of composition or this or that expression, but to such and such classes of people it will appear mean or ludicrous.' This mode of criticism so destructive of all sound unadulterated judgment is almost universal: I have therefore to request that the Reader would abide independently by his own feelings, and that if he finds himself affected he would not suffer such conjectures to interfere with his pleasure.*

Some people may find the book disturbing. But, all the same, it is an optimistic book and I hope that readers will find that it increases not only understanding but also hope.

Ann Dally
London and Graffham, 1974–5

* Preface to *Lyrical Ballads*, p. 270.

Introduction: The Three Types of Mother

Feel the dignity of a child. Do not feel superior to him, for you are not.

Robert Henri

Your children are not your children.
They come through you but not from you,
And though they are with you yet they belong not to you.
You may give them your love but not your thoughts,
For they have their own thoughts.
You may house their bodies but not their souls,
You may strive to be like them, but seek not to make them like you.
You are the bows from which your children as living arrows are sent forth.

Kahlil Gibran, *The Prophet*

He who would understand himself needs first to understand his mother ... When I was about seventeen a distinguished and pioneering headmaster, who was a family friend, visited my parents and made a remark I have never forgotten. 'I never cease to be amazed,' he said, 'at how much boys are influenced by their mothers. This is nearly always the clue to understanding their troubles.' In later years I came to realize that this influence is not confined to boys or to young people. It affects everyone.

This book describes different types of mothers, what they do and their enormous influence. Its emphasis is on the children in their adult lives and on the ways in which they can, through their own individual efforts, make the best or the worst of the mothering they received.

In most cases the influence of our mothers determines the sort of adults we become. Insight into these matters is important, not to enable us to blame our mothers for everything we have not become, but because a sympathetic understanding of our own and other mothers' characters and difficulties may be the best and surest way of coming to grips with our own. I hope that what I have to say will also interest those who are at present engaged actively in the business of being mothers and also those professionally concerned with mothers. I feel that it will have a special appeal to those people (who must form a large proportion of general readers) who, at some time in their lives, as parents, children or observers, have tried to understand the process of mothering, its joys and wonders, its sorrows and pitfalls.

At present big changes are taking place among mothers and in attitudes towards them. They are idealized, because their importance is recognized. They are turned into scapegoats and blamed for the problems of young people. There is a fierce conflict about whether or not a mother's continuous presence is 'necessary' to her child and whether a mother 'should' or 'should not' go out to work. In my opinion this conflict is absurd because the questions it poses are irrelevant. It would be just as absurd to ask 'Should children be brought up in the town or the country?', or 'Should young people go to university?' No general answers can be given to such questions so that, if the questions are formulated at all, this tends to be for political or for personal psychological reasons which do not relate to any individual mother or child. One might add that whether or not one asks such questions and what answers one gives depends to a large extent (though of course not totally) on the kind of mother one has had.

Changes are also taking place in the way many mothers feel about their children and behave towards them. It is, for instance, becoming fashionable not to have any. There is a growing feeling that people should only have them if they are suited to the parental role, capable of bringing up children in our difficult world, and prepared to put a great deal of themselves into it. There is hostility to those who do otherwise. There are increasing demands from women who are becoming aware that the role of wife and mother can be degrading and is often exploited. They are determined to get something better and many of their arguments make other people look at these matters in a new light. They also create anxiety among more traditional men and women. Young people are making new demands on their parents, many of whom are unable to meet them or to understand what is happening. Inevitably they feel they have failed. There is widespread uncertainty and bewilderment among parents. Mothers have never felt so guilty. There is no longer the former assurance about how to bring up children. This is the first generation of mothers who have been taught that having a good relationship with children is more important than imposing moral principles. Yet much of this seems to have gone sour. There has been much publicity about the 'Spock-marked generation' and Dr Spock himself has changed some of his views. No one has stepped forward to fill the gap – perhaps because of the very uncertainty that seems to have brought about the changes.

Mothers feel about their children in three ways. First, they may see their children as *part* of themselves, *enclosed* within the same boundaries. Second, they experience their children as *extensions* of themselves. Third, they know them as *separate* people.

Most mothers will recognize all three types of feeling even if they feel one type predominantly and one type weakly. Many have different patterns of feeling for different children, and sometimes these may appear to be totally different so that one child is regarded predominantly as an *enclosed* part, another as an instrument and a third is rejected. Most mothers can assess for themselves what they feel towards a particular child or in a particular situation, and this assessment is frequently (though not invariably) accurate. Moreover, most people know whether their mothers regard them as *parts* of themselves, as *extensions* of themselves, or as *separate* people. Again, the assessment is usually authentic although it may be inaccurate in detail.

Some mothers lack one or even two types of feeling, and some even regard their children (regardless of age or maturity) as entirely *part* of them, solely as an *extension* of themselves, or as totally *separate* beings. So we can divide mothers roughly into three types, according to the way in which they regard their children or a particular child.

These types are related to the three psychological stages of mothering. In the earliest months of her child's life a mother is likely to feel he is psychologically *part* of her. There is a special kind of bond and *rapport* that exists between a mother and her very young child. As he grows and becomes more independent, often around the age of two, she is likely to feel more that he is an *extension* of her than still actually a *part* of her. As he becomes a child rather than a baby, and an adolescent and adult rather than a child, she is increasingly conscious of him as a *separate* being independent of her. All through his life she will tend to revert to earlier types of feeling when circumstances trigger it. For instance when he is ill or in trouble she is likely to have an increase in *enclosure* feelings and when he achieves success she probably experiences an upsurge of feelings of *extension*.

The three psychological stages of mothering are based on the three physical stages of mothering. The first physical stage is the time when the child is *enclosed* in the mother. The second physical stage is when he is born but still physically dependent on her and is a kind of *extension* of her, and the third as he grows up and becomes a free person. The psychological stages follow the physical.

Most mothers are a mixture of the three types and as their children grow up they become aware of each stage as it rises and falls, is anticipated and lingers. Most mothers go through each psychological stage with each child in turn. Most are better at one stage than at others. Many have considerable difficulty with one or more stages. Many end up as predominantly one of the three types.

Whether your mother was or is an *enclosing* mother, an *extension* mother or a *separate* mother and how far she is a mixture of these is one of the most significant influences in your life. The type of mother your children have is one of the most significant influences in theirs. The influence of mothers is both positive and negative. Mothers have much to do with the moulding of their children and the development of their personalities. They also largely determine the problems and difficulties their children meet in life and how they overcome them. Those who wish to understand themselves need first to understand their mothers: those who wish to understand their children need to understand the mother of those children.

This is a book about mothers. Fathers differ from mothers but much of what I have written is also true of them. Many fathers go through the three psychological stages in the same way as do mothers. Sometimes the father is the more important parent to the child. The first stage, *enclosure*, is not often strongly developed in fathers but sometimes a father is more of an 'enclosing parent' to a child than is the mother. The second stage, *extension*, is often strongly developed in fathers and many adolescents and young people suffer huge problems and struggles because their fathers regard them as *extensions* of themselves rather than as independent people. Many fathers have difficulty in achieving the third stage and continue to regard their children as *extensions* of themselves. Some readers may find that what I have written applies as much or more to their fathers than to their mothers.

Thus most of what I have written in this book is applicable to a variety of family situations. For convenience I have mostly confined my observations to mothers and I leave the reader to make individual imaginative leaps to other relationships and situations as required.

Part I

1. The Three Stages of Mothering

This object I have endeavoured . . . to attain by various
means; by tracing the maternal passion through many of
its more subtle windings . . .
                    Wordsworth, Preface to *Lyrical Ballads*

Childhood is measured out by sounds and smells
And sights, before the dark of reason grows.
                    John Betjeman, *Summoned by Bells*, IV

PHYSICAL PRECEDES PSYCHOLOGICAL

Mothers go through three physical stages and each of these has its
psychological counterpart. In each case physical precedes psychological.

Pregnancy is the first physical stage, when the child is *enclosed*
in the mother and is part of her. Infancy is the second stage, when
the child is dependent on the mother and is an *extension* of her.
Childhood comes last, with increasing independence and freedom
of mother and child. After childhood there is normally no further
physical dependence.

The first psychological stage is the stage of *enclosure*. Its physical
counterpart is pregnancy but it starts and ends later. It begins with
the first awareness of the child's presence and it lasts throughout
infancy. It reflects the mother's healthy feeling towards her infant,
which is that he is *part* of her. So important is she in the child's
environment that we can say that virtually she is the child's environment. During this period both mother and child tend to be absorbed
in each other and the atmosphere and feelings which will dominate
the child's future life are created, or allowed to develop. The first
stage is largely a period of physical sensations and feelings of
security and insecurity. Its relics remain as such through the later
stages and during later life.

The stage of *enclosure* corresponds more closely than do the other
stages to the mothering of animals. It is the period when the child

is physically dependent on the mother, and it is usually intensive until the child is two to three years old. It then declines slowly. It is instinctive and can be disrupted easily by adverse conditions, either within the mother or outside. In western society today it is often weak or absent and may be distorted or replaced by an atmosphere which is anxious, intellectual or controlling.

The second psychological stage is the stage of *extension*. This corresponds to the physical stage of infancy, when dependence is at first total and diminishes slowly over two or three years. The beginnings and end of this psychological stage are variable in time but *extension* is usually strongest during the second to fourth years and often at least until adolescence. It represents the healthy relationship between a mother and her growing child. The mother is aware of the child as an *extension* of herself. Emotionally the child is intensely involved with the mother and is profoundly attached to her. He feels her as a sort of *matrix*, a supporting background that gives him confidence and enables him to develop and mature.

The stage of *extension* is peculiarly human. It has scarcely any counterpart in animals. It is the stage during which the child, though he could survive alone physically in an appropriate environment, is in practice dependent on his parents, who provide for him. At this stage complex human characteristics, or culture, are transmitted. From it come many of the attitudes, motives, identifications, specific interests and patterns of behaviour that remain throughout life. While retaining many of the feelings of the stage of *enclosure* the stage of *extension* is more concerned with skills and accomplishments, attitudes, identification, motivation and a gradual moulding to prepare for later life. It is the basis of language and custom, habitual and day-to-day behaviour, and also of later adult attachments between parents and children. Although the feelings that accompany these attachments are greatly influenced by the stage of *enclosure*, the fact of attachment, and often its mechanics, is largely the product of the stage of *extension*.

The first and second stages are usually separate and distinguishable, but sometimes and in some areas they merge. In some mothers and children and in some families there appears to be a kind of *enclosure–extension* complex or network in which it is impossible to distinguish one from the other. More will be said about this at the end of chapter 3.

The third stage is the stage of *separation*. This corresponds to the physical stage of childhood. Like the other two stages it is normally present from birth. In our society it usually predominates after the age of ten to twelve, but this is variable both as a total stage and in its many component parts. The variations and permutations of the stage of *separation* play an important part in the ways in which young people attain or fail to attain feelings of fulfilment and self-determination.

The stage of *separation* represents the healthy relationship that develops between a mother and her adolescent and adult children after they have passed successfully through the two earlier stages. Both mother and child are now free. They are attached to each other yet are *separate* people and recognize each other as such. There is respect as well as love. Both recognize that the child is mature and independent and that the mother too has her needs and her life apart from the child. The third stage concerns the emerging adult personality, increasingly harmonious, self-determined and responsible though often in practice overlaid by the storms, upheavals and disagreements of adolescence and adult life.

Each psychological stage of mothering comes later than the corresponding physical phase and is its counterpart. When the child is physically dependent on her rather than *enclosed* within her a mother is still likely to feel that he is *part* of her. When her child is physically independent and could, at least under some circumstances, survive alone, a mother is likely to feel that he is more an *extension* of herself. Only when a son or daughter is grown up, perhaps eighteen years old or more, is the mother–child couple likely to have developed fully to the stage of *separation*. They are then two people, developed and mature, inextricably bound to each other yet essentially *separate*.

Psychological ties between mother and child remain throughout life and beyond. This is true even when these ties appear to have been severed or are denied.

What a mother does is important throughout her child's life and her influence continues into later generations. She presents to the child whatever is in herself. Throughout his life the child absorbs it and reacts to it in his or her characteristic way. This process is involuntary and inevitable. It is also altered and modified by other aspects of the environment. This usually means father and the rest of the family, friends, neighbours, professional workers and social custom against a widening background of school, neighbourhood and country. What is imparted at each stage influences the development of the personality, basic feelings about the self and its relation to the world, the ways in which one can and can't make one's own way, the interplay of mind and body and their degree of harmony, the growing sense of continuity, both of time and of person, the capacity for self-expression, for work, for achieving and delaying satisfaction, for spontaneity, creativity, making all types of relationship with other people – transient, superficial, lasting and close. For most people it concerns ultimately the capacity to find suitable work and a way of life, to choose and win a suitable mate, make a home and raise children successfully and with satisfaction or, willingly, to pursue some other course. It also concerns qualities such as adaptability and the capacity to cope with new situations, courage, honesty, realism, acceptance, independence, resourcefulness and the ability to be alone. One might simply refer to the capacity to love.

A mother provides an environment in which her child can start life and to which he can learn to relate. What she actually does after producing the child can be divided into three parts and these are relevant to the three stages of mothering.

Her first function is nursing the child. This involves the care of the infant's body functions, particularly breathing, feeding and elimination. The atmosphere surrounding this care forms the background for her interaction with the child, which is the basis of their relationship and, ultimately, of the relationship between the child and the world about him. Nursing is the predominant function of the new mother and is linked most closely with the first psychological stage, *enclosure*. As the child grows older the nursing function changes to feeding and caring and gradually merges with the second function.

Her second function, usually shared with the father, is the provision of surroundings in which the child can develop. This means a home and family, protection from danger, food and facilities necessary for good development, the transmission and absorption of the culture of which the family is part, and adequate and realistic emotional and intellectual experience and stimulation. Together with good direct care, all this stimulates the development of a sense of self. This function is particularly associated with the second stage of mothering, the stage of *extension*.

Her third function is to stimulate, facilitate and guide the child in his relationship with the outside world. This has many aspects. In the early stages, for instance, it involves helping the child to understand and to deal with such dangers and threats as stairs, fire, traffic, attack and over-stimulation. Later it involves ideas and feelings, exploration and play, attitudes to strangers and outside influences. It involves enrichment, demonstration, teaching, launching and, often, leaving alone.

All three of these main functions of mothering or their derivatives are normally present or latent at each stage. At any given stage or moment one main function tends to predominate, but this can change, often temporarily or even momentarily, with circumstances.

INDIVIDUAL VARIATION

Few mothers are equally good at each stage. Most are best at one stage and most have one stage that they like least or are least good at. Many run into difficulties during at least one stage and some at all stages. Only seldom are the results of this disastrous. What happens at each stage has irrevocable repercussions on the child's personality and so on his whole future. At each stage different kinds of mothering lead to the development of different kinds of people. Most mothers compensate during one stage for failures during another and the result is normal variation. Failure or relative failure at any stage is seldom, if ever, without effect, but any damage done is usually absorbed into the personality, which may even be enriched thereby.

The way in which mother and child go through each psychological stage is of profound importance in forming the personality of the child and his feelings about himself, other people and the world. What happens to people at each stage of mothering influences them for the rest of their lives.

What happens to children at each stage depends partly on themselves and partly on their individual inheritance, on personalities and circumstances. A child born to a teenage mother will experience each stage differently from children born to the same mother ten or twenty or thirty years later, and these experiences are also different for the mother. The result is not necessarily better or worse but it is different. Children attract different experiences at each stage according to whether they are lively, intelligent, physically attractive, placid, stupid or ugly as well as a host of other characteristics. Mothers behave differently towards each child at each or any stage. Sometimes they behave very differently indeed. Many mothers go through phases of being particularly good or particularly bad at any stage. This may be for any of a number of reasons, personal, environmental or to do with the child.

Success at each stage depends on the influences and interactions appropriate to that stage occurring in the right quantity at the right time in the right way. But the word 'right' is not meant in a narrow way. At each stage there is an infinite variety of mothering that can be good enough for the child to develop, to be his own architect or builder.

Success is more likely if transactions between mother and child are straight rather than twisted, complete rather than fragmented, and coming from the whole mother acting with and for her child. All this of course depends on the mother, what sort of person she is and her background, especially her early experiences. It also depends on the child, what he is and how he reacts, and on the background against which the mother–child pair live and develop. True success, like perfection, is never attained, so everyone is bound to fail to some extent. Reaction to that failure is also important and in its turn influences the basic situation.

Variety abounds. Individual differences are wide. Mothers differ according to personality and circumstances. They go through each stage accordingly. They may even not reach it or may bypass it. The same is true of their children. Each mother and child has experiences infinitely different even from the experiences of the same mother and her other children.

In the normal course of mothering each stage merges harmoniously with the last stage and with the next. It is not possible to draw an exact dividing line. Each stage, however clearly defined, contains the healthy remains or beginnings of the other two stages. Each is contained in previous stages and anticipated and begun within them. Each remains in the stages that come after it, according to how things went at that earlier stage. So each stage contains the seeds or relics of other stages and, in so far as it does not, it is altered, perhaps damaged or impoverished, perhaps made unusual, eccentric or endowed with special qualities.

Sometimes these remnants and seeds need to grow. At each stage situations arise which demand reaching back to an earlier stage or forward to a stage as yet unreached. Doing this successfully is primarily an intuitive process. The capacity for it can only be learned in so far as people can learn to trust intuitive feelings, but it can easily be prevented or destroyed.

Intuition and imagination are important in motherhood. This means that the whole process is greatly influenced by the ways in which the mother is and is not in touch with those parts of her mind and feelings which are difficult to categorize or control. Mothers who are out of touch with these feelings or in whom they are awry have special difficulties, and so do their children. 'Being in touch' with feelings does not necessarily mean being fully conscious of them. But it does mean being aware of conflict rather than denying or burying it.

The ability to be aware of one's own feelings, to be imaginative or to follow intuition is difficult for modern men and women. Although it is a natural development, it is often lost. A rational, scientific age demands rational, scientific explanations and proof, so that, even when the voice of feeling is heard, unless it is supported by rational argument, it is often set aside. In the case of a mother, she is likely to set her feelings aside and ask her neighbour, the Health Visitor or the child care manual. But she would often do better to ignore the judgement of the outside world, suspend intellectual activity, which obscures imagination and intuition, and act in accordance with her feelings.

This does not mean that nothing can be learned from books, experts or the example of others, only that this kind of learning leads to certain kinds of mothering and particularly to loss of spontaneity. The children are affected accordingly.

Mothering has an instinctual basis, which means that it is influenced or controlled by inborn drives. But these inborn drives are complicated in their results and much influenced by experience. In other words, although they are inborn, the way they develop is much influenced by the environment. The quality of mothering depends on the mother's circumstances, both present and past. Most particularly it depends on the nature of the mothering that she herself received and the ways in which she reacted to it.

THE BASIC CONFLICT

What a mother *is* has much more effect than what she does or what she purports to be. This is why people do not usually change much, and why expert advice, manuals of child care, social work, psycho-therapy and so on are so limited in their influence that it is easy to doubt their value. But the contribution of these, though small, is not negligible. Most people can change a little, can learn, can strive towards greater understanding and truth. And some people can change a great deal.

What a mother is influences her child in a number of ways. First, she transmits herself directly in her character and feelings, both conscious and unconscious. Her anxieties, limitations, sensitivities and reactions affect her child, whether either of them is aware of it or not. In this way she communicates her personal myths and symbols, her feelings about herself, body, mind and soul, and the relations between them. She also communicates her basic attitudes – optimism or pessimism, suspicion or friendliness, involvement with the world or withdrawal from it, and her feelings, often hidden from herself, about her child. She transmits all these and many more according to her personality.

She also influences her child through the *rapport* which grows between them, which does not grow or which grows mischievously. In the *rapport* is interaction and the child also acts and reacts. Again, his mother influences this reaction and the growth of independence and of self, or she may thwart or stunt it.

The attachment of the child is his love. Inevitably he is attached and inevitably his love has to absorb whatever is there, which will then be part of that love. There may be hatred, resentment, envy, anxiety or falsity and any of these others may form part of his love. Some things can't be faced, may be too difficult to face, but they are still absorbed or transmitted and will complicate his life and his love.

So there is a basic conflict in mothering. The child is *part* of the mother, which means that each is necessary to the completeness of the other. Yet the child is also an independent person and so essentially *separate* from the mother. The mother is the child's environment. Yet she is also an independent person, established in her own environment and *separate* from the child.

Growing up successfully depends on the resolution of this conflict and this means both love and distance. Yet love tends towards closeness, integration and belonging and so conflicts with distance. There is always a tendency to avoid the conflict by developing either love or distance at the expense of the other, or to deny the conflict by pretending that one is the other. If the conflict is avoided there may be love with insufficient distance or distance with insufficient love. Both situations are hazardous. If the conflict is denied there will be confusion in the mind of the child about the nature of love and distance. He will lack the means to distinguish between them. Sometimes both love and distance are lacking and this is the worst of all. If the mother is totally centred on herself she is unable to love the child and any apparent love can only be self-enhancement. Yet she may be emotionally dependent on the child and unable to separate from him. The absence of both love and distance can lead to a stranglehold which can, and sometimes does, destroy the child.

Some mothers never even reach the conflict, in which case they never really go through the three stages but instead remain permanently in a state that is a kind of perverted *separation*. For the essence of motherliness is the ability to show tenderness and gentleness, to feel rapport and to value a loved person more than oneself, while respecting him as a *separate* person.

Most mothers resolve the conflict between love and distance. Most mothers are aware, deep in themselves, of the pain and effort that it involves, as well as the joys and satisfactions. Many are surprised to find how difficult it is, yet they achieve it just the same. In this they are often aided not only by their husbands but also by their children. Children can have a profound effect on the development of a mother, even into her senility. Through them she can learn what she can never otherwise learn and resolve conflicts which would never otherwise be solved. She would otherwise probably not even be aware of such conflicts and would herself be impoverished by lack of awareness.

The conflict between love and distance runs through the three stages of mothering. Even during the first stage, *enclosure*, the child needs to be respected as a person in his own right. Even when he is grown up and all ties are severed that ever will be severed, there are ways in which he is still *enclosed* within his mother and an *extension* of her. If a mother is unable to produce and provide these feelings, the child will be affected. For the child, the extent of his mother's capacity to contain the conflict between love and distance affects his future capacity in human relationships. His eventual ability to contain the conflict himself will govern his whole future life.

Thus the ability or inability to set at a distance and to respect in this way is handed down from mother to child and may be traced through several generations. One often discovers that possessive or neglectful mothers had mothers and grandmothers who were similar and one can see how the tendency will be repeated in their daughters.

Parents who form close relationships with their children without first setting them at a distance are so common that many people do not believe that children can be loved in any other way. Yet setting the other at a distance and respecting him as a person in his own right is essential if human relationships are to be constructive and enriching as well as close. This is as true when the relationship is with babies and children as it is between adults.

Enclosure that is too much and too exclusive brings love without distance. A surfeit of extension leads to rigid distancing with inflexible love. Too much separation minimizes love.

A mother is likely to develop some degree of emotional dependence on her children. Indeed, if she does not, the three stages are likely to be impoverished. But extreme dependence of a mother on her child or children prevents the normal development of the three stages and leads to an overemphasis on enclosure or extension or on both in a manner that precludes the development of freedom.

A relationship can exist between parents and children in which parents love and respect their children as separate people. They are in communication with them but recognize their own existence, rights and needs. In another type of relationship parents regard their children as part of themselves, to be treated, or used, accordingly. In yet another, children are regarded chiefly as part of a system, to which they are to be moulded, of which the parents themselves feel part.

The difference between these attitudes can be traced from birth and the type can often be predicted or guessed from a knowledge of those concerned. But it is not always easy to see, because each type of relationship can have many manifestations. The types may also be mixed and to some extent most close relationships between parent and child contain elements of each.

The appropriateness of each attitude over another is also much affected by cultural influences. In certain societies one type of relationship works best, in another another.

Most people who consider this distinction will recognize parents, their own or other people's, who never have achieved this 'distancing' and so can only love their children as *parts* or *extensions* of themselves. Even more complicated, a certain amount of this treating children as *part* of oneself is normal. It may be difficult to distinguish between pride in one's children's gifts or achievements and the feeling that the gift or achievement is one's own, particularly since the 'gift' may be inherited and the 'achievement' the indirect result of one's parental efforts. Conversely, it is difficult not to take our children's failure as our own, and many an unsuccessful or erring child has been punished or made to feel guilty because he has let down or 'disgraced' his parents.

No one can be certain of what goes on between a mother and child or in an infant's mind but, from a child's point of view, the three stages of mothering are both background and means to his own developing self, to his awareness of himself and to his feelings concerning his body and mind, surroundings and attachments. This involves a slow progression from a feeling of mother as environment, undifferentiated from himself, to an appreciation of mother as a person in her own right.

To sum up, in the stage of *enclosure* the mother is the environment. The child has no concept of himself. The environment is *cradling* and totally protective. Thus the child in a sense has perfect freedom because he is unaware of any restriction. As he achieves self-awareness he also becomes aware of mother. Then, if she leaves or he hears that she will, he suffers from *separation* anxiety. His relations with others are tenuous or non-existent.

In the stage of *extension* the mother provides the environment, or an important part of it, for her child who is himself and an *extension* of her. He has no idea of her as a person, though he can be forced into a pseudo-awareness of her which is actually a projection. His relationships with others are increasingly his own but still dominated by her. She, and, increasingly, other important figures too, provide his environment rather than form it as in the earliest stages. The environment is now directive and has structure. The child has a sense of himself supported by and pitted against the environment.

The stage of *separation* is symbiotic, and increasingly free. The child is aware and concerned. He recognizes his own needs apart from his mother and her needs apart from his. His relations with others are indelibly stamped with her mark, yet are as indisputably his own as he is himself. The *cradled* freedom of the stage of *enclosure* and the structured directiveness of the stage of *extension* have united to form a structured freedom that is an important part of the basis of adult life and relationships.

MOTHER AND CHILD

Each stage also brings its characteristic type of anxiety. The anxiety of the first stage concerns chiefly physical sensations and survival. The anxiety of the second stage is associated with pressure, guilt and shame. Anxiety of the third stage is associated with meaningless and loneliness.

From the beginning, and increasingly as he grows older, the child has opportunities to be himself, to develop himself, to express himself and to influence the way in which he is mothered.

Mothers develop too. They do this partly on their own and partly through the experience of being mothers. The idea that maturation stops with physical growth is misleading. Psychological maturity is not normally completed with the attainment of adulthood. It frequently continues even into old age. In most people it ceases slowly some time during adult life and is replaced by hardening. This involves a lack of flexibility and a loss of spontaneity and imagination. If this happens in early adult life or before, the result is an obsessional, rigid, controlling person, incapable of further development. The greatest rewards and satisfactions of adult life, and also probably the greatest suffering, are found in those who continue to mature into middle age and beyond.

Maturation in adult life, as at any other time, depends on the existence of an environment, including positive influences, suitable to the development of innate potentiality. Motherhood provides an environment not only for the child but also for the mother and it provides unique influences through which the mother can develop. The influence which the experience of bearing and rearing children has on a mother's maturity can be considerable or negligible. For many people it is one of the greatest influences on their whole lives and the greatest of all influences in their adult lives. It can be a strong maturing influence, a prolonged exercise in learning to see others as separate people and a training in learning to foresee the likely consequences of certain events or actions. It is also a training in responsibility, in delaying satisfaction, in making realistic decisions, in resolving conflicts and in the art of dealing with a number of different problems simultaneously. If all this can be achieved without loss of spontaneity, flexibility or imagination, then the experience of rearing children has truly had its best possible effect.

For a mother who is already mature enough to benefit from maternal experience, bearing and raising children is a reaffirmation of her own life and a reliving of her own experience. It offers opportunities to rectify what went wrong in her own upbringing. In passing through the three stages of mothering, perhaps several times over with several children, the mother can redevelop herself and broaden, deepen and expand her personality, understanding and imagination.

Sometimes the experience of motherhood and the things that go with it can be a considerable maturing experience to a mother who is rather immature or who has special difficulties. This is particularly true of those whose immaturity stems from lack of experience, through being very young, from having had a sheltered or an old-fashioned upbringing, or from difficulties in childhood. Henrik Ibsen has written about this in different ways in several of his plays. His own mother played with dolls until the experience of her husband's bankruptcy changed her, and this influenced her son profoundly. His plays show a preoccupation with growing up and the loss of 'ability to play with dolls'.

Another example was Mary, who found motherhood difficult. Her first child was born with a slightly deformed chest which was unimportant but caused much interest among doctors and made it especially difficult for Mary to achieve confidence with her child. She felt from the start that in not producing a 'perfect' child she had failed as a mother and she was always extremely anxious and devoted. She was continually conscious both of intuitive feelings about her children and of intellectual forces trying to stifle them by keeping anxiety at bay. However her children were strong and healthy and soon learned to help her. Even when their minor deviance or growing independence increased her anxiety, both mother and children were usually able to benefit from the experience. All three children eventually became free and independent people. Mary looked back over the years since they were born and marvelled not only at them, but at the way in which she had developed through them.

A constant background to the three stages of mothering is the ebb and flow of the mother's own development and destiny. Mothers change as their children grow. The satisfactory passage through the first two stages of mothering and the attainment of the third stage depend very much on the mother's capacity to mature and on her ability to benefit from the unique experiences offered to her by her children.

But if a mother uses her children as buttresses against the world, as instruments of self-enhancement or as an excuse to remain her own immature self, she may actually use motherhood as a means of failing to mature. This is of course much to her children's disadvantage.

Once she had a child Margaret felt free to refuse every demand made on her. Her husband had to do the shopping because she was frightened of leaving the pram outside. She would not go out in the evening because the baby 'needed' her. She nearly always refused to have sexual intercourse, saying that looking after the baby made her 'too tired'. Fifteen years later Margaret dominated the household, mostly from her bed. Her three children felt obliged to stay with her because she was so 'poorly'. They felt guilty if they went out to play and even when they went to school. Her husband frequently took time off to take Margaret to the doctor or the hospital. Sometimes she would get a fixed idea that one of the children was ill and then her husband had to take time off to take them both to the doctor. By now Margaret had severe anxiety whenever she left the house and was incapable of doing this alone. The children took it in turns to come home from school early to take her for a walk. Margaret had not matured at all during her years as a mother. Two of her children are already under psychiatrists and the third is thought by the school to have special emotional difficulties.

2. People and their Mothers

In the dark womb where I began
My mother's life made me a man.
John Masefield

There should be no mothers, only women.
George Bernard Shaw

We don't need mother and father any more. We only
need mothering and fathering.
David Cooper, *The Death of the Family*

My mother was a saint.
Richard Nixon, on resigning the Presidency

Those who cannot remember the past are condemned
to repeat it.
George Santayana, *The Life of Reason*

FEELINGS

Nearly all mothers have strong feelings about being mothers and
about the children they have produced. This is true even where the
period of motherhood seems long past or when the predominant
feeling has become dislike or indifference.

There is a modern tendency to blame parents, particularly
mothers, when children or young people are unhappy, disturbed
or give offence or when things go wrong in adult life. This tendency
is not new in our times but is characteristic of them. Things are
going wrong at present. Many young people are alienated from their
parents' world. Parents are less certain than before about what they
want for their children. Neurosis and mental upset are apparent as
never before. There is a widespread tendency to blame mother,
both as causative influence and as scapegoat.

Ours could be called an age of maternal anxiety and guilt. Many mothers feel anxious and guilty about what has happened to their children or about whether they are bringing them up right or have done their best by them. The external difficulties of modern living have meant that much more than formerly has depended on an individual mother's capacity to cope. Yet now she is uncertain. She is often cast in the role of scapegoat. No wonder she feels anxious and guilty. No wonder Dr Spock's recent 'recantation' was given widespread publicity.

Yet nearly all mothers try to do their best. There are many kinds of good or adequate mothering, and many kinds of adequate mothers. Mothers who are most successful do not usually try harder, and often try less hard, than those who are less successful. Mothers are individuals and they mother their children according to their own personalities. They have no other choice. Much also depends on the nature of the child and how this fits with the mother. There are many reasons why blaming mothers for what has gone wrong is usually not only pointless but also unfair. Probably doing one's best for one's children is part of the biological inheritance of mothers that we share with the rest of the animal world. It is not difficult to think of the ways in which we or our own mothers have failed. This is common sense in retrospect. It does not mean that we or our mothers are to blame or could have done better at the time.

It is normal for mothers to worry. All good mothers feel anxious sometimes and no one can be a good mother without a good deal of anxiety. Moreover, nearly all mothers feel guilty when things go wrong. This is normal. They also feel unhappy when their children are unhappy and when they hate and reject them.

What a mother is is much more important than what she does. This fact is usually omitted in books and articles on child care. One might add that what a mother does is more important than what she says. This does not mean that what she says is not important.

MOTHERS, BIOLOGICAL AND ACTUAL

Everyone has had two sorts of mother, one who gave birth and one who did everything else that a mother does. Sometimes they are not the same person. Sometimes they are many people.

The simplest division is seen in people who were adopted soon after birth, but often it is more complicated. Sometimes the 'mothering' mother was not a mother in any true sense at all. 'She' may have been several people at once or a series, a father, or even an institution. So when I write of mothers I include not only physical mothers but also adoptive mothers, foster mothers and all who act as parents or parent figures to children, sometimes including fathers, teachers and doctors. Their influence thrusts itself into those children's adult lives and is perpetuated in the lives of those to whom those children eventually become parents and grandparents. Sometimes the influence of a particular mother can be traced clearly through several generations. Through studying such families one comes to understand that, even in cases where it is not obvious, a mother's influence is enormous.

As this book is less concerned with the mother who gave birth than with the mother who did everything else, it seems sensible to write of the former first.

It has at times been thought that the function of the father's seed was merely to activate a potential child who already existed inside the mother. It has also been thought that the father plants his child in the mother who only contributes food and the right environment for growth. Both these views are wrong. Each parent contributes an equal amount of inherited material to the child. Thus characteristics such as colour of skin, eyes and hair, shape of different parts of the body, potential height and also probably to some extent intelligence, aptitudes and personality characteristics are inherited equally from both parents. Most of what is inherited does not depend on the sex of the parent. It depends on what happens to be transmitted to this particular child and on the relative strengths of different genes. Thus, if both parents carry genes for, say, red hair or blue eyes, it will be a matter of chance whether those of their children who inherit them will be boys or girls. And a child whose parents are Indian and blue-eyed European will inevitably have brown eyes regardless of whether the Indian parent is father or mother because brown is dominant over blue and Indians, unlike many brown-eyed Europeans, have no blue eyes in their ancestry.

Certain characteristics, including some inherited diseases, are 'sex-linked'. This means that they are carried on the sex chromosomes and so can only be transmitted by a particular parent in a particular way. An example of this is haemophilia which occurs only in males and is 'carried' by females who (unless they 'mutate' spontaneously) inherit the abnormality from their haemophilic fathers and transmit it to their sons and daughters (to the latter only in the same 'carrier' form in which it exists in themselves).

A mother who gives birth to a child, even if she never sees him again, has already contributed more to him than her average half-share of the child's inherited material. She also contributes the earliest environment in which the child has grown and developed. There is increasing evidence that her state of health and nutrition, and also to some extent her state of mind, influence the foetus. Drugs she takes during pregnancy, including nicotine from smoking, may damage the child. Anxiety experienced during the pregnancy may also affect the child and so may the experience of birth itself. Otto Rank, one of the early psychoanalysts, believed that all anxiety originated in anxiety generated during the experience of being born, and to some extent Freud went along with this idea. Nowadays it is demodé, but there is no doubt that drugs given during labour, or a period of prolonged deprivation of oxygen, such as occurs only too easily during birth, can have an extensive and lasting influence on the child. There is also increasing evidence about the importance of prenatal influences in the growing foetus, but the subject is still rather nebulous and much more research is needed before any conclusions can be reached. These influences may turn out to be the most important of all.

It seems superfluous to say that people are influenced by their mothers. But the extent, depth and subtlety of these influences are not always obvious for they can be unexpected, pervasive and often perverse. People are influenced by their mothers (and their fathers) all the time, all their lives and in a myriad different ways, most of which are subtle, unconscious and unsuspected.

Each individual, apart from his physical ancestry and family tree, has an ancestry of influences acting on him all his life through his mother and the imagery that she has created in his mind. This often dominates childhood, persists into adult life and is perpetuated in the lives of future generations.

All mothers exert a powerful influence over their children's lives. This is true of mothers dead and alive, helpful and unhelpful, wise and foolish, those who encourage and expand their children's development, those who allow them to go their own way and those who restrict them to such narrow limits that personality is crippled or mental illness becomes the only escape. It is true not only of mothers who have towered over their children and controlled them all their lives, but also of mothers who haven't really bothered, and of those who have loved, hated, protected, neglected, cherished, abused or defeated their children or have been loved, neglected, defeated or abused by their children in return. It is true of mothers whose children have turned against them and even of mothers who haven't been there at all. The absent or unknown mother can exert an influence as powerful as the parent who is real and known.

Most of our attitudes to ourselves and the world are conditioned by our parents and for most people in our culture this means largely mothers. By the time we are adult we have mostly absorbed our parents, who do not have to be present to exert their influence. Nor are we usually conscious of their presence in our personalities, though if, through introspection, we seek the origins of our feelings and attitudes they are usually traced back to early parental, particularly maternal, influences through the three stages.

WHAT DO WE GET FROM EACH STAGE?

The stage of *enclosure* is largely responsible for our basic feelings about the world and outlook on it. This includes optimism and pessimism, feelings of security and insecurity, and feelings about ourselves and our bodies, and about other people. A person who had a good first stage was harmoniously part of his mother. Such a person is firmly established as someone in his own right. He has few doubts about who he is or what he wants to do. He feels basically optimistic and secure even under difficult circumstances. He is at peace with his body and its functions and he knows its limits. He is likely to have a good intuitive understanding of any symptoms he may develop, both physical and mental, and about the feelings of other people. His intuition is developed and he trusts it. He is unlikely to have serious difficulty in sexual function or in human relationships. The closest of these are likely to be deep, mutual and lasting.

The stage of *extension* gives us our standards of morality, our feelings about body functions and health, food and cleanliness, punctuality and other habits of personality. It also colours our attitudes towards truth, towards other people and their feelings and towards strangers and new situations. From this stage too come many of our attitudes to society and to cultural activities as well as many of our skills and accomplishments.

A person who has experienced a good second stage is likely to be healthy without either effort or emphasis. *Mens sana in corpore sano* seems to come naturally to such a person. He is clean and considerate but not with excess or falsity. He is moral and truthful, at least to himself. These characteristics do not impinge or impose themselves on others. He has a strong inner code which directs him but also allows him freedom. He possesses social skill, at least within the limits of his culture, and he probably has many accomplishments.

The stage of *separation* gives us the freedom to allow the effects of the other two stages to settle and take root within us while allowing us to develop as ourselves. If the stage of *separation* is adequate children neither merely copy their parents in their attitudes nor merely react to them. They add much that is personal, deriving from themselves. They are also not immutable. But in examining and understanding how a particular person came to have a particular attitude to such matters, one can always find a strong early influence. Moreover, happiness or contentment in adult life depends on fulfilling wishes that arose in infancy and early childhood.

When the three stages of mothers have not run smoothly the results will show, often markedly and sometimes dramatically. A difficult stage of *enclosure* can leave a permanent sense of gloom or loss, overwhelming sensations of emptiness, or feelings of perpetual struggle between love and hate, good and bad, the life-affirming and the life-denying. Such feelings can become so much part of the personality that they feel basic to it. Kindred spirits may be found who have the same feelings. *Enclosure* feelings, or rather feelings left over or derived from the stage of *enclosure*, are often a basis of the way in which one reacts to others. One tends to be attracted to people similar to oneself in this respect and repelled by those who are different. Since one's *enclosure* feelings are mostly the basis of one's attitude to life and to the world, close similarities in *enclosure* feelings are found among people who have come together for this reason. The affinity is often in the escape chosen. This can take many forms, such as feelings about nature or art, preoccupation with self, or a kind of reversal, as when, for example, those whose stage of *enclosure* left them feeling uncared for ease their unhappy feelings by caring for others. It would be interesting to study this in relation to, just to name a few examples, politicians, social workers, actors and actresses, or those who specialize in different branches of medicine. One also sees this special 'affinity of *enclosure*' in those who adhere to the different points of view that at present divide the theories and practice of psychiatry.

Certain groups of people who stick by each other because of their basic similarity of *enclosure* feelings and who frequently discuss their basic interests with each other tend to form the view that their experience and the experience of their group is the inevitable human lot. If they are outward-looking they may develop a particular political or social point of view which seems to them to be the only possible correct one. Or it may be expressed in religious terms, perhaps as revealed truth or divine ordinance. A group of people given to introspection may study their own *enclosure* feelings and those of people similar to them and come up with a basic theory of human psychology. It is as though people seek out others who speak their own mother tongue, study the language and come to the conclusion that this language is all language. If the different schools of psychology, and still more of psychoanalysis, are studied from this point of view, the results and implications are fascinating. It would be irrelevant to pursue these thoughts further here. It would require another book.

A difficult stage of *extension* can leave behind such characteristics as lack of direction, motivation or spontaneity, or intense preoccupation with moral principles, body function or sexual activity, and all variety of opinions and feeling in matters concerning conscience, prejudice and affectation. Any of these can also be the basis of whom one likes and dislikes and the company one keeps. Close association on the basis of difficulties or peculiarities of the stage of *extension* are usually more obvious and often more overtly bizarre to the outside world than are associations based on peculiarities of the stage of *enclosure*. Examples would be close religious sects and the strange fraternities that sometimes grow up among those who share common experiences.

A difficult stage of *extension* often means that a person never truly manages to become himself. He therefore goes through life as a part or an *extension* of his mother and maybe also of his father and other people who were important in his early life. We shall meet examples of these later, in chapter 4.

So we might say that during the course of the three stages,

enclosure, extension and *separation*, mothers both limit and develop the potential of their children.

INFLUENCES

The first influence of mothers, and also of fathers, occurs in a number of ways. A child is gradually adapted to his mother's life and prepared for the life she expects him to lead. This includes feeling and emotional drive, defences against anxiety, language and types of reaction. It also includes types of attachment, codes and modes of behaviour, and the symbolic background that forms the basis of living.

Sometimes this is a closed process, admitting few influences outside the family and aimed at maintaining a *status quo*, usually of the parents' way of life and state of mind. The expense to the child is loss of potential, lack of individual growth, and narrowing of the personality. Sometimes the result can be neurosis or mental illness.

In other cases parental influence can be much more enriching and diverse, helping the young person towards finding satisfaction, for instance in gratification and the capacity to delay it, and also in attachments and relationships, in creative activity and accomplishments, in the capacity to deal with anxiety, frustration and loss, to recognize potential wherever it may lie and to develop it without overstimulating or causing anxiety.

To regard all these processes as 'languages' can be useful in understanding how they are learned. For they are all learned in a way that can be personally enriching or merely adaptive.

Inevitably one's mother tongue is that of one's parents or parent figures. It would be impossible for a child brought up by parents to have a mother tongue different from theirs. Unless outside influences are exceptionally strong (for example on certain immigrant families), a child will speak his language with the same dialect or accent as his parents, with similar intonation and idiosyncrasies and with the same range and limitation of vocabulary. He will also speak it in his own way, constructing his own sentences that are not necessarily those of his parents.

The same is true of metaphorical 'languages', which are patterns of emotional response, modes of relating to others, and all the symbolism that develops in family life. All these are absorbed and learned in much the same way as the actual 'mother tongue'.

There are aspects of language development in which the influence of parents, particularly mothers, has only recently been shown to be extensive. It has been shown that in the earliest years a mother unconsciously restricts or elaborates her child's linguistic development and capacity and therefore his capacity for educational development according to her own social and educational background. She may transmit a 'restricted' form of language from which, once adapted, it is difficult to expand. Or she may transmit an 'elaborated' form, which leads to other possibilities, both linguistic and imaginative. For instance, one mother might say 'Pick up the red ball and put it on the small table', whereas another less articulate would simply say 'Put it there' and supply the missing details with gestures. If a child asks 'Why do things fall when I drop them?', there is an immense difference in attitude and influence between a mother who explains the laws of gravity in a simplified form suitable to the child's level of intellectual development and the mother who answers 'They just do', or 'Well, why shouldn't they?'. Such differences, repeated in hundreds of ways many times a day as the child grows up, will have a profound influence on his development and personality. They affect not only his vocabulary and his linguistic development but also his feelings towards whatever is discussed and his attitudes towards them. If he is always encouraged or always snubbed when he asks a question, his curiosity and responses will develop accordingly. If a particular atmosphere emanates from his parents at the mention of certain subjects, this will affect him too. Neither he nor his parents may be consciously aware of this atmosphere or of the fact that they are different from anyone else in the matter. They may be unable to explain why there are certain silences or feelings in their relationships.

It never occurred to Susan, aged six, to leave her bedroom once her parents had kissed her goodnight. In later life she came to recognize that an odd kind of taboo had grown up in the family about it. Its strength was revealed one evening when she vomited repeatedly. She cried but no one heard her. Her parents were downstairs watching television. It did not occur to Susan to disturb them. She lay, wet and cold, until they came up to bed and heard her crying.

Emotional 'codes' and imagery seem to be transmitted from one generation to the next in much the same way as language. They are profoundly influenced by personality and circumstances and more indirectly by social class and education. A mother may transmit richness of language and poverty of emotion, or vice versa. Apart from direct genetic inheritance, which is also probably important, each person's character and basic attitudes are largely the product of influences from parents and parent figures who in their turn were the product of many influences, good and bad, suitable and unsuitable to the environment, strong and weak, expansive and restrictive, stretching back into the remote past. Most of these influences will never be known or understood, and most of them, like the genes of an individual ancestor, exert less influence as the number of intervening generations increases.

One might illustrate this from the same linguistic examples. In asking her child to put the ball on the table or in answering his question about things falling, quite apart from her linguistic attainments, a mother will reveal a multiplicity of personal feelings, moods and attitudes towards life, towards material things, towards the child himself and the relationship he is trying to make with the world. Her tone may be bored, exasperated, resigned, hostile, full of love or hate, joy or distaste or any other of many possible variations, both straightforward or devious. Repeated thousands of times in different ways this helps to form the subtle differences of human personality and behaviour. Because the young child sees most of mother and is attached to her, most of this influence comes from her.

The influence can be virtually unchanged from generation to generation. Not uncommonly one comes across families in whom a particular type of behaviour or relationship seems to have been 'handed down' almost in the manner of a physical characteristic such as height or hair colour. Happy family relationships, good mothering, capacity for friendship and successful marriages tend to run in families in this way. Strange patterns can also be perpetuated. For instance it is not uncommon to find members of one sex dominating several generations and branches of a family, while members of the other sex, those who marry into the family as well as those born into it, are submissive and weak.

The mother of five daughters in such a family remarked 'My sons-in-law don't know what they're in for until they're well and truly married. But eventually they all come to heel.' It is not surprising that her husband was known in her social circle as her 'puppy-dog' or that her only son, intelligent and sensitive, suffered a severe breakdown in late adolescence which left him unable to tolerate pressure or competitive existence. It is also not surprising that he married a young woman of powerful personality, who 'mothered' him, apparently to the satisfaction of both. His two-year-old daughter, by his own rather proud admission, 'already twists me round her little finger'.

A direct, unchanging influence can be more sinister. For instance, it is now well known that the practice of 'battering babies' often runs in families and can be traced through two or three generations and occasionally through as many as four or five. Battered children grow up to be battering parents. I believe that this fact has extensive implications and applies not only to physical 'battering' but also to the more subtle forms of cruelty, hostility and malice. Cruelty that is physical and visible is the tip of an iceberg.

Often the influence of parents on their children and later descendants is greatly influenced or modified by some inevitable situation or event. For instance the loss of a parent in childhood will always influence the child when he or she becomes a parent, though the effect is likely to be different in different people and to be itself influenced by other circumstances.

Thus one woman whose father had deserted the family when she was two years old and who was raised by a dominating mother could only have serious relationships with men who were greatly inferior to her in intelligence and ability, whom she felt she could control.

Another whose childhood circumstances were similar could only attach herself to much older men who were 'father figures' to her, and eventually married a man twenty years her senior.

A man whose father had been killed in the war when he was ten became used to being 'boss' at home, and when he grew up he had difficulty in taking orders from his superiors at work.

Another, who had watched his mother die slowly from disseminated sclerosis, i.e. 'creeping paralysis', was dominated by fear that he was developing some similar disorder and repeatedly produced symptoms which conformed with his picture of the disease.

So a huge variety of unperceived and mostly imperceptible influences act upon whatever was there before to produce the feelings and modes of behaviour that make up personality and way of life. The capacity to free oneself from parental influence and develop autonomously is also, to some extent, the result of parental influence. It may well be that the capacity to do this, like musical talent or the potentiality to grow very tall, is inborn and infinitely variable between one individual and another but, like other characteristics, can only be realized if circumstances allow. There are certain types of parental influence which crush the capacity for healthy development, either as an individual or in relation to others. Other types allow individuality and innate abilities and talents to flourish and relationships to flower. Still others lead to rebellion or complicated changes, in which case the influence of parents may be less obvious, though not necessarily less powerful.

To get some idea of the influence of mothers such as one might see quite easily in looking around, I have made a few notes on patients seen just before writing this chapter. They are typical rather than extreme or peculiar.

A man in his fifties cries in the night for his dead mother.

Another has a nervous breakdown on the death of his mother, ninety years old and senile.

A woman in her thirties can hardly bear to be apart from her mother, even for a few hours.

A married woman who was adopted in infancy spends years tracking down her true parents and commits crimes to obtain the information she seeks.

A talented artist thinks of his mother every time he tries to make love to his wife and is immediately impotent.

A successful businessman still feels deep resentment because his parents refused to allow him to go to university.

A woman has such strong feelings because her mother came from Finland that she feels immediately 'at home' in that country, though without speaking a word of the language.

Such reactions might be observed at any time, not only by a psychiatrist but by anyone who has occasion to know something of the feelings of those around. Even an apparent indifference or total ignorance conceals strong feelings. Anyone who reflects at all knows how strong these feelings are. In fact, every mother exerts so profound an influence on her children that it seems worthwhile to explore further. Those who wish to understand themselves and others better do well to study mothers, both their own and other people's.

PATTERNS OF CHILDHOOD

People are the sum of everything they have ever been and of all the experiences they have ever had. This concept is more imaginative and useful than looking at the past as influential but finished.

From the beginning, whatever happens to a person contributes to his personality. The same would be true of building a house or a road. In these too there are basic materials out of which the final product is constructed. The basic material of people is their genetic make-up, their inheritance. An experience does not have an effect on its own, but only by its effect on this basic material. The same experience is totally different to a cat, a fish or a human being, and so to a lesser extent it is different for each individual human being who has his own unique genetic structure. This is why man is more than the sum of his experiences.

Experiences that are longstanding, continuous or repeated contribute more than single experiences. Exceptions are experiences that overwhelm. Even then the ground is already prepared for the incident to have the effect it does by the nature of the person and by previous experiences that were longstanding, continuous or repeated often. Of course, some experiences are so catastrophic and overwhelm regardless of previous experiences, but these truly 'traumatic' experiences are rare beside the other so-called 'traumatic' experiences. Even total catastrophe is survived or dealt with according to the nature of that person at that time and so according to previous experiences.

The adult is formed from the youth, the ten-year-old, the

six-year-old, the toddler, the infant, the foetus and from the original germ cells that contain all the inherited material. The important things in life, those indefinable qualities which make life seem worth living or worthless, and which provide atmosphere and mood regardless of circumstance, seem to come largely from repeated and continual experience in early life.

The infant lives on in the adult, demanding what are basically the same gratifications. Patterns of infancy persist and can be seen all around. What pleases an adult, what brings gratification, happiness and a sense of well-being, are mostly adult forms of infant gratifications. These may be as diverse as physical closeness, aesthetic pleasures, feelings of security or satisfaction at producing something laboriously or triumphantly.

What brings people unhappiness and frustration, what brings neurosis and mental illness and wrecks the lives of people unable to find peace or satisfaction are infant problems. This is not to say that the problems of infancy are the cause of all later problems or of mental illness, only that often there is a close connection.

The patterns of infancy persist into adult life. You can see them all around and, provided they are not taken too literally, much can be learned. One adult is a jolly baby in harmony with himself and the world around. Another is accustomed to being the centre of attention and by his manner makes sure that he is. He probably knows that in moments of doubt he only has to roar loudly and he will get what he wants. Another may be obviously resigned to not having his needs provided and his lifelong despair either shows through or is hidden behind a mask. Another had a mother whose feelings were mixed and whose behaviour was inconsistent. Can he please her? He goes round forever with a slightly bewildered air as though uncertain of the best thing to do. Another is forever hungry either literally or metaphorically and nothing will satisfy him, another is a querulous baby who doesn't know what he wants and whom nothing pleases. He feels neglected whatever the true situation. Yet another is accustomed to being appreciated for what he is rather than for what he does; he joins in the general applause at his own excellence, and makes sure that he gets it. Another behaves as though brought up to concentrate on the process rather than on the product, and expects visible effort, regardless of results, to bring its reward.

The adult whose infant self feels mishandled and intruded upon is probably withdrawn in some corner, suspicious and touchy. The infant self who was controlled is fearful of making any mess at all and is likely to lay emphasis (as doubtless did his mother) on the importance of getting everything right, starting from body functions and body sensations and spreading to other areas of life.

Attitudes to unknown and new experiences also seem to originate in infancy. An infant (or adult) may feel anxious when faced with novelty and may do his best to make the new apparition or situation go away. Another excitedly explores it. Another is curious but vigilant and circumspect, and yet another denies the existence of anything new or to be explored.

Approach to the unknown includes feelings and attitudes towards what goes on behind one's back or when one isn't there.

Growing children increasingly become aware that things happen when they aren't there, over which they have no control, and for which they are not to blame. The development of this awareness involves confusion and strong feelings. This has been well worked out in psychoanalysis, and is known in its jargon as 'primal scene fantasy' because it is supposed to be concerned, either literally or metaphorically, with the child's interest in or concern about his parents' sexual intercourse. Sooner or later the child comes to realize that this takes place, or must at some time have taken place. It is of considerable interest to him and it links in an intense personal way with his general curiosity about the world. His attitude to the 'primal scene', originating in his mother's attitude, will carry over to his adult life and will typify his attitude to everything that goes on which he does not understand and cannot control. Adults unwittingly reveal their attitudes to these matters.

Freud worked out his theories at a time when there was much frustration and taboo about sex, and in a community whose neuroses centred primarily on sex. As a result much psychoanalytic writing seems to suggest that literal 'primal scene fantasies' are the basis of neurotic confusions. But, looking at our world today, it seems more convenient and constructive to see the concept of 'primal scene fantasy' as symbolic of an individual's conscious and unconscious reactions to everything that goes on behind his back — of which actual 'primal scene fantasy' about parents is only a part. Thus it is one of the most important factors in development and it makes a fundamental difference, which lasts throughout life, between those who like to explore and who really want to know and those who do not. Lack of curiosity can become a powerful defence against threat.

The influence of the infant's position in the family may also be obvious. You may be able to spot the imperious eldest, used to being bigger and stronger than everyone else, or the less confident, who has a fearful job keeping ahead of his younger brother. There is the younger brother, maybe hopelessly less good at everything than other people, or cocky and pushing while striving to catch up. There is the displaced infant, ever angry at the presence of the new baby, and the youngest infant who never had to cope with competition from below but who has a hard job proving that he's as big and grown-up as everybody else. There is the infant who is dominated by rivalry for the parents' affection and the infant who feels he is the ugly duckling of the family, different from everyone else.

Although such assessments are speculative, it usually happens that, if one has the opportunity to explore a person's past and there is sufficient evidence to do so with likely accuracy, one usually finds a pattern of infancy emerging which corresponds to the present person. This observation is frequently used or abused by armchair psychoanalysts judging historical characters. In practice these connections between infancy and adult life come out most clearly in direct, intimate conversation based on a strong, trusting relationship. Under such circumstances a clear picture usually emerges. There may be objective evidence to support it, and sometimes this comes to light only *after* one has made one's assessment. More often one achieves a curious memory or mental reconstruction of infancy which may or may not be literally true but which has its own truth, in that it feels right to both patient and investigator in a way that other interpretations do not. Of course this is no proof of objective reality but it is surprising how often information about what really happened, if it comes to light, corresponds to the psychic reconstruction. Even if it does not, which also sometimes happens, the sense of 'feeling right' cannot be discounted because it must somehow be explained. In other words, imaginatively it is true. This interesting phenomenon is a product of introspection on one side and observation or inspiration on the other. The feeling of 'that's right' is known to everyone who has ever done or experienced successful psychotherapy. During the process, if sufficiently searching and sensitive, the patient is likely to 'know' what he felt like as an infant. This 'knowledge' probably consists in no more than having a feeling, but it is a special kind of feeling because of the sense of truth and revelation to which it is attached. People with special talents or creative gifts, including many writers and poets, can sometimes achieve this 'knowledge' or 'insight' for themselves without assistance.

No one knows how much it matters whether these 'memories' are objectively true or not, and one may well ask what does it matter. Freud realized that *all* his women patients could not have been seduced by their fathers in childhood and so some of them must have been 'making it up', however unconsciously. But he also realized that this was just as important in its way as 'true' reality. Thus he made one of the great contributions to human knowledge.

Freud was not the first writer to realize the important effect that people's earliest experiences had on them or the way in which reality and imagination combine to make this effect. People have always known that early experience, background and upbringing are important in people's lives. Discerning people have also known that experience blends with feeling and imagination to form memories and their effects. Probably Wordsworth was the first writer to appreciate the subtlety and the enormous implications of these ideas. In Book II of *The Prelude* he describes how mother love conditions the way in which a child learns to perceive things, and how the resulting associations remain in his mind for always.

> Blest the infant Babe,
> (For with my best conjecture I would trace
> Our Being's early progress), blest the Babe,
> Nursed in his Mother's arms, who sinks to sleep,
> Rocked on his Mother's breast; who with his soul
> Drinks in the feelings of his Mother's eye!
> For him, in one dear Presence, there exists
> A virtue which irradiates and exalts
> Objects through widest intercourse of sense.
> No outcast he, bewildered and depressed:
> Along his infant veins are interfused
> The gravitation and the filial bond
> Of Nature that connect him with the world.
> Is there a flower, to which he points with hand
> Too weak to gather it, already love
> Drawn from love's purest earthly fount for him
> Hath beautified that flower – already shades
> Of pity cast from inward tenderness

Do fall around him upon aught that bears
Unsightly marks of violence or harm.
Emphatically such a Being lives,
Frail creature as he is, helpless as frail,
An inmate of this active universe:
For feeling has to him imparted power
That through the growing faculties of sense
Doth like an agent of the one great Mind
Create, creator and receiver both,
Working but in alliance with the works
Which it beholds – Such, verily, is the first
Poetic spirit of our human life,
By uniform control of after years,
In most, abated or suppressed; in some,
Through every change of growth and of decay,
Pre-eminent till death.*

No one can see precisely what sort of future will grow from the present, however well it is understood. No one can say for sure that a particular type of mother or a particular pattern of infancy will produce a particular type of adult. One may be able to make certain predictions based on probability and some of these may turn out to be accurate, but that is all. It can be compared with seeing a pile of bricks but having no idea what sort of building will be constructed from them. But certain predictions can be made with confidence. For instance, a pile of bricks will not make a house of stone or wood but it may make a brick house that is beautiful or ugly, stable or unstable, practical or inconvenient and so on. One's mother influences the process of development but so do many other people and circumstances, including what one is made of oneself.

But in looking back over the past, if sufficient information is available, one can see how the present has grown from it and how far it has been influenced by what might have been predictable and how far by unexpected events.

Everyone has strong feelings about mothers even if these feelings are of indifference or based on ignorance. Adults cannot shake off their mothers any more than children can. Mother forms an essential part of, and usually the basis of, the inner world in which and by which everyone lives, however little or much they are aware of it. At first one is joined with mother, later one absorbs her.

* 1850 Ed. Lines 234–65.

What is absorbed and the way this happens is the foundation of personality and individuality. It generates the fantasy factor in everyone's lives, the imaginative activity that underlies all thought, feeling and action.

We have seen that an absent, unknown or even a dead mother can exert an influence as strong as can any real or known mother. Sometimes the absent mother is actually stronger than the real mother because the fantasy she generates is unchecked by reality.

Everyone has a psychic representation of his own infancy of which he may or may not be aware, which may or may not correspond to objective reality and which is a powerful influence on his life.

All through their lives people repeat the behaviour of this psychic representation of infancy and tend to reconstruct its patterns. They often do this by manipulating the circumstances of their lives in order to fit the feelings they have and the result is that they tend to behave as they felt in the earliest years. They do this even when it appears to be against their interests. For instance someone whose mental representation of early life is of being angry and misunderstood will tend to provoke situations in which it then seems justified to feel angry and misunderstood. Someone who feels rejected and unloved is likely to set up situations in which others reject him with hostility. Someone whose psychic representation is of satisfaction in separating and controlling both parents may be adept in adult life at dealing with triangular situations in ways advantageous to himself, though he may be unhappy in the process. Someone who feels cradled in the arms of a loving mother or who longs to be, may find a substitute in adult life. This may be a wife but can also be a secretary, an institution or a job.

People try to set up the predominating environments of their childhood. The less aware they are of this the more it is likely to damage them. Since no one can really return to his mother's knee or womb, it is done symbolically. Many people brought up in a predominantly *cradling* environment often choose husbands or wives who will cradle and support, and find secure, undemanding jobs in which they can feel sheltered and safe. People brought up in a predominantly *directive* environment are controlled, and anxious about control and being controlled. They find controlling jobs and often act according to strict conscience. People brought up in unusual circumstances create correspondingly unusual situations.

Edward C.'s childhood environment was one of psychological catastrophe which he always managed to survive. His mother died when he was four and he was precipitated prematurely into what was largely an unsupporting environment. He learned to survive. He made sure that he kept on the right side of those who provided what he needed. He learned to do without what there seemed no chance of obtaining. He grew up competent, charming and successful within his limits. At the cost of part of his personality, he was surviving. His efficiency stood him in good stead during the war when time and again he found himself in a situation of catastrophe in which it seemed impossible that anyone could survive. Each time he was the sole survivor. But later in life, in his work and in his marriage, the pattern of recurrent catastrophe with survival repeated itself to an extent that was truly remarkable.

Maria's first memories were of trying to improve. Her mother was always trying to make her better at everything, striving towards the perfect child. Maria found it difficult to enjoy the moment instead of looking into the future when things ought to be better. She caught herself choosing occupations at which it was possible to improve, and turning activities less obviously suited to this role into competitions against herself or others. Giving a party, for instance, was to her a battlefield in which she struggled against the enemy (the guests) and emerged triumphant and somewhat improved. At the age of thirty she decided to take up piano lessons again, and she chose playing the piano deliberately so that she could just enjoy it. Inevitably she found herself striving to improve and competing with herself to practise each day.

Thus, all mothers exert a powerful influence over their children's lives and their children carry them round inside for the rest of their lives. This happens largely through fantasy, symbolic thinking and imagination. Each of the three stages, *enclosure, extension* and *separation*, leaves its psychic representation in the child's mind and forms part of his personality. Most of this is unconscious but, given sufficient patience and skill, it can usually be unravelled. The result is imaginative rather than factual but not therefore less authentic.

3. The First Stage: Enclosure

Sweet my child I live for thee.
Tennyson, *The Princess*

In the earliest phase we are dealing with a very special
state of the mother.
D. W. Winnicott, *Primary Maternal Preoccupation*

She was so deeply imbedded in my consciousness that
for the first year of school I seem to have believed that
each of my teachers was my mother in disguise.
Philip Roth, *Portnoy's Complaint*

The first psychological stage of motherhood is the counterpart of
pregnancy, though it usually begins and ends later. A mother may
feel that her child is *part* of her from the moment she is aware of
him inside, or imaginatively before he is even conceived. During
the last weeks of pregnancy the feelings of the first stage of motherhood are likely to increase markedly and reach their peak during
the first few weeks after birth.

Not all mothers develop these feelings in this way. Some need
time to become accustomed to the situation and for the feelings
to grow. Others never feel like this at all. Once developed, these
feelings usually predominate through the child's infancy, then
gradually give way to other, more independent feelings, but are
never quite lost. As long as the feelings of *enclosure* predominate, the
mother not only provides the child's environment but also is that
environment.

Many people grow up without ever having experienced the first
stage or only having known it to a very limited degree. Many of
these are successful people who might even deem themselves happy,
especially if their environment holds them comfortably and in a
manner that balances other experiences, particularly those of the
second stage of mothering. Many people who have never experienced

the first stage of mothering fit into society and get on with their lives. In some societies such people can fit in nearly perfectly and indeed are what is required by that society. But increasingly in our own society such people are unhappy, many are limited in feelings and personality and all of them are vulnerable to kinds of stress with which those who have been more fortunate can deal. The stage of *enclosure* is a vitally important stage and it is increasingly difficult or impossible to grow up complete in our society without experiencing it.

It is not essential that the experience of the stage of *enclosure* comes through the real mother, though it usually does. It is the stage that is least likely to be provided by father, adopted parent, foster parents, nanny or institution. But some substitute mothers 'tune in' easily to this stage, particularly when the baby arrives when only a few days or weeks old. It is not uncommon to find adoptive mothers, foster mothers or nannies who have a special talent for this stage of mothering and who take on a series of young babies success-fully and give them a better start in life than they could have had from their natural mothers. Some young mothers in the richer sections of the community, who themselves lack the feeling or way of life necessary to provide their infants with adequate first stage mothering, have a talent for choosing a nanny or mother-substitute who is particularly well suited for this. This is probably an import-ant reason why many members of the upper class, traditionally raised without close contact with their mothers, grow up healthy and undamaged. Many grandmothers and aunts also seem able to develop *enclosure* feelings when necessary, and this saves many children whose mothers go out to work, are ill or have other difficulties.

Not every natural mother has the feelings necessary for a healthy first stage. It depends partly on her circumstances, her husband, home and environment, but most of all on the way in which she herself is made and the way she experienced the first stage in her own infancy. Although differences are found between generations, on the whole women mother in the way in which they themselves were mothered, however hard they try to do otherwise. A mother whose own infancy was lacking in first stage mothering with its appropriate feelings of *enclosure* will be unlikely to provide this kind of beginning for her own child, though she may do much better than her own mother.

The feelings associated with the first stage of mothering are sometimes referred to as 'going broody'. This intense, conscious and also unconscious identification which a mother makes with her infant has also been called by Winnicott 'primary maternal pre-occupation'. The feelings are nearly always confined to women and usually to biological mothers. It seems likely that there is a physiological basis to the feelings, probably mediated by the hormonal changes of pregnancy and lactation. Similar relationships can be seen in animals. The stage of *enclosure* is very like the mothering of animals, particularly mammals. Mothers who have experienced strong feelings during the stage of *enclosure* often feel them again momentarily in sympathy with, say, a bitch or a mother-cat with a litter, or a mare with a foal.

In harmony with the child's physical dependence, the mother feels that he is part of her. She identifies with him totally, continuously and harmoniously in a unique *rapport* which may totally disregard the surroundings and even have a healing quality. We have a record of the early Christian martyr Saint Perpetua who died in AD 203. She wrote of her experiences in prison:

And so I managed to have my [newborn] child stay with me in prison: straightway I became better and was relieved by the task of looking after my little baby: and the prison suddenly was made for me a palace, and I would rather have been there than anywhere else.*

D. H. Lawrence also describes the development of *enclosure* feelings under difficult circumstances. Mrs Morel was lying in bed after giving birth, unhappy about her unwanted child and her gross, drunken husband:

In her arms lay the delicate baby. Its deep blue eyes, always looking up at her unblinking, seemed to draw her innermost thoughts out of her. She no longer loved her husband; she had not wanted this child to come, and there it lay in her arms and pulled at her heart. She felt as if the navel string that had connected its frail little body with hers had not been broken. A wave of hot love went over her to the infant. She held it close to her face and breast. With all her force, with all her soul, she would make up to it for having brought it into the world unloved. She would love it all the more now it was here; carry it in her love. Its clear, knowing eyes gave her pain and fear. Did it know all about her? When it lay under her heart, had it been listening then? Was there a reproach in the look? She felt the marrow melt in her bones, with fear and pain.†

* Quoted in Peter Brown, *Augustine of Hippo*, p. 159.
† *Sons and Lovers*, p. 37.

This unique *rapport* includes suffering as well as joy, for example the infant's crying, and the acceptance of occasional feelings of hostility, such as a sudden impulse, probably felt at times by most mothers of young babies, to smother it or throw it out of the window.

In this way the mother is in touch with the infant and responds to his feelings and actions. She protects him from situations with which he is unable to deal and she provides a setting in which he can explore and discover the world.

In our society an immature mother is unlikely to be able to cope successfully with a young baby, especially if she is feckless by nature and unsupported.

Janet, eighteen years old, was unable to organize her life in any conventional manner. She only did what she wanted to do and she never did anything that bored her. An immature unmarried mother, she kept her child largely, I think, because she thought he would bring her amusement and satisfaction. She lived in a fantasy world into which the crying baby intruded. Her temperament was changeable and she expected her child to accommodate himself to her moods. It didn't work. She got into more and more of a muddle with her baby, frequently became hysterical and eventually broke down. In the end she decided to have the baby adopted, much to the relief of those concerned with her.

But an immature mother is not necessarily a bad mother. Unlike the later stages of mothering, the stage of *enclosure* can be successful in a mother who is herself immature and may be little more than a child. Above all things, the stage of *enclosure* requires spontaneity and imagination and these are often stronger and less eroded than in more mature mothers.

Lorraine was a feckless nineteen-year-old who somehow acquired a baby. She wasn't sure who the father was but she found someone to support her and the child. She was irresponsible with money and unable to foresee that if she squandered what she had today there would be none tomorrow. She was incapable of buying food for more than one meal at a time. Milk bottles accumulated in her apartment because she never had the foresight to put them out the night before and she never got up early enough for the milkman in the morning. Yet her baby thrived. When he was born she developed strong and healthy *enclosure* feelings. She understood him. She knew when and how to feed him. She knew when he needed to sleep and when he needed a cuddle. She didn't know how to bath him but when she felt he needed it she undressed herself as well and got into the bath with him. He was a large, cheerful, happy baby who looked as though he had had a splendid start and was ready to cope with whatever life held in store for him. I felt that they would probably mature together. But she is likely to cause him trouble later on.

Not all the children of immature mothers have such a good start. Fecklessness such as that of Lorraine's often goes with inadequate mothering, especially if the mother is self-centred and unable to develop *enclosure* feelings.

All through a successful first stage of mothering there is a gradual onward movement towards the next stages. Winnicott calls this 'graduated failure of the environment', but 'failure' is an unfortunate word to use for something which is a sign of success. Normal signs of this include family pride and a sense of the past, fantasies about the infant's future that are mild and flexible and, to some extent, pride in the baby's achievements, an early recognition of the baby as a separate being and appreciation of his individuality. But if these feelings and fantasies are strong at this early stage they are probably being used as a substitute for the first stage mothering rather than as a normal fragment of it.

An example of a mother involved in the stage of *enclosure* and with remnants of this during the stage of *extension* is Lady Middleton in *Sense and Sensibility*. Jane Austen concentrates on this aspect of her life and her personality. She was 'not more than six or seven and twenty' and her intense involvement with her children made her appear to be lacking in 'frankness and warmth' and she 'had nothing to say for herself beyond the most commonplace inquiry or remark'.

A fond mother, though in pursuit of praise for her children, the most rapacious of human beings, is likewise the most credulous; her demands are exorbitant, but she will swallow anything.

The important results in adult life of a successful first stage include a sense of self and a capacity for self-awareness. Winnicott writes:

The peculiar identification of the mother with the child enables the infant to begin to exist, to have experiences, to build a personal ego, to ride instincts, and to meet with all the difficulties inherent in life. All this feels real to the infant who becomes able to have a self.

Also from the first stage come basic feelings about the world, appropriate senses of optimism and pessimism, of security and insecurity, what Laing has called 'primary ontological security', a sense of the need for vigilance along with the confidence and ability to relax, a sense of harmony and continuity, the ability to use imagination freely, to cope realistically with the physical world and with bodily feelings and functions. From it too comes the capacity for close contact with another person, both physical and psychological. To some extent the sense of curiosity and the capacity to explore new territory is also rooted in this stage of mothering.

The infant is at the mercy of whatever happens at this early stage. He has no means of assessing what is taking place. He absorbs whatever is success or failure, whatever is true or false. Inevitably he becomes attatched to whatever is presented to him. Inevitably his experiences during this first stage will determine his later ability to detect the mode of experiences. Trust and distrust, falsification, denial, amplification will, if they occur, be 'built in' to his personality. For adequate development this needs to be based on genuine feelings of goodwill and to accord to a large extent with what he will later recognize as external reality.

Not every devoted mother is capable of the feelings of the first stage. She may be more at home with other stages and has to compensate for her difficulties with the first stage by other means. She may be a good mother in every other way and she may be good at making up to the child what they have missed together. In practice this may mean a benevolent predominance of second stage, *extension* mothering, and this will be discussed later on. Or it may mean an attempt to develop *enclosure* feelings through intellectual effort.

Whole cultures and sub-cultures can be built in which *extension* replaces *enclosure* and these can be highly successful. The results are different from those in which *enclosure* plays a part but not necessarily worse. The replacement of *enclosure* by *extension* is likely to be more successful in an environment where this is customary or expected than in one where it is not.

Attempts by mothers to develop *enclosure* feelings through

intellectual effort in order to compensate for lack of instinctive feelings are particularly common at present, especially among those who are educated and articulate. This is partly because important discoveries about the early mother–child bond have coincided with a period of improvement in women's education together with the widespread encouragement of mothers to look after their own babies. The result is that many mothers have been made aware of these matters intellectually and often this stirs faint memories and vestiges of instinctual feeling. This can stimulate fantasies, for instance, that breastfeeding is the basis of the bond. Many such mothers make a deliberate policy of breastfeeding their babies. Sometimes they have fantasies about the umbilical cord, perhaps that someone is trying to pull it out, and they develop desires to *enclose* rather than spontaneous feelings of *enclosure*. But the lack of *rapport* often means that the baby goes on crying and this may provoke rage. This is a sequence of feelings and events that can lead to baby-battering.

In my own practice, intellectual attempts to develop *enclosure* feelings are particularly common among young American mothers, many of whom have a striking lack of confidence in themselves as mothers combined with considerable ability to describe it in words.

Mrs Harting was thirty-three years old, American and married to an Englishman. There were two children, Harriet aged three and a baby boy, six months old. Mrs Harting came to consult me about Harriet. She began by saying, 'I feel I have a behaviour problem on my hands.' Harriet was whining all the time and Mrs Harting didn't know what to do about it. She said, 'I have no idea how to handle the problem or how to behave. I feel jittery about whether I'm right or wrong.'

Harriet's had been a difficult birth in a hospital in which contact between mother and child was not encouraged. Mrs Harting tried to breastfeed 'but it was like being rubbed with sandpaper'. She liked the idea of being a mother but felt that she had no gift for it, and this made her feel a failure. She felt better when she was out of the house visiting art galleries or sitting on committees. She had read Dr Spock and other baby books but she liked to have the personal advice of an expert in what she did for her children.

A striking feature about Mrs Harting was her lack of the kind of confidence that comes from the feeling of knowing what one's children need. She seemed to lack all feelings of *enclosure* and most feelings of *extension*, yet she was desperately trying to develop them. She *knew* intellectually that the children were hers and she felt responsible for them. She felt that motherhood was 'a project that I had to do'. Only by achieving a kind of intellectual understanding and control could she keep her family going.

The physical basis of feelings of psychological *enclosure* are very much lacking in the lives of many Americans. This goes right through the whole process of mothering. At least until recently most British babies have been delivered by midwives and spent their early days close to their mothers. Even though breastfeeding is declining, a baby is still likely to be fed fairly haphazardly from a bottle. He probably attends the infant welfare centre and is fed much the same as everyone else's baby. His mother may get a little advice from the Health Visitor or from other mothers. The baby is not, unless his family is wealthy, delivered by his personal obstetrician, nor does he have his special 'formula' (the very word suggests the antithesis of *enclosure*) devised by his personal paediatrician and altered in composition from week to week. From the start the American infant's world tends to be more 'scientific' than that of the European infant. Much of what is normally achieved by the feelings that go with the *enclosure* stages of motherhood is done by the mental activity that replaces it. Since psychotherapy encourages mental activity, vicious circles are often formed, and both mother and child are denied the opportunity to develop the healthy feelings that go with early mothering. This is America's tragedy, but something not dissimilar is happening in Britain. The modern trend in childbirth in Britain is towards quicker deliveries organized at times that suit the staff of the hospital. This does not help the development of *enclosure* feelings.

Anyone who has experienced a satisfactory stage of *enclosure* probably has it for ever, linked in later childhood with special feelings closely connected with love and often with nature. Wordsworth's poetry is full of it. Others, usually less fortunate, seem to have had glimpses or they have feelings about it and seek it.

'Are you my mama?' asked the child. He had no idea what a mama might be, but he knew at once that he needed one badly.

'Good heavens!' said the elephant. 'Of course I'm not your mama. I was simply singing words I once heard.'*

Sometimes there is a yearning, perhaps for what has never been achieved.

> My genial spirits fail;
> And what can these avail
> To lift the smothering weight from off my breast?
> It were a vain endeavour,
> Though I should gaze for ever
> On that green light that lingers in the west:
> I may not hope from outer forms to win
> The passion and the life, whose fountains are within.†

Some people who are vaguely aware of what they have missed try to achieve a kind of *enclosure* situation or *cradling* environment. This may be in relationships such as marriage or parenthood (and this is one way in which parents can become emotionally dependent on their children), it may be in work or in possessions, such as a house or a collection, or a hobby.

ENCLOSING MOTHERS

Sometimes the only difficulty in the first stage of mothering is an excess of it. This goes with an inability to encourage the beginnings of *separation* and sometimes of *extension* too, so that there is failure to pass on to these stages at the appropriate times. Such predominance of the stage of *enclosure* and its prolongation at the expense of other stages can be advantageous under certain circumstances. It is, for instance, characteristic of groups and minorities with a history of persecution, such as the Greek and Jewish peoples. As such it probably has some survival value. But under the circumstances that commonly exist in the western world an excessive or prolonged stage of *enclosure* can lead to excessive dependence on the mother and an inability to develop normal independence.

The chief characteristic of a mother of predominantly *enclosing* type is an intense and overwhelming feeling of love of her child and an identification with him, often to the exclusion of all other interests. She is conscious that the child is part of her and, for much

* Russell Hoban, *The Mouse and his Child*, p. 20.
† Coleridge, *Dejection: an Ode.*

longer than with other mother–child couples, the child is unaware of the possibility of being separate from his mother. She identifies with her children to such an extent that she breathes with them, laughs with them, cries, sighs and stays with them. Even in separation she remains with them in spirit. She is also likely to provide them with food in a manner which not only expresses her love but also both symbolizes that this love is a part of themselves and demands their submission to it.

I would refuse to eat, and my mother would find herself unable to submit to such willfulness – and such idiocy. And unable to for my own good. She is only asking me to do something for my own good – and still I say no? Wouldn't she give me the food out of her own mouth, don't I know that by now?

But I don't want the food from her mouth. I don't even want the food from my plate – that's the point.

Please! a child with my potential! my accomplishments! my future! – all the gifts God has lavished upon me, of beauty, of brains, am I to be allowed to think I can just starve myself to death for no good reason in the world?

Do I want people to look down on a skinny little boy all my life, or to look up to a man?

Do I want to be pushed around and made fun of, do I want to be skin and bones that people can knock over with a sneeze, or do I want to command respect?

Which do I want to be when I grow up, weak or strong, a success or a failure, a man or a mouse?

I just don't want to eat, I answer.*

Food is often linked to the special kind of control which *enclosure* mothers exert over their children, often by using special kinds of threats which are only effective because of the child's involvement and identification with the mother. One mother is most anxious that her son does not eat lobster. Ever. She tells him: 'There are plenty of good things to eat in the world without eating a thing like lobster and running the risk of having paralyzed hands for the rest of your life.'† And when he refuses to eat at all:

So my mother sits down in a chair beside me with a long bread knife in her hand. It is made of stainless steel, and has little sawlike teeth. Which do I want to be, weak or strong, a man or a mouse?

* Philip Roth, *Portnoy's Complaint,* p. 15f.
† ibid., p. 105.

Doctor, why, why oh why oh why oh why does a mother pull a knife on her own son? I am six, seven years old, how do I know she really wouldn't use it?*

Excessive control by *enclosing* mothers starts at the birth of the child as a rather extreme form of normal maternal preoccupation. Such a mother seems almost to live her child's life for him. To her each feed, each episode of crying, each bowel movement and each weighing is an event to be noted, analysed and discussed in all its minutiae. As the child grows the mother is involved in every detail of development and often worries about whether everything is proceeding normally, calls the doctor whenever she detects a slight variation in some function. She retains responsibility for what he eats, and this is often of great importance to her. As he gets older she continues to organize his life. She not only buys his clothes but she chooses which he will wear each day and lays them out. She gets him ready for school, checks his books as though they were hers, goes through his homework in her own mind if not actually with him, knows exactly what he has learned and how much he knows. He has no experience of doing these things on his own and the idea of doing so is intolerable to him. I once asked a man of thirty what he would do if he came home from work one day and found that his mother had left a pound note on the table with a note saying 'This is to buy food for your supper.' He told me he would be totally unable to cope with the situation and he burst into tears at the very idea.

Excessive control of children by their mothers can take many forms, but it always has the same effect. This is the prevention of free development leading to lack of growth of self, failure of independence, inability to explore and loss of spontaneity. The children are unable to do the work they need to do on their own in order to grow up as authentic people, firm in the sense of self and able to set themselves into their surroundings.

The commonest and mildest form of excessive control is not necessarily disastrous in its effects. This is the failure of parents to make themselves dispensable as the child grows older. In mothers this is usually associated with a difficulty in transition from second to third stages of mothering. All mothers who are predominantly *enclosing* mothers tend to run into this problem. They include many who achieve *separation* in the end.

* ibid., p. 16.

An example of this was Mrs Troy. She fought with her teenage daughter for five years over almost every issue on which it is possible for an adolescent to rebel. Meanwhile she kept a tight control on her 'goody-goody' son, who was two years younger. Gradually Mrs Troy realized that her daughter had won every battle they had ever fought. She left school early, refused to take exams she regarded as unnecessary, had insisted on a career about which her parents were doubtful and was making a success of it, came and went as she pleased and slept with her boyfriend, with whom she was happy. Mrs Troy looked at her son and saw how hard he worked at his books to please his parents, how little he did of anything else, how small was his experience of the world and how afraid he was of venturing into new experiences. Mrs Troy underwent a personal revolution, gained confidence in her daughter and sought her aid in drawing the boy out of his shell. The daughter suggested that Mrs Troy leave her son alone to find things out for himself and to make his own mistakes, and Mrs Troy followed this advice. Mrs Troy took up new interests and began a study course for a recognized qualification, thus shifting some of her emotional investment in her children back on to herself with benefit all round.

This kind of excessive control that responds so easily to the right experience is likely to be due to the mother's excessive or inappropriate emotional investment in the child. Mothers who have been deeply involved with their children during the first two stages of mothering may find the stage of *separation* hard to achieve.

Excessive control of children by their mothers may be part of the mother–child relationship at any of the three stages, or it may virtually replace the relationship at any stage. It tends to occur particularly when there is imbalance between the stages, when the predominance of one stage is inappropriate because of the child's age, or when at any stage there is virtual absence of the other two stages.

'My mother loves me with a sort of philosophical violence,' said Peter, a sixteen-year-old boy who was finding it increasingly difficult to leave home and go to school where he was expected to do well in A levels. He felt he had never been an independent person at all. His mother was conscious of and tended to comment on everything he did, every move he made, everything he ate. She seemed almost to be aware of what he thought. Peter was conscious of her consciousness, felt he was dependent on it, resented it and also resented her remarks. He had also become excessively conscious of himself through remarks which she made. All his body functions seemed to impinge. He was aware of his heart beating, his tummy rumbling, his lungs inflating. He was also aware of an anxiety that flooded over him and made it difficult for him to get up in the morning, go to school or do his homework. He spent most of his time trying to ease the anxiety by tidying his room and checking that everything was in its place. He had a belief which he knew was irrational that by doing this he prevented his parents from invading him.

Peter was experiencing typical symptoms of excessive control of a type that was based on the first stage of mothering, the typical anxiety associated with this stage, both in its excess and in its deficiency. Peter's mother was very much an *enclosure* mother. She had two children, both boys, and freely admitted that since they were born almost all her energy had been taken up with living through them and experiencing their lives with them. She felt that they were still parts of her and she could not imagine it any other way.

A less extreme example of excessive *enclosure* and the kind which many people can recognize was Mrs Fox. She had always been very close to her children, particularly to her daughter Clare, who wanted to follow in her mother's footsteps by going to Oxbridge. Clare was highly intelligent and there seemed little doubt that she would achieve this. As the entrance examination approached, mother and daughter became increasingly involved together in the preparations. They discussed every step in Clare's preparation for the examination and went through every essay together. During the final weeks Clare became depressed and unable to concentrate. She seemed to forget most of what she knew and had lost her zest and the ability to deal with the subject. All her mother's efforts and encouragement failed to rouse her from this state of mind and she failed the examination. The following year the whole performance was repeated and eventually Clare decided to go to another university.

Throughout their children's lives many *enclosing* mothers emphasize *being* rather than *doing*. Such a mother is more interested in what her child is than in what he does, and she is more interested in what he does than in what he achieves. She is more likely to be pleased at his having curly hair than at his learning to walk. She takes more interest in his being intelligent than in his using his intelligence. She has more pride in his being musical than in his achievements on the piano. What he is is part of her. What he does is largely done by her. He is permanently wrapped round with loving care, and probably incapable of actually doing anything very much.

This direct support or control of his personality and daily functioning is undermining to the growing child. The constant emphasis on and praise of his personality and talents is uncomfortable and binding. He hardly knows where hers end and his begin. He has little or no opportunity to make choices, use judgement or develop inner standards. He is likely to feel anxiety fixed on whatever his mother has emphasized, perhaps body functions, or some personal quality. Because she still controls him he is unable to step outside it. As he grows up he may run into difficulties from his emphasis on being rather than achieving.

Donald, aged twenty-eight, felt anxious whenever he was asked to do anything. Unaided and unprompted, he could produce work of high quality but, if any demand was made on him, he collapsed in a state of confusion. This meant that he was not making progress in his career. His most powerful childhood memories were of his mother praising his looks and his talents both to him and to her friends. But she had dressed him until he was six years old and had tied his shoelaces for much longer. Even when he was at university, which he attended from home, she chose his courses, bought his books and regulated his hours.

When such a person is faced with competition he may tend to take the line 'If I don't try, I can't fail, and I shall still be the same, which is what makes me feel comfortable.' So he will tend to opt out of competitive situations and may even develop a drive to fail in worldly situations, which underneath is an attempt to reassure himself that whatever he does he is still the wonderful boy who is part of his mother. His inability to choose and judge may show in adult life. Some adults are incapable of choosing their own clothes, job or even food without help. Some are incapable of making decisions, of standing alone. Excessive control by an enclosing mother often leads to adult submissiveness and sexual impotence. Thus a highly intelligent person may be unable to achieve anything other than being a highly intelligent person.

A man had been found as a child to have perfect pitch and his enclosing mother had reacted joyfully to this in such a way that prevented him from developing his musical talent or benefiting from a musical education. He grew up semi-ignorant of what he heard and unable to play any musical instrument.

Some sons of excessively enclosing mothers grow up to be permanent patients in psychoanalysis, organized and paid for by their mothers. This kind of enclosing control can be particularly strong when the mother has money. I have known several such mothers bring up their sons to be admired but to be incapable of actually doing anything. The result is that the incapable youth or man sits around being admired by his mother and wholly dependent on her for support. As one of them put it: 'It's as though I am forever tinkering with the engine while my mother drives the car.'

Such situations are often perpetuated in the choice of a wife who replaces the mother in almost every way. The equation of wife with mother is also likely to increase the likelihood of sexual impotence. One does not have sex with one's mother.

The concomitant fear is of annihilation. If you are not sure of your own boundaries you are bound to feel anxious and uncertain, particularly when you find youself in situations where clear personal boundaries and a sense of self are required. Your personal boundaries will be confused if you grow up with the feeling that you are part of your mother. They will also be confused if you have never had the feeling of being part of your mother. In this way the anxiety of the first stage, enclosure, links with the anxiety of the third stage, separation. Anxiety that is rooted in the stage of enclosure can be much the same when the mother is over-enclosing as when the initial identification between mother and child never becomes established.

Nigel, aged nine, refused to go to sleep at night in case he died. Unless he could actually feel his heart beating he was terrified that it had stopped. He felt that any separation from his mother might lead to his being poisoned. He could not bear her even to visit the bathroom without him.

This is a typical example of anxiety of enclosure. The anxiety is about existence itself and the child feels trapped. He could have a totally *enclosing* mother or a mother lacking in *enclosure* feelings. In fact, Nigel's mother knew that she had never managed to make contact with him and had never felt in harmony with him.

ABNORMAL ENCLOSURE

Sometimes a mother causes her child to become totally identified with her and to remain so for ever.

One of the worst cases I ever saw was a man of thirty-five, of good intelligence, who was unable to do anything except wait for his mother to feed him, talk to him and take him out (which was usually to the psychiatrist of her current choice). His only method of communication, if such it can be called, was to describe in detail every event which had occurred since the previous visit, particularly functions and sensations of his own body. He appeared to be unaware of and showed no interest in whether he was holding the attention of the person to whom he spoke.

Another patient who could be regarded as an extreme example of total identification was an American divorcee with two young children. She seemed totally to *enclose* her elder daughter Anna, who was seven. She lived every minute of the day through Anna, slept with her in the same bed, shared every meal, took her to school each morning and was aware of every minute of the child's timetable. All day she thought of nothing but Anna and what she was doing at that particular moment, and each lunch-time and each evening Anna had to recount every moment of the day. The mother made frequent and unwelcome visits to the school and complained vociferously to the teachers with arguments that were both intelligent and irrelevant. The reason for her psychiatric consultation with me was her desire to find a perfect school for Anna and she was prepared to centre her entire life on this and to discuss it endlessly with all forms of 'expert'. During the previous summer she had crossed the Atlantic with the child six times and had visited innumerable schools in different parts of Europe and America. She finally chose America and so, unfortunately, I had no opportunity to follow Anna's progress.

When the *enclosing* mother is intrusive the results can be catastrophic. This sometimes leads to severe feelings of annihilation in adult life, to an intense preoccupation with body functions (hypochondria) or to a permanent need for an *enclosing* 'womb' which may take the form of a wife, a job, an institution or even a club or hobby.

These extreme cases require a life-and-death struggle if the child is to escape and he may find this impossible to initiate or to complete. Occasionally he actually kills himself. Sometimes he makes some suicidal gesture that is a desperate attempt to alter the situation. Frequently the choice is submission. Sometimes the struggle seems more of the child's own making, or what he makes of his difficult circumstances, for example Hamlet.

Enclosure can become abnormal because of unacceptable feelings. These may be the mother's anxiety, her emotional dependence on the child, hostility, desire for control or perverse sexuality.

Many mothers with abnormal feelings have a good deal of understanding of their predicament and often struggle to be normal. Most have a strong desire to do their best for their children. But inevitably they are drawn into a kind of deviousness because they cannot be honest with their children about the way they feel.

Kathryn had been neglected in infancy and probably also physically ill-treated by her drug-addict mother. She felt she had a tenuous hold on life, suffered from a strong sense of futility, was frequently depressed, and had made several suicidal attempts. When her first baby was born she managed well for several months, breastfed successfully and coped with the baby without too much difficulty during both day and night. Even when the baby was difficult she was not excessively upset. But gradually she developed sadistic feelings about him and kept imagining herself burning him on the kitchen stove or with a red-hot poker. She devised various tortures for him and thought of putting out his eyes. She noticed that these fantasies were particularly strong at times when the baby was well-behaved and easy to manage. She never actually did anything hurtful to him and she continued to care for him lovingly and efficiently though she was upset and frequently tearful about her hateful fantasy life and her fear that she might put it into practice.

Mary felt terrified that her son, aged six, might want to leave home. She was aware that she was dependent on him emotionally and found it hard to endure the hours when he was away at school. She was terrified that he would make friends of his own age and want to spend time with them. Yet all the time she knew that for his own sake he needed to be independent of her with companions of his own age. Her life was a struggle between her feelings and what she felt was right.

In fantasy it is possible for a mother to have a variety of feelings towards the 'enclosed' child. If she does not feel straightforward love, acceptance and preoccupation she may have different feelings. There can be hostile enclosure, and she may even feel that she is enclosing a foreign body. There can be rejecting enclosure, clinging, dependent enclosure, persecutory enclosure, persecuted enclosure, and enclosure full of fears. And the child absorbs it all.

Feelings of enclosure along with feelings of rejection lead to sad, guilty, backward-looking people. Where feelings of enclosure were weak the child is at the mercy of the second stage. A weak stage of enclosure followed by a strong stage of extension depends on the source of the strength. Strength which comes from the personality of a parent is likely to make it difficult for the child to exert his own necessary influence on his own development and so is likely to lead to neurotic difficulties or distorted personality.

When there is abnormality of enclosure it can be useful to discover precisely what part of the mother the child represents. Sometimes this turns out to be the face she puts on for the world and has little to do with the real person underneath. One may then find a child who is dressed to match her mother's dress and trained to behave in a way that will enhance the mother's relationships. Daisy in The Great Gatsby treats her child like this. In extreme cases a marked discrepancy may develop between the mother's fantasy about the part of her that the child represents and the real situation. The child swallows the image of himself that is the mother's wish-fulfilment.

A new stepmother brought her small daughter to live with her husband's four children. She emphasized constantly that her child was cleverer and prettier than the others, though it was obvious to everyone that this was untrue. The child was thus forced into the dilemma of either accepting what her mother said and ignoring the evidence of her own and others' senses, or disbelieving her mother, which would be upsetting and disloyal. The mother also imposed household duties on the stepchildren but only pretended to do so on her own daughter. The girl grew up isolated with an unreal fantasy that she was cleverer and prettier than other people and that she wasn't expected to help.

Sometimes the child represents that part of the mother which has never separated from her own mother. In this case the mother uses the child as a repository for her own anxieties. The child is likely to suffer from a form of 'separation anxiety', which is really the mother's anxiety about *separation*. Such mothers often exert subtle control over their children which makes it difficult or impossible for them to do what they would otherwise do easily or spontaneously. For instance the child may 'refuse' to go to school and the real reason for this is that the mother is frightened of *separating* from the child and transmits this anxiety to the child who then experiences it as his own anxiety. Or the child may 'refuse' to behave in a civilized way towards his brother or sister because, underneath, the mother is frightened that friendship between the children will exclude her.

Sometimes the child represents a part of the mother that she finds unacceptable. Thus she may be charming and well-behaved herself and no one can understand why her children are so awful. If they spoil other people's comfort and pleasure and damage or destroy their property, the mother is subtly gaining the satisfactions in which her conscience would forbid her to indulge directly. Sometimes the mother's anxieties are passed directly to the child, as in the case quoted by Winnicott* of the little boy, sent up to out-patients by his mother, who said, 'Please, doctor, my mother says I've got tummy-ache.'

In the more bizarre identifications between mother and child it becomes difficult to separate *enclosure* from *extension*, just as in other areas of life *extensions* of ourselves, our houses, cars, work, hobbies, etc., can seem as though they are parts of ourselves, sometimes abnormally so.

TRANSITION FROM ENCLOSURE TO EXTENSION

Normal transition from the stage of *enclosure* to the stage of *extension* takes place so slowly and easily that it is scarcely noticeable. The

* D. W. Winnicott, *Collected Papers.*

mother gradually becomes less identified with the child, less protective towards him, more involved with life outside and increasingly concerned with adapting the child to it. She continues to be involved and protective but also moulds and guides. She is also increasingly aware of her child as a *separate* person with his own feelings, interests and needs. While entering the stage of *extension* she is also preparing for the later stage of *separation*.

Mothers who are by nature strongly *enclosing* often have difficulty in making this transition. Some never make it at all, and cannot even think of their children except as *parts* of themselves. Some can cope with the stage of *extension* but exclude its essential seeds of *separation*. Occasionally a mother who has been fairly successful during the stage of *enclosure* is totally unequipped for the stage of *extension* and proceeds directly from *enclosure* to *separation*. In such a case a small child who has been surrounded securely with love and *rapport* is suddenly cast into the world as a *separate* being. This is more likely to be an emotional than a physical rejection. Such a mother often disguises her rejection by having a new baby and becoming involved with it.

Time and again one sees the children of *enclosing* mothers having to make their own bid for independence, and when they love their mothers, perhaps more than anything in the whole world, this can be hard.

St Augustine, at the age of twenty-eight, could only break away by tricking his mother and slipping off at night in a ship across the Mediterrranean. His mother, Monica, was a typical *enclosing* mother of the more stable type. He tells us in his *Confessions*: 'She loved to have me with her as is the way with mothers, but far more than most mothers.'* When one of her sons went astray 'She acted as if she was undergoing again the pangs of childbirth.'† 'I have no words to express the love she had for me . . . I just cannot see how she could have been healed if my death in sin had come to pierce the entrails of her love.' She was, he says, the voice of God in his early life.‡ Through the *enclosure* feelings absorbed from his mother Augustine seems to have felt about God rather as Wordsworth felt about nature.

* *Confessions.*
† ibid.
‡ ibid.

St Augustine may have escaped by tricking his mother but many children of *enclosing* mothers require much more than this. D. H. Lawrence, whose novels have an autobiographical feel about them, describes this convincingly. Throughout *Sons and Lovers* Mrs Morel controls her son Paul to an extreme degree and strives to keep that control. Only after the death of his mother is Paul able to struggle seriously against her:

Paul felt crumpled up and lonely. His mother had really supported his life. He had loved her; they two had, in fact, faced the world together. Now she was gone, and for ever behind him was the gap in life, the tear in the veil, through which his life seemed to drift slowly, as if he were drawn towards death. He wanted someone of their own free initiative to help him. The lesser things he began to let go from him, for fear of this big thing, the lapse towards death, following in the wake of his beloved.*

Paul becomes depressed. Everything seems different and unreal and pointless. The only thing that seems real is the 'thick darkness of the night', which brings memories of his mother. But eventually he makes the enormous effort required to break away:

'Mother!' he whimpered – 'mother!'
She was the only thing that held him up, himself, amid all this. And she was gone, intermingled herself. He wanted her to touch him, have him alongside with her.
But no, he would not give in. Turning sharply, he walked towards the city's gold phosphorescence. His fists were shut, his mouth set fast. He would not take that direction, to the darkness, to follow her. He walked towards the faintly humming, glowing town, quickly.†

In a different generation and culture we see Alex Portnoy struggling to escape from his mother on the analyst's couch. He describes how another boy of similar background has already found his own and only escape, or supreme fusing which is what the *enclosed* child longs for.

When I was still very much my mother's papoose . . . there was a suicide in our building. A fifteen-year-old boy . . . hanged himself from the shower head in the bathroom. 'With those golden hands!' the women wailed, referring of course to his piano playing – 'With that talent!' Followed by, 'You couldn't look for a boy more in love with his mother than Ronald!' . . . There is a note pinned to the dead young pianist's short-sleeved shirt . . .

* *Sons and Lovers*, p. 409.
† ibid., pp. 422–3.

Mrs. Blumenthal called. Please bring your mah-jongg rules to the game tonight. Ronald. Now how's that for good to the last drop? How's that for a good boy, a thoughtful boy, a kind and courteous and well-behaved boy?*

Here we are again approaching the area that is not so much exaggerated enclosing as abnormal *enclosure*, leading to extreme or bizarre attempts to progress. These lead to difficulties in making adult relationships, particularly sexual relationships.

Most mothers emerge from the stage of *enclosure* when the child is two to three years old. The process is slow, often marked by milestones pointing towards the later stages, *extension* and *separation*. The identification with the infant that is the chief characteristic of the stage of *enclosure* is strong but not total. From the birth of her child onwards the mother begins to impose herself and her culture on her child, mostly unconsciously. He is already an *extension* of her and has to learn to fit in. This is the beginning of the stage of *extension*. Many mothers are also aware from the moment of birth that the child is a *separate* being. Often this is brought home by the independent activities of the child. He may yell for food or comfort and is totally dependent on his mother for these, but he also snuffles, yawns, murmurs and hiccups in a typically human way. These activities are unrelated to his mother and by them he demonstrates his *separateness* just as much as when, some months later, he will learn to shake his head and assert his independence by the positive use of the negative. From birth onwards both she and the child experience all three stages, so that 'emerging' from the stage of *enclosure* to 'entering' the stage of *extension* means only that a relationship that is predominantly *enclosing* gradually becomes one that is predominantly one of *extension*.

* Philip Roth, *Portnoy's Complaint*, pp. 108, 110 and *135*.

4. The Second Stage: Extension

Train up a child in the way he should go: and when
he is old, he will not depart from it.

Proverbs 22:6

How can a bird that is born for joy
Sit in a cage and sing?

William Blake

The second psychological stage of motherhood is the counterpart
of infancy, the period during which dependence diminishes slowly
over several years. Its roots lie in the earliest weeks, when the
healthy mother is more preoccupied with the first stage, *enclosure*.
The stage of *extension* usually becomes predominant when the child
is about two years old. It reaches its peak between four and eight
years later and slowly declines with approaching adolescence and
increasing independence. The ages at which it occurs are variable.
In practice the stage of *extension* may begin at any time from birth or
not at all. It may end almost as soon as it has begun or it may
last throughout life. It corresponds to the stage of independent
existence but physical dependence. The mother no longer feels the
child so much as an *enclosure* but more as an *extension* of herself. The
child feels the mother as a supporting and guiding background as
he copes with his own exploration and fantasy. The mother supplies
what is needed but not more. She lets him do on his own what he
can and wishes to do. She sets standards which he can reach. She
guides but neither forces him nor holds him back. She probably
experienced the stage of *enclosure* alone but she is likely to share the
stage of *extension* with the father, often so closely that it is impossible
to assess the influence of each.

The stage of *extension* is what most people remember as their
childhood.

At this stage both parents usually feel and show considerable pride
in the child, in his existence, his attributes and his achievements.

Both usually devote a great deal of time and energy to him and their way of life and expenditure is likely to be dominated by his needs or by what they think will be best for him. As a result they experience a feeling of personal enrichment. Life for them has a purpose. Their child's future seems immensely important.

Freud seems to have believed that the stage of *extension* is the essence of parenthood: 'If we look at the attitude of affectionate parents towards their children we have to recognize that it is a revival and reproduction of their own narcissism . . .', and again: 'Parental love, which is so moving and at bottom so childish, is *nothing but the parents'* narcissism born again'* (my italics).

In a traditional society, or one whose changes are slow and scarcely noticeable, there is no need to develop beyond the stage of *extension*. In such a society people belong and know where they belong. It may contain evils and disadvantages but there is no sense of isolation and no need to be *separate*. People fit in and are *extensions* of the society in which they live.

The change from a world of belonging to a world of change has been going on at least since the Middle Ages, but the rate of change has accelerated markedly in recent years. Western society now seems much less stable than it did in Freud's day. Today more is needed than parental *extension*. This will be discussed further in chapter 4 on insecurity.

What does a person gain from a satisfactory stage of *extension*? Its benefits include self-confidence, a feeling of security in social settings and about one's own abilities and achievements, skills and accomplishments, good feelings about those with whom one is in contact and feelings of harmony about the outside world. There is also pride in achievement, self-control, the development of talent and skills, conscience and the senses of morality and humour. This is the stage at which a child, though constantly learning and exploring, has no experience or knowledge outside his immediate environment. So he identifies with that environment, which usually means his parents. He absorbs feelings from them. He acquires their standards and values. He learns from them, both knowledge and practical skills.

A healthy stage of *extension* also contains the remnants of the previous stage, *enclosure*, and the beginnings of the next stage, *separation*.

* S. Freud, *On Narcissism*, chapter 4, p. 4.

Basic feelings towards the world, other people and self remain from the previous stage and are for both mother and child the foundation of the stage of *extension*. With this goes an underlying *rapport* and closeness which changes with increasing independence. It embraces occasional rebellion and irritation, but remains as an awareness of needs and ability, the imparting of confidence, optimism, a sense of security and also as a capacity for regression or return to the previous stage at suitable moments.

Also present during this stage is awareness of the next stage. There is a growing sense of the reality of a *separate* being and toler-ance and respect of this along with acceptance of differences and a desire to bring out the emerging person rather than develop the *extension* of the parent. Eventual independence and *separation* is anticipated with equanimity.

Marked features of the stage of *extension* are parental pride, control, the working out and imposition of boundaries and limits, a fitting into a pattern or system. At its best it gives the child a sense of belonging. Therefore the stage of *extension* predominates and works best in certain kinds of traditional upbringing, usually dominated by family. Over most of the Third World it remains the customary pattern, probably tending to be so in any unchanging society. In the west it lingers in pockets, for instance in the traditional middle classes.

EXTENSION AS PART OF A SYSTEM

There are still many parents in the west who regard their children as part of the system of which they themselves are also or would like to be part. All parents hope that their children will grow up to fit into and be part of some form of society. This may be the society in which they themselves live or one in which they think they live or would like to live. Or their expectations may be based on hypothetical ideas about what society will be like or ought to be like for their children.

These parental wishes may be flexible or rigid, realistic or fanciful. But in the world as it is today a clear or inflexible picture of what the child is expected to become or to adapt to is likely to make difficulties for the child, particularly during the difficult transition between adolescence and adulthood. One still finds people who have the idea that children must be moulded to the old order as a means of defending it (i.e., defending their parents) against the new. It is shown in such attitudes as insularity ('Wogs begin at Calais'), or class hostility ('I wouldn't like him to play with "common" children' or 'A posh accent! We'll soon take him down a peg or two').

The idea that children must be moulded to a system helped us to rule our empire. It makes for difficulties nowadays. So do other ideas involving the moulding of children to bygone systems. Today such an upbringing can bring people to the psychiatrist because they have been brought up to fit only into a world that no longer exists. Nevertheless the idea that children must be moulded is still widespread, largely because it is still necessary. Children need to be fit for society and so they need to be fitted for society. But the problem now is what sort of society and what is 'fit' and 'fitted'. It is no longer how to make children submit to society but how to help them to survive in it.

In a traditional society each person grows to play a predetermined part and develops as part of a stable environment. The child develops as did the parent. The parent is part of the society into which the child grows and himself plays a predetermined role in it.

In such a system no one has to relate to anyone else except as part of an assigned or chosen role. The people in it, provided they conform more or less, have no need to confront either themselves or others, nor to question basic attitudes nor to be original, imaginative or individually spontaneous. They live much as did their forefathers and as they expect their descendants to live, and with the same values, expectations, feelings and reactions.

In this country it is not the custom to see the imposition of a traditional system of family domination to anything like the same extent as exists, for instance, in Mediterranean countries. Recently I have seen as patients two Arabs and a Greek, who live in Britain and find themselves in financial difficulties and mental confusion from the moral obligation to send money home for the education of brothers. One would be very unlikely to encounter this situation in a western European. Among British people the system imposed is much more likely to be one of following a family tradition in education, occupation, social and sexual customs, marrying within the group, and so on. Even so, there is likely to be overemphasis on the stage of *extension* at the expense of the other stages. All is geared to the system and there is little room for individual variation. There is often a feeling that the child must go to a particular school or have a particular training. The mother of a four-year-old said to me seriously the other day, 'We bought this house so that he can bring his friends home when he goes to x school,' and it did not seem to have occurred to her that circumstances might change or the boy might not be suitable for the highly academic school they had in mind. Such mothers are likely to be part of the system themselves and only secondly and inadequately people in their own right. She may want to 'get him off my hands' by seeing him safely into the system. Or she regards only certain attitudes, professions, accents, ways of behaving and so on as tolerable.

Wordsworth, deeply entrenched in enclosure feelings, seems to have viewed a desirable stage of extension as one with as little maternal pressure and control as possible. In The Prelude (Book v) he describes a child pressured by extension-type mothering and turned into a 'model of a child', immensely knowledgeable, tender and wiser every day, yet with 'unnatural growth' supported only by vanity and not in harmony either with himself or with nature.

In Wordsworth's time a country childhood probably needed little pressure or personal effort from the parents. Nowadays most children need a great deal of personal effort from their parents during the stage of extension. This is why our society is full of people whose parents overdid the stage of extension and never got beyond it and people whose parents were unable to cope with the stage of extension and left most of it to outside forces, for better or for worse.

The problems of the stage of extension are particularly acute in our society at present. Probably fewer pressures of extension are required from parents than before. Many of the apparent troubles of young people result from their own necessary attempts to break through to the stage of separation so as to achieve independence. Yet the stage of extension is still vital to development. It is further complicated by the fact that our society is changing so rapidly that no one knows what kind of forces of extension are needed.

A magnificent account of mothering of the extension-type based on a social system has been written by H. G. Wells.* His mother had been trained as a lady's maid and she did not have 'the mental flexibility to rise to new occasions . . . By nature and upbringing alike she belonged to that middle class of dependents who occupied situations, performed strictly defined duties, gave or failed to give

* Experiment in Autobiography, Vol. 1.

satisfaction and had no ideas at all outside that dependence. . . .
She clung most desperately to the values she had learnt at Miss
Riley's finishing school; she learnt nothing and forgot nothing
through those dark years spent for the most part in the under-
ground kitchen. . . . She was engaged in a desperate single-handed
battle . . . to keep up appearances.' Wells goes on to tell us: 'I
was never to mix with common children, who might teach me
naughty words' and 'I began to wonder what went on in her brain
when I was in my early teens and I have wondered ever since'.*
He puts this extension-type of mothering in a wider setting and his
mother becomes

a symbol of the blind and groping parental solicitude of that age, a
solicitude which enslaved and hampered where it sought to aid and
establish; and my individual story merges into the story of the handicapped
intelligence of our species, blundering heavily towards the realization and
handling of vast changes and still vaster dangers and opportunities. My
mother becomes a million mothers and my brothers a countless brother-
hood. My life is a sample life and not an exceptional one; its distinctive
merit has been its expressiveness; its living interest lies in that.†

When times change a rigid system no longer provides a secure
framework for life and it no longer supports in the old way.
Anxiety increases. Individuals or whole communities develop fear
of change and resistance to change. This may or may not be recognized openly. The cultural background often becomes the basis for
reactionary tendencies and bewilderment in the older generation
and rebellion, bewilderment or neurosis in young people.

Many of the patients I have seen who have been brought up or
who have brought up their own families to fit into a rigid system
have belonged to the traditional ruling class, with its exclusive
restrictions, strengths and denials and its hidden methods of
communication. If the system works, the traditions and attitudes
that once ruled an empire, or perhaps kept revolution or the papacy
at bay, are perpetuated, often with much power and worldly
success. But if the system does not work, problems arise. For
instance, such parents or teachers may try to force unwilling or
bewildered adolescents to adopt their own values and way of life.
In doing this they often reveal or conceal strong anxiety about what
is happening and what they feel might happen. They feel that, if

* Experiment in Autobiography, Vol. I, pp. 59, 65, 69 and 73.
† ibid., pp. 134–5.

they do not succeed in producing replicas of themselves, their children will be failures which will reflect on them as parents so that they too will be failures. Worse still, the children may become 'drop-outs' or drug addicts, which creates an even more disturbing reflection. Such attitudes can lead to acute conflict in the young person, who either rebels and may do exactly what his parents most fear, or else retreats to a position from which he cannot cope. The system into which he is being forced is not relevant in the outside world and he is unable to resolve the conflict.

One mother never really got over the fact that her son did not stay in the navy as had all his male ancestors. Instead, as soon as his war service was over, he left and went to university. Years later, when he was a successful professional man, his mother still bewailed his defection. 'If you had only stayed,' she would wail, 'you would have had another stripe by now.'

Another mother said to me seriously: 'It's such a pity that one has to send one's boys to boarding school when they are eight. I'm sure it's bad for them but one knows that, if one doesn't send them, they'll never get on in the world.' It did not surprise me that by the time her boy was twelve he was being given tranquillizers and antidepressant drugs from the school doctor.

Alfred, aged fifteen and three-quarters, arrived for an emergency appointment after several anxious letters and telephone calls from parents, backed up by a doctor's letter which said that the boy was 'keeping bad company', 'telling lies', seemed to be 'on drugs', was 'beyond control' and 'constantly hostile' to his parents and all authority. The doctor wrote that Alfred's father was 'particularly depressed about the visible failure of his son'.

But Alfred told rather a different story, which was in fact confirmed by the parents when they were asked to describe exactly what the boy had been doing.

Although his sixteenth birthday was not far off, Alfred was never allowed out in the evening. Even in the daytime he was only allowed to go out for purposes which were first approved by his parents. He had to say exactly where he was going, with whom and what time he would be home. If he was even a minute late his father would be pacing up and down in anxiety and anger. He was only allowed to meet certain boys approved

by his parents, and never any girls, for fear of 'sex'. This was in
1974.

A stronger boy would have rebelled long before. Alfred
was friendly and rather nervous. He loved his parents and
greatly admired his father, even when he was in conflict with
him and felt that he did not understand. He was on the brink
of the modern teenage sub-culture, nervous of plunging into it
and made even more nervous by seeing that any attempt to link
with his own age group would distress his parents to a degree
that alarmed him. He attended a school that was well known for
its intolerant attitude to the current ideas and ideals of the
younger generation. He had not been in serious trouble at school
and had passed required examinations. His 'drug-taking' turned
out to have been one marijuana cigarette shared with friends
at a party nine months before. The 'bad company' consisted
of boys who held left-wing political views. Alfred's father, a
successful businessman, aided by his conforming wife, tried to
control the whole of the boy's development. They could not
bear the idea that 'standards might slip'. They felt it imperative
that the boy follow in his father's footsteps. They could not
tolerate Alfred's own ideas of leaving school. They felt sure that
they were liberal parents because they allowed him to wear his
hair over his ears.

The clue to these parents' behaviour was their own sense of
insecurity and fear of loss of control. This stemmed, as I learned
gradually, from their own relationship and their own back-
grounds and parents. They refused to allow the boy more
freedom and said, 'If we allow Alfred out in the evening, our
whole family life will be threatened and perhaps destroyed.'

Alfred had a tough time developing and finding his own feet
despite his parents. He had to come to terms with his parents'
terror and insecurity as well as with his own. His independence
was partly achieved through an increased understanding of his
parents' feelings of insecurity about him. In a way he had to
learn to be more adult than his parents, giving them comfort
and reassurance to allay parental anxiety.

A frequent problem of those whose stage of *extension* has been
powerful and controlling is that even when they long to achieve
independence and freedom a part of them also wants to be con-

trolled. This makes it even more difficult to break free from their parents. One often finds however that they do achieve it in the end, usually somewhat later than average and often acquiring considerable understanding on the way. Often they are actually aided and abetted by their parents who, controlling though they are, often have a good deal of insight into the problem and indeed often suffered from similar problems themselves. A controlling *extension*-type mother, who was having great difficulty through her teenage daughter's attempts at independence, admitted to me that she herself had not felt free from her own parents until she was over thirty.

Sometimes parents try not so much to force a child into a mould as to protect him or her from the dangers of the world.

Wendy, aged sixteen, was brought up by her mother, a lady of powerful personality. Wendy looked about twelve, scarcely spoke above a whisper, and suffered from anorexia nervosa, which is a form of food refusal with relentless pursuit of thinness. She never went out except *en famille*. She had never been in a bus or train, a town or a shop by herself. She had no close friends at school and the only friend at home whom her mother allowed her to see also suffered from anorexia nervosa. Wendy had artistic talent and would have liked to go to the local art school but this, mother said, was out of the question. There were, apparently, some 'rough types' there and even some 'coloureds'. Wendy must, of course, go to parties and these must be approved by her mother and, preferably, given by her mother's friends. Wendy hated parties, which was not surprising considering her physical and emotional insecurity and her inability to make contact with people of her own age.

Sometimes inadequacy or lack of ability on the part of the young person makes it difficult or impossible for him to follow in father's footsteps, even when he wishes to. For instance our world no longer accepts the natural right of young aristocrats, or even young rugger players, to attend establishments such as Trinity or Christ Church simply because these are part of the family tradition.

David made several attempts while at his public school to pass the examinations necessary before he could be accepted at the famous Oxbridge college attended by his father and several generations before him, in those days without question or proof of ability. But David could not make the grade. His parents were astonished ('Nothing like this has ever disgraced our family before'), and made no allowance for the changes that have taken place in university entrance requirements. They came to the conclusion that their son was a moron and a public disgrace. David was crushed. No alternative seemed possible to him. Life seemed futile and lacking in enjoyment. To his father's anger, despair and shame, David became a 'drop-out', an alcoholic and, eventually, a junkie.

On leaving school, Charles entered his father's firm at the lowest level, destined for rapid promotion. However, his lack of ability and energy and his frequent disappearances on pleasurable excursions cut short a career which, a generation before, might have prospered. His parents, especially his mother, said that he had 'let the side down'. No one seems to have tried to find out what he was good at or capable of, what he might really enjoy doing, or how he might fit into the modern world. He, too, 'dropped out'.

One of the ways in which people with neurotic personalities display their inadequacies is by rigidity and lack of adaptability. Clinging to the past is often a form of rigidity and it is not always easy to distinguish between cultural customs, simple thoughtlessness and neurosis. But in all the cases described above there has been a lack of consideration of the young person as someone in his or her own right, and lack of sensitivity to his personal needs. There has also been an attempt to fit him into a traditional system that is no longer appropriate, an absence of appreciation of the person and a failure to confirm that person.

PERSONAL EXTENSION

Sometimes a prominent stage of *extension* is not supported by a traditional system. The child may be regarded as an *extension* not of a social system but of his parents' own personal system, such as a family business, or an internal belief of the parents.

In a situation rather like *Dombey and Son* a business couple longed for a son who would one day go into business with his father and eventually take it over. When their son was born they were overjoyed and would tell the boy stories of the great days he would have when he was in business with his father. But the boy grew up with other ideas and became a university don. His parents never got over their disappointment. As their son described it, 'My parents only ever saw me as an extension of the business.'

A devout couple felt that the greatest contribution they could make to God would be to produce a son who would devote himself to God and perhaps become a minister. They directed their efforts towards this. But the boy preferred mammon and eventually started his own betting shop.

A pretty young girl, recently married, was longing to produce a pretty little girl like herself, as her sister had done. But she gave birth to an ugly boy who seems unable to help or please her.

A middle-aged woman seemed to believe that her son was her property. She would summon him from his nearby home whenever she wished to see him and she made a point of snubbing his wife, who she had originally chosen for her son.

Another dominating woman lived with her thirty-five-year-old unmarried daughter who hurried home from work each day to spend her spare time with her mother, who never allowed her to go out during the evenings or at weekends.

Sara's mother couldn't stop talking about sex when her daughter became engaged. She described to her with gusto the intimate details of her own unsatisfactory sex life with the girl's father. When the daughter visited a Family Planning Clinic her mother, who had never used contraceptives herself, was fascinated. She demanded first of all to see the appliance with which her daughter had been fitted, then to watch her insert it, and finally to insert it herself.

These vignettes all illustrate parents' emphasis on the second stage of mothering at the expense of the other stages. The children are regarded as *extensions* of the parents rather than as people in their own right. Although in each case *extension* feelings are strong, the parents have failed to provide environments that are flexible, personal, sensitive or imaginative. If the parent fails so totally it is likely that there was also failure at the earliest, *enclosure*, stage, when the child was small and vulnerable. There is no germ of the third stage, *separation*, no idea of setting at a distance in the way that is necessary if human relationships are to be constructive and satisfying as well as close. For the child the extent of his parents' capacity to create this distance will condition his future capacity for human relationships. His capacity to create it for himself will govern his future life.

AMBITION

Ambition is part of the normal stage of *extension*. In most cases parents who have ambition for their children produce successful children whose talents are developed and potentialities fulfilled. A parent with low expectations for a child is likely to produce a child of low achievement. Most parents develop some talents in their children successfully and leave others undeveloped. Most of us, if we look into ourselves, know where this is true. We can develop for ourselves many of those talents which were left undeveloped by our parents. This is often the better way. Parents cannot possibly provide the special conditions necessary to develop all the talents possessed by their children. Much has to be left to the children themselves.

Insufficient *extension* is a form of neglect and may result in the child's failure to achieve what he could have achieved.

There is an important difference between ambition that is part of a normal second stage and ambition which is part of extension-type mothering (or fathering). Normal second stage ambition is geared to what is best for the child. Ambition that is part of extension-type mothering gratifies some inner need of the mother, who uses the child as an *extension* of herself. Thus both may aim high or low, far or near. If one has a child with the potential of Mozart it is not unrealistic to aim high and attempt to provide the most suitable environment to nurture the genius. Such a child needs it, will benefit from it and will suffer if he does not get it. But, even if one's child is a genius, satisfying his genius is not his only need and for the parent to use that genius as an *extension* of himself is just as excessive and unsuitable as to use children of smaller talent. James

Mill was an example of an *extension*-type parent who drove his brilliant son to develop his talent at the expense of himself as a person. The young John Stuart Mill read Greek at the age of three, but he grew up to be an unhappy, lopsided person.

Thus the value of a parent setting high standards which the child can attain depends on what is best for the child and this nearly always means that the parent, entrenched in the stage of *extension*, can reach beyond it to the stage of *separation*. Those who cannot do this are *ipso facto* extension-type parents.

George is a neurotic and able man of humble origins. He has managed, by the skilful use of psychiatrists and drugs, to avoid nervous breakdown and to become the successful managing director of a big company. He has a teenage son, John, whom, he frankly admits, he regards as part of himself. It is essential to George's equilibrium, if not to his son's, that the boy shall be first in everything he attempts. This consists chiefly of school work and golf. When John came home, having been top in all school subjects except one, George was upset and conducted a prolonged and emotional inquiry into this failure. John is also a county golf player and aims at higher things. During matches, though George does not play himself, he stands near his son urging him on, shouting his advice and assuring him that 'winning' is the only thing that matters. He frankly admits that he is incapable of any other course of action and he willingly pays psychiatrists' fees so that his son can be helped to understand and to deal with the situation. John, who is more stable than his father, copes with the situation with skill and understanding. But his father's ambition gives him many problems.

Mothers are often socially ambitious for their daughters.

Typical of these was the mother of Christine. Her mother was determined that Christine, who was seventeen, should rise in the social scale. She made elaborate plans for her to meet 'nice' people and planned details of clothes, entertainments and social events. Meanwhile Christine was busy starving herself. She was undersized and immature in everything except intellect. She had three good A levels but her periods had not yet started. She could talk intelligently in the company of middle-aged people but had scarcely ever met a boy of her own age. She had never held hands, let alone kissed. Any thought of physical contact made her retch. The thought of parties terrified her. Only when her mother was persuaded, with considerable difficulty, that Christine was unsuited to her plans and would be far happier staying at school and working for university did Christine's physical and mental condition improve. Eventually the mother gave way with a good grace and was helpful to Christine in the girl's own, more realistic ambitions.

CONTROL

Mothers who are going through the stage of *extension*, all mothers of predominantly *extension*-type and many of those who are weak in the stage of *extension* are all deeply concerned with questions of control, both excess and lack of it. This is the stage at which control is or is not attained and future patterns of control are laid down. Preoccupation with the subject stems from fear of loss of control.

A certain amount of control is necessary in bringing up children if they are to be safe physically and to feel safe psychologically. Obviously one must control a toddler so that he does not play with fire, poke his fingers into electric sockets, run in the road and so on. The amount of direct control needed to achieve physical safety depends on how easily the child can endanger himself and is likely to do so. If no roads, fires or electric sockets are available, direct control will be less necessary, but is still exerted, for it is often a measure of the mother's personality rather than of rational need. Failure to achieve the amount of physical control that is necessary for safety is usually a sign of weakness at the stage of *extension*.

Control that is necessary for feeling safe psychologically is more complicated. Sometimes small children who have not yet learned to control their own reactions to their feelings feel a need to have this done for them. For instance a small child who is having a tantrum may feel safer if his mother holds and restrains him than if he is left to thrash about on his own. A rebellious teenager may drive his parents to despair by his failure to conform to their standards, yet he may at the same time be longing for them to control him because, although he struggles so hard, he feels lost having to do things for himself. Parents who are frightened of imposing authority or of exerting control sometimes fail their children in this. Such parents are often strong in extension feelings and long for their children to conform to the system but they are weak in the practice of extension.

This occurred in the Sand family. When the younger son Richard was sixteen he started truanting from school, smoking cannabis every day, associating with 'drop-outs', failing to wash or to comply in any way with his mother's orderly household. There were frequent rows at home. The parents were frightened of him. They felt guilty and feared that the way they had brought the boy up had confused him and prevented him from finding himself. They were convinced that they should interfere as little as possible. They gave way as far as they could yet he always pushed them further till they could stand it no more. For instance the more his mother tried to be flexible about meal-times, the less reliable he became. The more his mother tried to tidy up and clean after him, the untidier and dirtier he became. The more tolerant his father was of his behaviour and that of his friends the worse he became and brought home ever more scruffy and badly behaved friends. Sometimes the boy broke down and cried and said that his life was pointless and hopeless. His parents were in despair. However it was obvious that Richard was trying to test himself and trying to find some standard. It was suggested that a certain amount of kindly firmness should replace variable permissiveness and that certain attitudes and behaviour should not be tolerated, even if it meant that Richard sometimes missed a meal or even left home. His mother was alarmed at these thoughts but gradually saw the point. The result was an improvement in Richard's behaviour and in family relationships. There were even occasions when Richard was recognizably sensitive to his mother's feelings, which had never been the case before. He still lounged about, smoked cannabis and kept eccentric hours, but he began to talk seriously about passing examinations and training for a career. When last heard of he had persuaded his father to go with him to an evening course of lectures on Transcendental Meditation.

Failure to control is not the same as having no need to control. Some parents seem to gain their children's co-operation so that the whole concept of control seems irrelevant. Provided this is authentic it is of course desirable. The parents are relaxed and spontaneous and so are the children, who are able to develop in their own way. Sometimes a family appears to be like this on the surface, whereas underneath subtle controlling forces are operating, making the children feel that they are *extensions* of their parents.

The H. family was an example of this. Both parents were clever and literary and much of the conversation at home was on literary subjects. They had three children who all seemed to be remarkably successful and problem-free. The eldest won a scholarship to his father's college and the second child did the same at her mother's college. Both chose to read English though the parents said they would have been happy to see them study other subjects. Both got Firsts, like their parents, followed by research grants and travel scholarships to America. All the family's friends marvelled at the way in which the children seemed to follow effortlessly in their parents' footsteps and choose to do exactly what parents would like their children to do. When the youngest child won his English scholarship to the same college, it seemed too good to be true. But at this point the façade cracked. The elder boy broke down and it was soon obvious that his sister was likely to do the same. He became unable to take even small decisions in his life, broke down and wept at the smallest frustration and devoted all his time to petty activity such as washing up and polishing the letterbox. He said that he felt he had never really had a chance to develop as a person. He didn't know who he was or what he wanted in life. He loved his parents but felt they were always talking about literary topics and avoiding everything personal. He couldn't break free from them. Going along with their wishes had always been so easy for him that only now, at the age of twenty-five, was he beginning to question it.

There is at present a school of thought which advocates constant stimulation of the child, virtually from birth. The result of this is likely to be a raised IQ, educational efficiency and the avoidance of many of the ill-effects of boredom and lack of stimulation. But the technique can be a subtle form of control and if it is used by mothers of the *extension* type who tend to lack spontaneity and sensitivity, it may induce in the child not only loss of his own spontaneity and sensitivity but also lifelong anxiety, probably linked with mental activity.

Most healthy families go through stages when the parents feel that one or more of the children is out of control. This may occur at any age. With babies common problems are food, excreta and general behaviour. With adolescents the common areas of disagreement include co-operation in household affairs and duties, hours and company kept, associates, sexual habits, ideas, clothes, deportment and cleanliness. At present these problems are particularly acute in the western world and there seems almost to be a sorority of teenagers' mothers who sympathize with and support each other, sometimes even vying with each other for the most horrifying 'Aren't they dreadful' story. Should they be allowed to come in at any time? How can I find out whether she is on the pill? Should she be allowed to sleep with her boyfriend in the house? How can I persuade them not to bring their friends in and eat up all the food in the house? and not to spend the entire evening on the telephone? How can I get them to do anything I want them to do?

Failure to control children is a distortion of the stage of *extension*. It may be more than simple inability to do or to perceive what is necessary. There may be a serious lack of *rapport*, or weakness, in the parent, whose child absorbs the weakness. Sometimes failure to control may be due to neglect on the part of the parent or to excessively strong rebellion on the part of the child. Or it may be due to failure at the stage of *enclosure* in which case it is often a subtle kind of collusion between parents and child. A mother who allows her child to mess and damage someone else's property or attack other children, or whose uncontrolled child makes adult conversation impossible, may be using the child to express her own hidden feelings. Often she herself is polite and self-controlled. No one can think why she has such a dreadful child or why she apparently has so little control over him. In reality she may be exerting a powerful control of a devious and rather sinister kind, and is using the child to balance her own feelings in a way that is not at all in his interest. Sometimes the child is used as a weapon against someone else, and this may require no more than simply letting him be himself in surroundings where it suits her purpose. On a number of occasions I have known a mother bring her child to my consulting rooms. The result is usually that no work is done and thus discussion of painful subjects is avoided, which is sometimes the reason why the child was brought. Usually she produces an excuse, 'I'm terribly sorry I had to bring him but he wasn't very well last night/the au *pair* is out/I thought you might like to see him.' It is of course impossible to do psychiatric work when a child is either yelling in the waiting room, clamouring for his mother's attention or wrecking the consulting room.

Excessive control at the second stage of mothering also often involves a relentless concern with minutiae and it also tends to lead to submissiveness and lack of spontaneity. But, symbolically, 'extension' control, in which the mother is controlling an *extension* of herself, is different from 'enclosure' control, in which she is controlling a *part* of herself. A *part* of oneself may be active or passive and it is important that it exists in harmony with the rest. But an *extension* has a purpose and is a means of achievement and something one tends to use. *Extension* mothers who control excessively rule through fear or through guilt or through both. Here the fear induced in the child is not so much of annihilation as of violence, sex, loss of love, spontaneity or of generally losing control. Or sometimes the mother sets such high standards that the child spends the rest of his (or often her) life trying to keep up to them.

> Thomas, aged thirty-seven and unmarried, lived alone and had withdrawn from all personal contacts. He suffered from nightmares, attacks of panic and a strong fear of all forms of violence. He felt that all his life he had been dominated by fear of his mother and, although she had died some years before, the fear persisted. His mother had been a violent woman. Thomas's earliest memory of this violence was of an incident that happened when he was four years old. In his own words he 'had a terrible battle' with his younger brother and shortly afterwards the younger boy developed diabetes. Thomas was instantly blamed for this and, in his own words, his mother 'beat the living daylights out of me'. After this Thomas was frequently violent towards his brother, and his mother retaliated by shouting at him that he was 'naughty and nasty' and beating him. As the boys grew older, the younger had only to say 'Thomas hit me' to provoke an outburst of violence from the mother. As he grew up his mind was constantly filled with visions of violence and he had an unusually strong dislike of all forms of hunting and shooting.

It is well known that parents of both sexes who come to the notice of doctors, social workers and courts of law for 'battering' their children and doing serious physical damage to them tend to demand absolute obedience from their children, together with 'a pathetic demand for clearly expressed love'. As one writer has put it (Renvoize [1974]) the doctor often sees 'a clean, tidy mother and a clean, tidy baby'.

These excessively controlling mothers and families who violate their children psychologically if not physically have been much criticized in recent years, particularly by those who believe that mental illness is not an entity in itself but a defence against such mothers and also by those who are hostile to the family. Some of these seem to equate families of this controlling type with families in general. An example is David Cooper:

> The family specializes in the formation of roles for its members rather than laying down the conditions for the true assumption of identity.
> She glues, say, her son on to herself to be that bit of her self that she feels to be missing ... The son, even if he 'succeeds' in leaving home ... may never become more personally complete than her because he has experienced himself during the most critical years of his 'formation as an appendage to her body ... and to her mind'.*

Extension mothers who have a strong need to control their children are often rigid in personality. Their need to control is rooted in the fear of what might happen if control is lost. The basic fear is usually of making a mess, indulging in some powerful sexual activity or of doing violence. Mothers who have acquired some psychological sophistication may be aware of a desire to do these things.

This can often be followed directly from one generation to the next. The person who exerts great control to avoid mess, powerful sexuality or violence is likely to have had a parent who did the same and is likely to pass it on to his or her own children.

The need to exert this type of *extension* control can also often be apparent almost from the time of the child's birth. These are the mothers who boast about the early age at which their child passed milestones, achieved toilet-training or developed in speech. Such mothers tend to make demands on their children which the children cannot understand. The child can then retain his mother's approval only by learning what he is required to do, without understanding it. This prevents spontaneity and personal development, leads to lack of personal values and ultimately to rigidity in the child.

* *The Death of the Family*, p. 25.

Jean was eight years old and advanced for her age. She had been toilet-trained at a year, learned to read at three and was now neat and organized in everything she did. She was top of the class and never gave any trouble. Apart from rather severe eczema she gave no cause for worry. Her mother was also neat and highly organized. 'I like my house to run like clockwork,' she said. 'At least I can rely on Jean to clean her teeth without being told.'

But Jean gave me an uneasy feeling and I knew that all was not well. A psychiatrist sees too many disturbed adults who were like Jean in childhood to believe that this is normal. But Jean was not the patient. She only came with her mother because her younger brother William was referred by the family doctor because he was 'out of control'. William was seven, rude, disobedient, dirty, offensive to his mother and free with his use of four letter words. He was clearly not going to allow himself to be a controlled *extension* of his mother and he was protesting with his whole self. Although he was going through a tiresome stage, I believe that of the two children he was by far the healthier. He was lively, spontaneous and a person in his own right, asserting himself because he was trying out his self. Some children seem to be irrepressible in spirit.

Controlling mothers of the *extension* type can be deceptively 'modern' in outlook for they often keep up to date assiduously. If the current popular theories say that separation in early childhood leads to neurosis, they will make sure that they are never separated from their children. If 'permissive' is the 'in' word and 'authoritarian' the out-of-date word, they will be obsessionally 'permissive', regardless of the effect on the child, which they are unlikely to notice. One of the most marked characteristics of these parents is their lack of imagination and spontaneity which inevitably involves insensitivity to their children that lies behind their inability to adjust to altered circumstances.

CONTINGENT LOVE

Strong *extension*-type mothering is often part of contingent love. The mother's response to her child is selective. Action, thought and mood are separated. The emphasis may be on any one or on a combination of many things, including motive, effort, results, method, 'being', appearance and selective perception. The child learns to please his mother and therefore to retain her love by orienting himself in the way she propels him. In adult life there are people who continually make efforts apparently regardless of results; many such people are found among bureaucrats and so-called 'dedicated' workers. There are also people geared to achieving results regardless of method, for example ruthless salesmen and politicians. There are people who concentrate exclusively on method, for example those who occupy themselves in research which has little content or aim but which is beautifully designed. Unbalanced concentration on the process rather than on the product or vice versa is a typical result of strong *extension*-type mothering and the form it takes depends on the circumstances. Concentration on performance and results regardless of method and process is common in those who appear to cope with life but actually do so at other people's expense. Concentration on appearances above all else is characteristic of another type of *extension* mothering, described earlier in the chapter.

In all these the core is liable to be lost and emphasis is on the shell. In many cases *extension* totally replaces *enclosure*.

EXTENSION AS ENCLOSURE

Sometimes a mother does not relate to the infant with that part of her instinctual and intuitive self that enables her to *enclose* him as is necessary to a successful first stage. Instead she imposes on him some other part of herself or of her husband or family aimed at control, achievement, allaying her own anxiety or enlarging her (and her husband's) sphere of operation. Some parents attempt to impose a personal or family pattern on even a young infant. They may, for instance, give him his father's christian name or one that is patently absurd. They may anxiously await signs of existent family characteristics and talents to emerge, put the child down for a particular school or club, disregarding possible variations in his future development. Or a mother may dress an infant in a way that enhances her own appearance or which appears in some way to glorify her. Such actions are rarely accompaniments of a successful first stage of mothering.

Some parents exercise a kind of control over their children that is

a mixture of *enclosure* and *extension*. For instance they may be forbidden
to watch television or to read comics. Or the parents may vet films
before allowing their children to see them. One girl was taken
out half-way through *Camelot* while the plot was still happy. Her
mother could not bear her to stay on to the end and witness the
break-up of the marriage, etc.

Sometimes a twisted stage of *extension* tries to embrace both
other stages. In such a case the mother is also unable either to
identify with her child or to let him go.

Mrs W. was an impressive lady of wealthy Eastern European
origins. After the war she gathered her surviving relatives
together and exerted power over them. Many were dependent
on her. Her own four children were part of her empire. She
ruled them as *extensions* of herself, she chose their careers, their
wives, their houses. An unusual trait was that, although she was
passionately Jewish herself, she insisted, and organized, that all
her children married non-Jews. It seemed that she felt that the
presence of other Jewish people in her family would be a threat
to her omnipotence. Quiet and inoffensive non-Jewish young
people were more to her liking. But of course these quiet,
conforming young men and women eventually matured and
rebelled. All the marriages broke up. Mrs W.'s own children all
had difficulty in coping with ordinary life, they were all centred
on their mother, unable to take decisions and inclined to become
obsessed with personal interests at the expense of what others
might consider more important. One of them became obsessed
with raising money for distant famines until his own wife left
him. Another became addicted to psychoanalysis and underwent
one analysis after another, each of a different school. The whole
family history is a sad story of people struggling to make contact
with origins that constantly repel them.

David's mother was always trying to participate in his body
functions as if this was her only means of communicating with
her son, who was the centre of her life. She was deeply involved
with everything he ate and with his stomach, gut and bowels.
He was grown up before she stopped asking him whether he
had 'been', and at the age of thirty-five he still lived with her
and submitted automatically every evening to her close question-

ing on such matters as his day at the office, and what he had eaten for lunch. I felt that she treated him as an *extension* that was *enclosed* within her. As a result of this he felt unable to function socially, professionally or sexually. He had no existence as a separate being.

SELF-ENHANCEMENT

Self-centred people are only aware of others in so far as they concern themselves. When they become mothers they organize their children to enhance their own looks, personalities or worldly success. Such a mother usually likes the idea of producing a child who will bring her credit. She is unaware of the needs of the child. Like all children of *extension* mothers the child tends to respond by trying to please the mother. He does this by trying to become the sort of person he imagines that she wants him to be.

These maternal feelings are to some extent present in all normal mothers as well as in those who are unusually self-centred. Some mothers, like Daisy in *The Great Gatsby*, dress their children to offset themselves. Some make them recite or perform to their friends, or dress them up to be little waiters and waitresses to adorn a dinner party. Often such mothers strongly deny anything concerning their children that does not suit them. For instance Clare was caught stealing at school. The evidence was incontrovertible. Her mother refused to believe it on the grounds that 'She is my daughter and I know that no daughter of mine could do such a thing'. She preferred to believe that the other children or even teachers had framed her daughter.

Some mothers who regard their children as self-enhancing *extensions* of themselves are obsessional about the child's achievement. They may be dedicated to some kind of personal success with the child, such as extensive linguistic development, exceptionally early reading, or the fostering of some talent. Such mothers try to gain credit for themselves from the child. They may idealize the child, misinterpret evidence and exert pressure.

Miss Jones was bringing up an illegitimate son alone and experienced this as a challenge. She was determined to show the world what she could do. One day, when the boy was eight, a teacher remarked casually to Miss Jones that her son had a good ear and seemed to be musical. Immediately Miss Jones mapped out in her imagination a great musical career for her son. She wrote to all the music schools, tried to get the local education authority to pay for extra lessons to bring out his special talent, and talked about it a great deal both to the boy and to her acquaintances. Everyone else could see long before Miss Jones that the boy was not fulfilling his musical promise, if indeed he ever had any. Finally he was rejected by a school that laid emphasis on musical education on the grounds of insufficient talent. Immediately Miss Jones was making plans for him to become a famous doctor.

Some mothers use their children to enhance their own social position or success. This is a variety of self-enhancing *extension* mothering that children are most likely to see through.

Margot is preparing for her wedding, which is being organized by her mother who sees it as an opportunity to demonstrate her power in the district and to further her social position. She has taken the utmost care to invite 'all the right people', and she tends to argue if Margot suggests the name of someone whom she, as the bride, would like to invite. Margot and her fiancé would have liked a quiet wedding with the guests consisting largely of their personal friends. Margot is annoyed at the way in which her mother is trying to turn the wedding to her own social advantage. However she is philosophical and has decided to hand over the day to her mother in return for what she hopes will be a lifetime of freedom. Margot has escaped from her unenviable role of instrument to her mother. She is free and independent and has her own life, and is in command of herself.

To some extent all self-enhancing mothers act deviously and pretend that what they do is for the child's good. They have to do this because this is what society demands.

WEAK EXTENSION

Some mothers are weak at the *extension* stage. This may be because they have not progressed beyond the stage of *enclosure*. I have already described mothers who do not reach the stage of *extension* because they are capable only of *enclosure*. There are also others who, after what is apparently a successful stage of *enclosure* which is now ending, are unable to go through to the next stage. They may lack the necessary feelings and characteristics, and this may show in a variety of ways. They may have a personal dislike of the difficulties of the second stage such as finding the child's company tedious. Some mothers, even though they can live harmoniously with babies, find small children intolerably boring, especially their conversation and their need for repetition. As a result the mother, who is often literate and educated herself, may fail to talk to the child or to stimulate him. As one such mother put it, 'I really can't bear the conversation of anyone under the age of five.' She was going through a difficult period with children aged two and three although she had greatly enjoyed their babyhood.

Other mothers may be happy conversing with very young children but find their behaviour intolerable. They may be unable to accept their growing independence, which may seem threatening to them after the years of babyhood over which they felt they had control. More commonly they dislike the mess. The mess of babies can be largely controlled, contained in napkins and in small eating areas. The mess of toddlers is endless and ubiquitous. Mothers who have strong feelings about mess and fears of losing control find this difficult. Some of them suffer considerable strain. Some of them are remarkably successful (if one can use such a word to describe it), passing on to their small children their own deep fears of mess and, as we have seen, these are the strong *extension*-type mothers. But others, with the same fear and distaste in relation to mess, find that they are unable to control it at all. Weak and helpless they look on in bewilderment and the stage of *extension* is passed in a state of impotent chaos.

There are other mothers, also weak in the stage of *extension*, who are strongly *separate* by nature. They may or may not have been able to feel the baby as part of themselves but they are unable to regard other people, even their own small children, as *extensions* of themselves. One such mother described how once her child could talk her whole feeling towards him changed. She felt he was now a person in his own right, entirely *separate* from her. She knew intellectually that he was still dependent on her and she felt morally obliged to be responsible for him, but she did not in any way identify with him or feel him as an *extension* of herself. Sometimes, when the stage of *extension* is reached, the child is rejected outright. Occasionally a mother may walk out on the child or, more frequently, neglect him for a new baby. Usually the rejection is subtle and may take the form of lack of pride or interest in the child, little attempt to understand him or help him to develop, learn or gain control.

The effects of these attitudes on the child include loss of orientation and feelings of strangeness or even of being a foreign body. Sometimes the child develops a kind of reversed narcissism, feeling ugly in relation to everyone else's beauty, feeling that he has failed and caused disappointment or been discarded, or feeling that he is the wrong sex. It can also induce in the child a loss of spontaneity and also a kind of pathological self-preoccupation. There may be excessive masturbation and a lack of interest outside the self. There may be an overdeveloped and premature sense of autonomy, or a feeling of belonging to a system rather than being a person.

Sometimes the stage of *extension* appears to proceed normally and adequately but it ends prematurely or does not extend into the stage of *separation* as is usual. Most mothers continue to feel proud and supportive towards their children long after those children are adults, and most mothers are prepared to resume the stages of *extension* and *enclosure* at times when these are needed. But some mothers are unwilling or unable to do this. For them the maternal tie is more or less cut at the end of the stage of *extension*. Sometimes this is mostly to do with the personality of the mother, sometimes with the behaviour of the child and often an interaction between the two.

Sometimes there is insufficiency in the stage of *extension* following inadequacy of the first stage. There are mothers who are *separate* mothers from the time the child is born. These really belong to the next chapter.

TRANSITION FROM EXTENSION TO SEPARATION

The transition from the stage of *extension* to the stage of *separation* usually takes place during the child's adolescence. It is the period when the mother, unless she has younger children on whom to concentrate and through whom to delay the final *separation*, has to face herself, decide who she is and what she wants to be and do for the rest of her life. If she has enjoyed being a mother or if she has used her children to defend herself against her own inadequacies and inability to cope with life, she will experience a sense of loss.

Unless she is already established as a person in her own right or is by nature a *separate* mother, she is likely to experience anxiety, which may be an attempt to ward off the third stage. She may also feel depression and despair, as if the next stage holds no future. Many of the problems attributed to the 'change of life' are actually problems about giving up the stage of *extension* for the stage of *separation*.

5. The Third Stage: Separation

A mother who is really a mother is never free.
Honoré de Balzac

A child's a plaything for an hour.
Mary Lamb, *Parental Recollections*

The stage of *separation*, reached after healthy stages of *enclosure* and *extension*, is the ultimate mutual achievement of mother and child. Many never reach it. Whole cultures don't require it. In our society at present there is a special need for it. This is because survival, both social and psychological, is less certain and less automatic than formerly and so depends greatly on individual development. There are special reasons why this is so in an advanced technological society and in a rapidly changing world. Many of our present problems are associated with a failure to achieve the third stage.

The stage of *separation* is the psychological counterpart of childhood. Childhood is the state of having recently become physically independent of parents. In our society the stage of *separation* usually predominates after the age of eleven or twelve. Mother and child are still strongly attached to each other but are free. Each now recognizes the other as a separate individual. These feelings increase on both sides until the child is grown up and the pattern is set for the future relationship between two adults, each living their own lives, making their own successes and mistakes, until death. The childish dependent relationship gives way to the adult relationship, which is independent with a personal link. Home, from being in itself the environment, supplying total support and a good deal of control, becomes the background to the environment, supportive, caring, advisory rather than controlling, and not interfering. The outside world is no longer a place unknown to be gazed upon from the security of the home environment but the place in which one has to find out who one is and what one wants to be and in which one has to establish oneself to find one's place, and make one's own decisions and mistakes. The sense of security is now carried within the self and no longer needs the constant support from outside that is necessary to a young child. With this inner sense of security comes freedom for exploration, adventure and increasing mastery. Between mother and child there is increasing respect for the individual, an increasing interest in what is new and different and a sense of personal enrichment and freedom on both sides.

In the last chapter I suggested that Freud had little or no idea of the stage of *separation*. His view was traditional, i.e. he had no expectation of great change between one generation and the next. He held the views of his time and culture about women, and felt that a woman's relationship with her son was the highest achievement of which she is capable. He wrote:

A mother is only brought unlimited satisfaction by her relation to a son; this is altogether the most perfect, the most free from ambivalence of all human relationships. A mother can transfer to her son the ambition which she has been obliged to suppress in herself.*

As the distance between Freud's world and ours increases such statements, increasingly, seem to be anachronistic or relevant only to a particular section of the community rather than basically or eternally true. The Viennese middle classes on whom Freud worked out his theories did not need to reach the stage of *separation* in the way it is needed today. In societies where women are generally regarded as inferior to men it is difficult to achieve the stage of *separation*. A woman who regards herself as inferior to men or who is regarded by her family as such is not likely to be capable of achieving this stage of *separation* because among its essential ingredients are personal respect and a sense of distance.

In Freud's lifetime Martin Buber, another Jewish writer, described these matters differently. In I and Thou (1923) he defines what he calls the I–Thou relationship, which involves essentially a respect for the other based on distance. Later he developed the theme in a slightly different way (*Distance and Relation* [1937]). He believes that human life is built up in a twofold movement: firstly, 'the primal setting at a distance' and secondly, 'entering into relation'. One can only enter into relationship with a being which has been set at a

* *New Introductory Lectures*, p. 168.

distance, he says, and thus 'become an independent opposite', and he calls this process 'distancing', and believes that it is the necessary preliminary to a satisfactory life:

> In human society, at all its levels, persons confirm one another in a practical way, to some extent or other, in their personal qualities and capacities and in a society members confirm one another . . . The basis of man's life with men is twofold, and it is one – the wish of every man to be confirmed as what he is, even as what he can become, by men; and the innate capacity in man to confirm his fellow-men in this way. That this capacity lies so immeasurably fallow constitutes the real weakness of the human race: actual humanity exists only where this capacity unfolds. On the other hand, of course, an empty claim for confirmation, without devotion for being, again and again mars the truth of life between man and man.

A healthy stage of *separation* does not predominate until the child is ready for it, and it is based on previous healthy stages of *enclosure* and *extension*, the remnants of which remain as part of the stage of *separation*.

The remnants of the stage of *enclosure* which are found in the healthy state of *separation* include a sense of self, of security, and a capacity for *rapport* and self-awareness. Moreover the mother is always aware that in some ways her child is still part of her, however adult he is and however much she is conscious of him as a separate person. If he suffers, she suffers. If he is ill, she feels the pain. If he is unhappy, it afflicts her too. There remains the capacity to return to an earlier stage at appropriate times, for example during illness or crisis.

The stage of *extension* persists into a healthy stage of *separation* in the form of constructive pride, beliefs, moral values and the potentiality for reversal of roles. As the mother becomes old and the child middle-aged there is normally some reversal of their former roles and in some cases this can be marked or extreme. 'She's like a child. I have to look after her,' is a not uncommon feeling or statement by a middle-aged son or daughter.

More than the two other stages, the development of the stage of *separation* is associated with anxiety, pain and a sense of loss. The first stage, *enclosure*, is of course established automatically and if it is normal there is no pain attached to it and it has nothing to lose. A normal second stage, *extension*, blends with the first and may be difficult to distinguish from it. Pain and anxiety may be experienced during this stage but they are not associated with establishing the stage itself. They may distort it, prolong it or prevent further development. But the stage of *separation* involves a gap and it is probably impossible for it to develop normally without anxiety, pain and a sense of loss. It follows that those who are incapable of enduring anxiety, pain and a sense of loss are incapable of achieving a normal stage of *separation*.

Much of the anxiety, pain and sense of loss that is part of the development of the stage of *separation* is similar in both mother and child. It concerns *separation* and facing the future. Both mother and child are likely to react to this in whatever way became customary to them in the past, going right back to infancy. So infantile anxiety and maternal anxiety turn out to be the same in origin and much the same in feeling. In addition the young person has to deal with the anxiety associated with the rapid changes in body and development of mind. The world is unknown to him and his future is uncertain. His anxiety is likely to be greater than his mother's. Hers is likely to be greater with a first and last child than with middle children. It is likely to be greatest when she has become emotionally dependent on her children. If her anxiety is considerable it will increase that of her child's and may cripple him and prevent him from attaining independence.

The pain associated with the establishment of the stage of *separation* in both mother and young person is the pain of severing old ties. The sense of loss is for the loss of the baby and small child, the loss of dependence, the loss of the closeness of the past, the safety of *enclosure* and the satisfaction of *extension*. The pair may be tempted to stick together, to avoid the bad feelings, the pain and anxiety. Many examples will be found in these pages.

In normal mother–child couples the pain and anxiety and loss are accompanied by anticipatory joy and exploratory satisfaction, particularly for those whose enjoyment of what is new is unimpaired. There is also a growing sense of freedom and an increased flexibility and capacity for choice. But all these can add to the burdens of those who cannot face what is new and different or who find choice a problem. At present, when society is changing so rapidly that each generation is very different from the last, the mothers and children who manage best are those who can endure the difficulties of their mutual period of change.

Certain characteristics are necessary before anyone can achieve the stage of *separation*. This applies both to mothers and to their children.

The first necessary characteristic is the capacity to regard other people as *separate* persons. This is the result either of having been regarded as *separate* oneself or else of exceptional mental powers resulting in one's own achievement of that state. For most people it is largely a function of the way in which their mothers were themselves mothered. If the mother's mother continued to regard her as a part or as an *extension* of herself beyond the normal age, she is likely to have difficulty in regarding herself, and therefore her child, as *separate*. The achievement of *separation* on one's own requires special talents, perception, concentration and capacity to endure anxiety and suffering. Anyone who can achieve it is likely to be exceptional in quality and personality. H. G. Wells in his auto-biography describes his own escape from his *extension*-type mother and his achievement of personal distance. He attributed it to 'a broken leg and some books and pictures'. In fact, as a result of his accident, he found himself in the freedom of a beautiful country house and its excellent library. Here he developed his own inde-pendence in a way that would have been impossible in the restrictive environment of his own family.

Other people have found their freedom and themselves in physical freedom and the availability of other, interested adults. The most important of these adults are probably teachers. Many young people have found their eyes opened and the world at their feet as the result of an inspiring teacher at school and university. Some teachers have a genuine vocation for playing this role.

The second characteristic necessary for achieving the stage of *separation* is the ability to foresee the likely consequences of events and actions. This is largely a measure of the capacity for observation and assessment, a sense of logical sequence and little tendency to falsify experience for personal gain.

The third characteristic necessary for achieving the stage of *separation* is an understanding of time and place which underlies the capacity to delay satisfaction and to tolerate anxiety and frustration. Without this there can be no distancing and no respect.

The mother who has strong feelings of *enclosure* and *extension* and yet who manages to achieve the stage of *separation* is likely to be the best mother of all. She has a firmer basis of *enclosure* than most of those who achieve *separation* more easily, and this gives her child security and a sense of harmony. She has a strong sense of *extension*, for this was the way she escaped from over-*enclosure*, and this gives her child wider security and a sense of family and community. Yet, on top of all this, she now loves and appreciates her child as a *separate* person, perhaps very different from her and different from her earlier hopes and dreams. She rejoices for him. She has matured as a mother.

Here is an example of a mother who had to struggle to reach the stage of *separation*. Sandra had grown up in a family with little love or affection. Her father was insensitive, overpowering and impossible to communicate with. 'If I asked him even for simple information,' she said, 'he would shout at me and tell me not to be impertinent.' Her mother was withdrawn and *separate*. Her two brothers were much older and away from home during most of her childhood. She longed for children of her own, whom she could love and who would love her. After her marriage she became happy as never before. She had four babies in rapid succession. For years she felt that she wanted to live for ever with a toddler at her skirts. As a mother she had found her strength, her vocation and her security. The children were *part* of her. The children were *extensions* of her. She loved it all and her husband and children loved her. But one day she was faced with teenage rebellion. Her older children left home. She felt bereft and insecure and for several years she was treated by her doctor for 'depression'. But gradually she came to understand the truth, to recognize that her children were *separate* beings who were loved but who must lead their own lives. Her emotional dependence on them, a compensation for the lack of love in her own childhood, was delaying not only their maturity but also her own. Sandra grew up herself. She became more independent. She took up outside interests. She enjoyed life more. Her children enjoyed her more.

Some mothers cannot reach the stage of *separation*. They include those who are still and perhaps permanently absorbed in the earlier stages of *enclosure* and *extension*. Many are unable to appreciate or even to imagine their children as other than *parts* or *extensions* of themselves. Others appear to be aware of the importance of the stage of *separation* but only pay lip-service to it. As one such mother said solemnly, 'It's important that they make their own decisions but it's more important that they make decisions we approve of.'

Many mothers have strong personal motives for not reaching, or allowing their children to reach, the stage of *separation*. This may be because they themselves depend emotionally on their children.

Mrs Foster, an *extension* mother, was a devoted wife and mother. The family lived in the suburbs, rather a long way from shops, schools and public transport. Mr Foster worked long hours and Mrs Foster's entire life centred on the children. Every day she walked with them to school, twenty minutes each way, morning and afternoon. She insisted that they came home to lunch, to make sure, she said, that they ate properly, but in reality to fill her time with their care. She boasted that she walked eight miles every day. She refused to allow them to cross the road alone even at pedestrian crossings. She also kept herself constantly involved in their lives. She entertained their many friends but had none of her own. She looked after the garden and the children's many pets. People admired her and commented on her devotion to her family but others could see she seemed to live in a fantasy world of frenzy for her children. She had no life of her own and no resources to fall back on. Tension arose between her and her husband. When her children grew up and left home her life was empty. She lost interest in her house, garden and animals and neglected them. She tried to break up her son's marriage. She became desperate, hysterical and finally secretly alcoholic. When her alcoholism was discovered and attempts were made to help her she tried to use it as a means of persuading her daughter to give up her job in London and come home to look after her. She showed no interest in her treatment except in so far as she could use it to bring her children home.

Many mothers who display this kind of emotional pattern break down sooner than did Mrs Foster, perhaps when the last child goes to school. They may insist on their children coming home to midday dinner, and they may even induce in the children a dislike of school food or an inability to eat anything except at home. Their children, if they are ever to be free, have to do the work themselves.

SEPARATE MOTHERS

For some mothers *separateness* is a state that exists in them rather than a stage that has been achieved. In a way they do not go through the three stages but are permanently *separate*.

In chapter 1 we saw that there is a basic conflict in mothering. The child is an independent person and yet is part of the mother. The mother is an independent person and yet is the child's environment. This conflict of love and distance has to be resolved before the real person can emerge. Far from resolving it, these mothers never even reach it. They include those who are unable to regard other people as persons, unable to foresee the likely consequences of events and actions or unable to delay satisfaction or to tolerate anxiety and frustration. These mothers are unable to value a loved person more than themselves or to respect anyone as an independent being.

One young mother often left her young children alone in the house when she went out with her friends.

Another was longing for her son to go to school because she wanted him out of the way. 'He'll be off my hands' was the way she put it.

A married couple departed on their holiday abroad three days before their nineteen-year-old son was due to be committed for trial on a serious charge.

Another mother feared what the neighbours might think if they knew that her son was mentally ill. Even though she had been told that he was in danger of committing suicide, she tried to persuade him to discharge himself from hospital against medical advice because she was ashamed of his being there.

These are all examples of mothers who were predominantly *separate* mothers, i.e. they had not reached the *separate* state via early stages, or had only done so to a very limited extent. Sometimes the background to the *separate* mother is determined by the traditions of social class.

My mother always seemed to be a fairy princess: a radiant being possessed of limitless riches and power . . . She shone for me like the evening star. I loved her dearly – but at a distance. My nurse was my confidante . . .*

Sometimes the mother is clearly working out her own problems or appears to be lacking in maternal feelings.

My mother rarely came up on deck and in general avoided us. She remained as silent as ever. To this day I remember her tall, handsome figure, her grim, dark face with its heavy crown of fair braids – all her strength and hardness, seen as though through a fog or a bright cloud. And across the years comes the unfriendly gleam of her grey eyes, . . .†

A young woman who had recently given birth to her first baby, turned against him. 'My husband doesn't love me,' she said defiantly. 'So why should I love the baby?'

'My children are still at the stage of only needing to be fed at one end and wiped at the other, so why should I bother to be there?' This remark was made by a woman doctor with a successful professional career ahead of her. Luckily not many mothers are as callous or obtuse as she. Even when they know that they are unsuited to full-time mothering or even to being mothers at all, most mothers put a great deal of effort and love into their children, and there may be benefit to all because the mother is being honest to herself about her own needs.

Struggling to be a good mother without the appropriate feelings usually means using mental activity as a substitute. This usually involves trying to deal with anxiety by intellectualization. Sometimes the development of authentic maternal feelings is actually prevented by intellectual activity. These mothers are usually diligent and many of them are frequent attenders of general practitioners, paediatricians, clinics and social workers. They buy baby books and magazines galore, thrive on the whole idea of 'techniques' of baby and child care, and are always searching for advice from outside rather than for their own feelings and intuition. They tend to fall for the current conventional wisdom in child care and, if they manage to find and use their feelings at all, they do this by intellectual means which in turn tend to block their feelings. Common questions asked by such mothers are 'How do you think I

* Winston Churchill, *My Early Life*, p. 12.
† Maxim Gorky, *Childhood*, p. 14.

ought to deal with this problem?', or even the more abstract 'How much should one think about mothering?' There is a tendency to overvalue thought because of lack of feeling or failure to be in touch with feeling. Intellectualization is a powerful personality trait and, if it is troublesome, it is usually difficult (and also exhausting) for a psychiatrist to tackle successfully. Intellectuality as a problem in this sense seems to be commoner in Americans than in British people. It is probably linked with the American habit of attending psychiatrists and believing in them. One of the hazards of psychotherapy is that, unless it is practised with unusual skill, it tends to encourage intellectual understanding. Although this is often a prerequisite to emotional understanding and development, it is also a powerful defence against achieving it. There are few patients who induce a feeling of helplessness and hopelessness in the doctor as much as the patient (often American) who has had years of 'therapy', knows all the answers in theory and is unable to do anything about them. In such a patient the defences against true understanding seem to have become part of the structure of the personality and are often so highly organized that one can do little to help.

Many intellectual mothers are anxious about their children's mental development. They watch the baby closely for every milestone, compare his progress and conceptual capacity with what the books say and with that of other children and do all they can to increase his vocabulary. Intellectual mothers know that at present experts in child care insist that rigid toilet-training is bad for a child so in this they tend to be rigidly permissive. But most experts at present are keen on language development. 'Bathe your child in language from the time he is born' is today's conventional wisdom. The intellectual mother tends to obey this with delight. She may take a pride in the size of her child's vocabulary or make sure that he learns a certain number of words each day. She takes great trouble to prepare him for school and to help him once he is there. She probably has a programme of reading to him and keeps abreast with developments in children's literature. Feeling, *rapport* and spontaneity tend to be smothered by words.

Mental activity is the most important means by which an infant or child makes up for inadequacies of mothering and for other deficiencies in his environment. This is why children of good intellectual capacity on the whole survive deprivation better than those less gifted. They are better able to solve problems and find their own way out. But they often have to carry the burden of an intellectuality of the kind I have been describing which may, like most character traits, develop either as a reaction to difficulty or else in direct imitation, usually of a parent.

Grace was born and raised in Manhattan, the only child of unwilling parents. Her father was in business and her mother was a successful actress who was seldom at home and had little time or feeling for Grace. Grace spent much of her childhood alone and lonely. Her parents were not intellectual but her grandmother, who lived near by, had many books. Grace became an avid reader. 'Everything I know, I learned from books,' she said. She did outstandingly well at school and won a scholarship to a famous women's college. There she had her first breakdown, followed by seven years of psychoanalysis. She had read all Freud's works and most of the published psychoanalytical literature. She had had long discussions with her analyst on such topics as the value of mental stimulation in infancy and the effects of career mothers on the Electra complex. She obtained an academic post and married another academic. When she became pregnant she found the process 'interesting' but she did not care for infants. She tried to talk to her baby from birth but was irritated by his lack of response. 'I can't bear anything under six,' she said. 'After that at least you can talk to them.' Her child was highly intelligent and by the time he was about six mother and son had a close, interdependent *rapport* based entirely on verbal interaction. They avoided physical contact and engaged in earnest conversation on such topics as the American constitution and space travel.

Grace is an example of intellectuality developed as a defence against loneliness and lack of emotional contact. Her own mother was a *separate* mother. Her son is an example of intellectuality developed by direct absorption from his mother and imitation of her. The mother indicated to him the only way in which she felt she could make a *rapport* with him and he complied.

Not all children are so compliant.

Jennifer is a young Englishwoman who reminded me of Grace. Of impeccable academic background, she gave up the chance of a university fellowship to marry. Jennifer very much wanted children and as her husband had an excellent job she had no need to work. She spent a few hours most days writing a learned book and this satisfied her intellectual needs. The rest of her time she devoted to her family, on whom she tried to impose a formidable intellectual control. She would have loved to introduce the children to literature and discuss intellectual matters with them, but they resisted this. One of them developed severe asthma and much of the energy of both mother and child became involved in managing this. The second child, a six-year-old boy, became unruly and unmanageable. Although he had a high IQ (women of Jennifer's type usually know their children's IQs), he was not interested in reading or learning. He was most interested in making a noise, asserting himself, and obtaining illicit food. Jennifer was bewildered and frantic. She tried to reason with him but when she talked to him he either ran away or put his hands over his ears. He made dangerous expeditions to forbidden places such as the bus station and across the main road and told his mother that since no harm had come to him it showed that she was wrong. Jennifer tried in vain to explain to him the significance of fallacies of relevance. She herself confused her priorities. She was just as upset when she found biscuits hidden in his room (because, she said, he had taken them without permission and because it increased the likelihood of mice in the house) as she was when he ran dangerously across the main road. Her maternal feelings were not absent or entirely unavailable but they were stifled by her thought processes, and in effect these made her a *separate* mother, without *rapport*.

Many intellectual mothers never really go through either of the first two stages of mothering. Such a mother never feels her children as part of her, or as *extensions* of her. From birth, and often before, she regards them as *separate*. She is likely to emphasize the importance of the child being a person in his own right, and she is often coldly clinical in her appraisal of him. She is often a rather rigid person and unable to show warmth or spontaneity. She may behave towards her child more as a psychotherapist than a mother, and conducts the relationship with her child by producing 'interpretations' rather than reactions. Indeed many such people take up the profession of psychotherapy or gravitate towards it.

Mrs J. was a psychoanalyst. One day she read a paper at a meeting of a professional society. In it she described in clinical language a near-psychotic child whom she had treated. It was the story of a lonely, isolated, disturbed, frightened child and the way in which Mrs J. 'interpreted' to him whatever he did and how dependent he became on her. There was no suggestion of warmth or personal involvement. Only later did her colleagues learn that the boy described in Mrs J.'s paper was her own son.

Some mothers are *separate* only because they are absent, perhaps even dead. An absent mother is *ipso facto separate* and her child's relationship with her is his own fantasy, thus stimulating his mental activity. A mother who is partially absent, perhaps through work or social custom, is not necessarily *separate*. She may have close feelings of *rapport* with her children and may be successful in all three stages of mothering, particularly if she was not absent too much during the first stage.

Mothers who are absent in spirit are more likely to be *separate* in the sense used here than are mothers who are absent for part of the time. They may be more involved in their own interests and emotional needs than in those of their children. One woman told me 'For five years I sat outside the pub while my mother was inside until one day a man came up and gave me a dirty postcard.' Sometimes the mother is neurotic and self-absorbed. A *separate* mother was remembered thus by her son: 'You could come into a room and feel it was empty. She just sat there looking beautiful.'

Some *separate* mothers use their children as instruments or toys and in so destructive a way that one could not even say that they are regarding them as parts of themselves. Edith Sitwell seems to have had such a mother: 'My eighteen-year-old mother had thought she was being endowed with a new doll – one that would open and shut its eyes at her bidding, and say "Papa", "Mama". I was un-satisfactory in those ways, as in every other.'

Some of these mothers also have a need to control excessively. Edith Sitwell's tried to do this by continually making threats, such as that she would throw little Edith out of the window. These are some of the saddest and most disastrous of all mother–child couples. If one needs to control someone whom one regards basically as *separate* from oneself one develops a manipulative relationship and uses that person for one's own ends in a way that can have no value for anyone. The person who has been over-controlled by a mother who regards him as part of herself is likely to feel smothered, but he is probably loved and usually achieves some kind of harmony with his mother. The person who has been over-controlled by a mother who regards him as an *extension* of herself may end up adapted contentedly to the same system that supports his parents and gives them their *raison d'être*. But the person who is over-controlled by a mother who regards him as *separate*, is not loved, but is being used as a thing and dehumanized. This is particularly true when the part of the mother that is controlling is also the part of her that regards him as *separate*. It is less true when a mother who has achieved the stage of *separation* has retained a certain need for control that is left over from one of the earlier stages.

Mrs K. was quite a different type of mother. She had taken little interest in her twin daughters and felt that they were no part of her. They had been brought up from birth by her sister, who cared for them well. Mrs K. and her husband parted. She drifted round the country with a series of men, and finally settled down. By now her daughters were eleven years old and at this stage it seems to have occurred to Mrs K. that they would need little care and could be useful to her. She claimed them, took them to live with her, bought them identical dresses to match one of hers, proudly showed them off to her friends, expected them to do all the housework and shopping, and vigorously opposed all attempts by their foster parents to keep contact with them. Mrs K. is an example of how the stages of mothering can vary not only in quality but also in the order in which they are experienced. Mrs K. regarded her children as *separate* when a normal mother would have been going through the stages of *enclosure* and *extension*. When they were at the age when ordinary devoted mothers are gradually developing into the stage of *separation*, Mrs K. was moving backwards and, by exerting her particular kind of control, was forming what was really a travesty of the stage of *extension*, devoid of advantage for the children.

Like Mrs K., Mrs E. had never been through the first two stages of mothering. After her first child was born she declared proudly to her friends and relatives that she had no 'mother instinct'. She left the upbringing of her son and daughter to whoever would take an interest in them and her husband played a much more maternal role in the children's lives than she did. When they went to school she seldom bothered to attend school functions and during the holidays she did as little as possible for them. Her daughter described her childhood as 'lonely and boring', and the children hardly knew their mother at all. But after their father died and they were both married, their mother, now ageing and weakening, began to take an active interest in them and to interfere, sometimes forcibly and grossly, in their lives. She played on the guilt feelings locked up inside her children left over from their sad, deprived childhood and began to dominate their lives to her own advantage.

Some mothers are not really lacking in the capacity to achieve the stage of *separation* but tend to act prematurely. Often this is when under strain. During the war many children suffered from the feeling that they had to look after mother and be responsible for her while Daddy was away at the war.

Robert, aged nine, was brought to the doctor because he could not sleep. It turned out that he was so terrified that something might happen to his mother while his father was away that he felt he must not relax his vigilance at all. He was terrified of going to sleep in case someone kidnapped her.

A woman with a difficult marriage or financial problems may turn a child into a confidante and say things which the child is really too young to bear. An example of a mother talking to a child about her personal problems with disastrous results is described by Thomas Hardy in *Jude the Obscure*:

... 'Mother, *what* shall we do to-morrow!'
'I don't know!' said Sue despondently. 'I am afraid this will trouble your father.'
'I wish father was quite well, and there had been room for him! Then it wouldn't matter so much! Poor father!'
'It wouldn't!'
'Can I do anything?'
'No! All is trouble, adversity and suffering!'
'Father went away to give us children room, didn't he?'
'Partly.'
'It would be better to be out of the world than in it, wouldn't it?'
'It would almost, dear.'

"Tis because of us children, too, isn't it, that you can't get a good lodging?'

'Well – people do object to children sometimes.'

'Then if children make so much trouble, why do people have 'em?'

'O – because it is a law of nature.'

'But we don't ask to be born?'

'No indeed.' . . .

'I think that whenever children be born that are not wanted they should be killed directly, before their souls come to 'em, and not allowed to grow big and walk about!'

Sue did not reply. She was doubtfully pondering how to treat this too reflective child.

She at last concluded that, so far as circumstances permitted, she would be honest and candid with one who entered into her difficulties like an aged friend.

'There is going to be another in our family soon,' she hesitatingly remarked.

'How?'

'There is going to be another baby.'

'What!' The boy jumped up wildly. 'O God, mother, you've never a-sent for another; and such trouble with what you've got!'

'Yes, I have, I am sorry to say!' murmured Sue, her eyes glistening with suspended tears.

The boy burst out weeping. 'O you don't care, you don't care!' he cried in bitter reproach. 'How *ever* could you, mother, be so wicked and cruel as this, when you needn't have done it till we was better off, and father well! – to bring us all into *more* trouble! No room for us, and father a-forced to go away, and we turned out tomorrow; and yet you be going to have another of us soon! . . . 'Tis done o'purpose! – 'tis – 'tis!' He walked up and down sobbing.

'Y-you must forgive me, little Jude!' she pleaded, . . .

Next day little Jude hangs the other children and himself, leaving a piece of paper on which was written: *Done because we are too menny.*

Some mothers use their children as instruments to enhance themselves. If they are very immature they regard their children as toys, to be played with, picked up and dropped, put away and ignored according to the feelings of the moment. The child is bewildered and confused. One moment he is loved and the centre of attention. The next minute his mother appears to have forgotten him and is pursuing some other interest.

Somewhat more sophisticated mothers may use the child's

development as a means of enhancing their own positions or security. One mother cut short her child's holiday with friends on the grounds that the child insisted on returning to attend a theatre group of which she was a member. In reality the child had no wish to leave the seaside for this purpose, but the mother liked to tell her friends how keen her daughter was on her weekly attendance at the group. A mother may use a child as a convenient slave in the house, as a scapegoat for her own misdeeds or as a pawn in the manipulations by which she is trying to accomplish her ends.

Mothers who *separate* from their children prematurely or inappropriately force them into escape routes. These include excessive mental activity, compulsive masturbation or its substitutes, escapist obsessions, physical illness, denial of reality and falsification of experience, escape into fantasy and seeking substitute mothers. Some of these children find their real selves and can cope with life. Others are not so lucky.

The children of *separate* mothers have characteristic feelings which tend to stay with them all their lives. They tend to feel solitary, without close contact with others, out of harmony with the world. This comes largely from the lack of the first stage, *enclosure*. They may be noticeably withdrawn or else apparently socially adapted but only with the shell of themselves. They also tend to be purposeless and drifting, largely because they were not submitted to *directive* second stage mothering, which might have given them a system in which to fit. They are very much on their own, out on a limb. On the other hand they have not been submitted to the smothering aspects of the stage of *enclosure* or to the impinging, intrusive aspects of the stage of *extension*. As a result they are free if they are capable of using that freedom. Some are not free because they are forever tied to relationships that they were unable to achieve. Some see no purpose in their freedom. Some try to tie themselves, perhaps by imprisoning themselves in their own minds, or by adopting a cause, a belief, a religion that directs them and offers a semblance of *enclosure*. Some escape into themselves. Thus Edith Sitwell:

My childhood, when I was not being bullied by my mother, resembled, before the birth of my two much-loved brothers, that of the child in Rimbaud's *Enfance* − I was an arrogant young being − who had 'neither family nor courtiers ... The staring azure and greenery which is her kingdom runs along level shores which the shipless waves have called by names ferociously Greek, Slav, and Celtic.

'On the forest-verge, where dream-flowers tinkle, glitter, and shine, sits the young girl, clothed by the passing shadows of the rainbows, by the shadows of the flowers and sea.'

This was my inner life, when I was a child of, say, twelve – it was then untouched by the brutish outer life in which my outer world was extinguished.*

Some spend much time in trying to understand what has happened, what has gone wrong and where they are not free. This was the method of young Anne Frank, a girl of fourteen in hiding with her family from the Germans, and forced prematurely to look truthfully into herself. 'I can't really love Mummy in a dependent child-like way – I just don't have that feeling', and 'I felt sorry for Mummy ... her tactless remarks and her crude jokes which I don't find at all funny, have now made me insensitive to any love from her side.'†

Coping with a mother who is *separate* usually involves finding a substitute mother. For obvious reasons, children who have access to other adults do better in this than those with little or none. Some manage to provide their own substitutes, to be their own mother. Thus Anne Frank: 'I only look at her as a mother, she just doesn't succeed in being that to me; I have to be my own mother.'‡

To some extent becoming their own mothers has to be done by all who achieve individuality and manage to become people in their own right. But some have to do it to an extreme degree if they are to survive at all.

As long as she could remember, Susanne had felt that she was more knowledgeable and mature than her mother. Her parents had provided well for her physically, but had left a huge psychological gulf between them and their child. Susanne was psychologically equipped to fill it herself. She was clever and imaginative and succoured herself in an imaginary world where she was queen and reigned supreme. She did well academically but all this was only achieved at a cost to her personality and sometimes to her sensitivity. She had rather a loud, strident

* Edith Sitwell, *Taken Care Of*, p. 38.
† *The Diary of Anne Frank*, p. 73.
‡ ibid., p. 48.

voice, was grossly and apparently unconsciously overweight, made no concession to feminity and wore men's shoes, no make-up and allowed her eyebrows to meet in the middle.

Sometimes a mother or a social agency deliberately finds a substitute mother for a child. Luckily in our society many substitute mothers are better mothers and more real to the children than are biological mothers, though this is only slowly being recognized by the law. Common substitute mothers include adoptive mothers, foster mothers, stepmothers and relatives or others who act as mother figures early in a child's life. They also include professionals and employees such as nannies, mothers' helps, *au pairs*, psycho-therapists and those relationships which arise more casually, often between a woman who is actively (though often unconsciously) seeking a relationship with a child and a child who is actively seeking a mother substitute or a partial mother substitute. Often the woman is a relative or teacher.

Substitute mothering can be part of a whole way of life as in the nanny tradition of the British middle and upper classes. The presence of a loving nanny and a nursery creates a special world of childhood that may be more satisfactory than anything the mother could have provided on her own. A middle-class family nowadays is more likely to employ an *au pair* than a nanny. This is likely to mean that every six months or so a new foreign girl joins the household with little English and even less interest in forming attachments with the young children of the family. But there are exceptions. Many *au pair* girls respond magnificently to children and derive much satisfaction from their relationships with them. Such girls can be life-saving to children who, unable to make full relationships with their own mothers, actively seek mother substitutes to fill the gap. Luckily, in our society, although there are many mothers who are unable to provide for their children everything that some mothers can provide, and whose children are therefore in this sense 'deprived', there are also many women who are 'deprived' in the sense that their mothering instincts and capacities are underemployed and they are therefore open to new relationships which can be rewarding on both sides. Some of these become official foster mothers or work professionally with children. Many just live in the community and are available to children who need them.

Tina was fond of her mother but found her unable to provide either the emotional support or the intellectual stimulation that she needed. Luckily for Tina the atmosphere in the family was free and few restrictions were imposed on friendships outside. Tina learned to satisfy her needs not, as so many do, and her sister did, by self-comfort and masturbation, but by making a series of strong relationships with older women, each of which provided some element that was lacking in her own relationship with her mother, while maintaining a warm, if somewhat super-ficial, relationship with her own mother. Tina grew up to be strong and stable with much warmth and a capacity to make strong, enduring relationships. She is a good example of the way in which the solution to problems or their lack of solution depends not only on the circumstances but also on the character and quality of the person.

Another method of survival or escape is caring for others. The infant's need to be cared for is turned into an adult's need to care. Great sympathy and ability to identify with others is often a result of learning to adapt to mother and not to offend or irritate her. Either or a combination of these often produces the people who eventually turn into other people's substitute mothers and so, by their own deprivation, help to overcome the deprivations of others.

Part II

6. The World Outside

We seem to have created a difficult social soil in which to grow families.

Sir Keith Joseph

Every man remembers his childhood as a kind of mythical age, just as every nation's childhood is its mythical age.

Giacomo Leopardi

Beyond the mother are other types of environment. The child has access to them to a greater or lesser extent, but always increasing.

A mother's influence is greatest when there is no alternative and no escape. This is why the first stage is the most powerful.

FATHER AND FAMILY

The first alternative and escape is usually father. He may play a part from the beginning, perhaps even a maternal role. Nowadays it is often father who gets up in the night to feed and attend to an infant. His influence is usually most pronounced during the second stage, extension, in which he may predominate and often sets the tone for the whole family.

Father plays an important role in his own right. Sometimes he may play the part of mother but the child needs him also as father. He protects, supports and guides. He shows the way, imposes necessary controls and boundaries, offers alternatives and plays an essential part in the conflict which is itself essential.

Just as in mothering there is a basic conflict between love and distance, so there are basic conflicts in being a child. Love and distance; himself and his mother versus his mother and father; his escape to his father versus his ties with his mother; these are just a few.

Along with father there is also the family group, brothers and sisters. When there is *rapport* between siblings, many individual mother–child difficulties are smoothed over. Brothers and sisters who can talk freely and intimately often learn a great deal about their mothers, and therefore about themselves, simply by hearing about the home situation and family relationships from a slightly different viewpoint. Contact with a brother or sister, usually older, can have a profound effect. Often the older child can provide what the mother lacks and the child needs.

In the Z. family the three daughters had been largely mothered by their father. Their mother was cold, controlling and lacking in warmth or maternal feeling. When the youngest child, Yvonne, was eight years old, the father died. The eldest girl, Freda, took over the role of mother to Yvonne. The three girls lived with their mother but it was remarkable how Yvonne always ran to Freda for help and advice, talked constantly about Freda when she wasn't there, and implored Freda to take her out, attend school events and generally perform the functions normally expected of a mother. On occasions Yvonne would accidentally refer to Freda as 'Mummy' and when she noticed herself doing this she would laugh nervously and explain, 'It's funny. I keep thinking Freda is my mother.'

Other people in a child's environment may act as substitute mothers and this is one way in which the environment can dilute a mother's influence and may protect her and help her to be a better mother or have the opposite effect. Schoolgirl 'crushes' are sometimes of this type. The child is desperately seeking something that is lacking in her own mother.

Some mothers cannot tolerate their children having close relationships with one another. They may space their families so that the gap between each child is too great for childhood intimacy, thus achieving the aim of separate relationship with or control over each child. Some do it to children who are close in age and could obviously be friendly and companionable. For her own security such a mother has to be at the centre, radiating bonds with each child separately and making sure that few are formed between child and child. This of course makes it difficult for the child to form bonds elsewhere. If the mother is at heart a *separate* mother or has *separate* tendencies she may even play off one child against another and create or maintain hostility between them.

Other mitigating influences include school and neighbourhood. School includes not only teachers and children but also its institutional framework, the discipline and freedom of formal learning, and the prospects of what may develop from it. Neighbourhood includes the degree of freedom of movement, safety, the availability of other people, their suitability and willingness to make relationships, and the influence of these.

Last but not least is the child himself. So often in the last resort it lies within him to make the most of his mother and his environment and to help or hinder her in making the most of herself. To some extent the child is the environment that he also creates for himself.

THREE TYPES OF ENVIRONMENT

Just as there are three main types of mother, who regard their children as *parts* of themselves, as *extensions* of themselves or as *separate* people, there are also three main types of environment: *cradling*, *directive* and *unsupporting*. They correspond to the three types of mothering, overlap with them and are even to some extent the same. As with the three types of mothering, they mingle with and merge into each other and no type is likely to be found in its pure form. The three types of environment also correspond to the three stages of development. The stage of *enclosure*, when the child is psychologically part of the mother, provides the *cradling* environment that most of us experienced during infancy. The stage of *extension*, when the child is psychologically an *extension* of the mother, provides the *directive* environment that forms and controls us during childhood. Together these types of environment can be almost totally *supporting*. When this is so, a mother has no need to develop beyond the second stage and the individual will remain adjusted to the *supporting* environment.

An *enclosing* mother tends to make a *cradling* environment, perpetuate it, and engender hunger for this type of environment which may dominate her children throughout their lives. An *extension* type of mother makes a *directive* environment and her children will be happiest in situations in which there are rules to be kept. A *separate* mother who has not adequately been through the other stages will tend to produce an environment that her children experience as *unsupporting* or meaningless.

A *cradling* environment does not impinge and so one is not usually aware of it. A *directive* environment impinges but adaptation to it means unawareness both of this impingement and of possible alternatives. This unawareness of environmental support and restriction makes matters worse when it fails. Failure of the *supportive* environment means that damage and neglect, or both, are virtually unavoidable.

In a world that changes rapidly, as ours does, the environment no longer supports as it does when change is slow. When the needs of one generation differ markedly from those of the last and the next, environments that are purely *cradling* or *directive* are bound to fail and so become *unsupporting* and a source of conflict. Difficulty in establishing independence, in separating one's own from one's parents' wishes, may be a serious handicap. Those who grow up in families whose attitude is that children are *parts* or *extensions* of parents tend to meet particular difficulties as they grow up in the modern world. They often have a feeling of special security within the family and great difficulty in making their way outside it, in what for them is now an *unsupporting* environment.

The stage of *separation*, when the child becomes psychologically independent of the mother, makes an environment that leaves us free to make what we can of it. But if we are not to flounder we have to be capable of using that freedom. This means imposing ourselves on it and doing much of the work for ourselves. If we are tied emotionally to a *cradling* or *directive* environment, we will be unable to do this. We are also likely to run into difficulties if the stages of *enclosure* and of *extension* failed to provide sufficient support at the appropriate times.

Because of the rate of change, the environment no longer supports in the way it used to do. This is one reason why it is particularly difficult to be an adequate mother in the modern world.

We go through each stage well or badly according to our needs and circumstances. We may or may not be able to cope with each stage as it comes to us, or we may emerge from any stage better or worse off than we were before.

INNER AND OUTER WORLDS

Each of us lives with two backgrounds, the inner world and the outer world. The inner is the world of our known and unknown selves. This is fantasy yet it can be more real than any concrete reality. It is the world that grows from inheritance through experience.

The outside world is where we move and have our being. To some extent we may choose and control it, and to some extent it is unaffected by what we do.

We are all in touch with both worlds and in constant interplay with each. Lying between them, we balance, match, imbibe, contribute, struggle, fight and make peace. We all have to find our own equilibrium between inner and outer world and this equilibrium changes constantly, no matter how hard we may try to hold one or the other still. The way in which we continually adapt our inner life to the world outside, are controlled by it and impose ourselves on it, and also the extent to which we create it, are products of ourselves as individuals and of our early environment, which is usually mostly the mother.

Most of us grow up in surroundings which are predominantly one of the three main types, *cradling*, *directive* or *unsupportive*, according to the type of mother and the type of family we have had. We are then best fitted for that type of environment. The more the type predominates, the better we are fitted for that type and the less fitted we are for any other.

CRADLING ENVIRONMENTS

A *cradling* environment is the outward symbol of the stage of *enclosure*. It holds and protects. It is complete in itself. It supports freedom only within its *cradling* ambience. It supports ambition only reciprocally with the child's desires. It neither knows nor wants what is beyond itself.

Hugh's mother died suddenly when he was eight years old. The family lived in the country and was poor. Throughout his childhood Hugh was left free to follow his desires and enjoy the outside world. For him this meant nature and its beauties. As he grew up he gradually became aware that nature had become part of him as his mother was part of him. He was aware of the fusion of his feelings with nature in a unity not only of objects but also of time, and he became aware of a direct connection between this and his remembered feelings and experiences with his mother. In adult life he came to understand how important these feelings about nature were, how they had *cradled* and sustained him through the loss of his mother and afterwards and had also conditioned his attitude to mankind throughout his long life. Significantly, his favourite lines of poetry were

> A motion and a spirit, that impels
> All thinking things, all objects of all thoughts
> And rolls through all things . . .*

Wordsworth had in fact had many of the same kind of experiences as Hugh so it is not surprising that Hugh felt an affinity. Like Wordsworth he also became increasingly religious as he grew older.

This kind of religious feeling sometimes seems to go with a mergency of feelings about nature and memories of a lost mother. Wordsworth wrote, in *Ode on Intimations of Immortality*:

> Our birth is but a sleep and a forgetting:
> The Soul that rises with us, our life's Star,
>   Hath had elsewhere its setting,
>   And cometh from afar:
>   Not in entire forgetfulness,
>   And not in utter nakedness,
> But trailing clouds of glory do we come
>   From God, who is our home:

More than a century later this difference recurs elsewhere. The writer Romain Rolland in a letter to his friend Sigmund Freud referred to his 'oceanic feeling', the mystical, cosmic emotion which he believed to be the true source of religious sentiments. Freud could not discover this feeling in himself but he interpreted it as a regression 'to an early phase of ego-feeling'. In *Civilization and its Discontents* he writes:

Originally the ego includes everything, later it detaches from itself the outside world. The ego-feeling we are aware of now is thus only a shrunken vestige of a more extensive feeling – a feeling which embraced the universe and expressed an inseparable connexion of the ego with the external world. If we may suppose that this primary ego-feeling has been preserved in the minds of many people – to a greater or lesser extent – it would co-exist like a sort of counterpart with the narrower and more sharply outlined ego-

* Wordsworth, *Tintern Abbey*.

feeling of maturity, and the ideational content belonging to it would be precisely the notion of limitless extension and oneness with the universe – the same feeling as that described by my friend as 'oceanic'.

Freud held the view that religious ideas are 'illusions, fulfillments of the oldest, strongest, and most urgent wishes of mankind'. In The Future of an Illusion he interprets God as a response to recognition of human helplessness:

the terrifying impression of helplessness in childhood aroused the need for protection – for protection through love – which was provided by the father, and the recognition that this helplessness lasts throughout life made it necessary to cling to the existence of a father, but this time a more powerful one.

Freud had a powerful father. He also lived in an age of patriarchy. It is not surprising that he was not fully aware of the mother and the stages she goes through with her child. Since that time beliefs have changed. A dominating powerful role is no longer expected of fathers. Theologians have been busy coping with the problems this brings them, and we hear much more about God inside us than about God 'out there'. The attempt to liberate Christianity from the dominating Father has also helped to destroy many of the emotional aspects of Christianity which used to provide support. This puts still more responsibility on to the mother. Moreover psycho-analytic theory and psychological thinking generally have become much more oriented towards the mother. Religious feeling and maternal environment are sometimes equated in womb-theories, based on the idea that the womb is the only perfect environment and after one is cast out from it paradise can never be regained. Wordsworth's idea of a glorious heavenly pre-existence is echoed by Coleridge in Kubla Khan and by many other poets, including James Joyce in Ulysses: 'Before born babe bliss had. Within womb won he worship. Whatever in that one case done commodiously was.' Also, by W. H. Auden:

> If it form the one landscape that we, the inconstant ones,
>   Are consistently homesick for, this is chiefly
> Because it dissolves in water. Mark these rounded slopes
>   With their surface fragrance of thyme, and, beneath,
> A secret system of caves and conduits; hear the springs
>   That spurt out everywhere with a chuckle,
> Each filling a private pool for its fish and carving
>   Its own little ravine whose cliffs entertain

> The butterfly and the lizard; examine this region
> Of short distances and definite places:
> What could be more like Mother . . .*

Whether mother's womb or mother's arms, we come back to
mother in the earliest part of life. Those who are aware of the
'oceanic feeling' or the 'visionary gleam' also seem to be aware of
its loss. Wordsworth was very aware of his mother, and not only
of the stage of *enclosure* merging with nature but also of it developing
into the stage of *extension*, a sense of loss. In Book II of *The Prelude* he
wrote:

> For now a trouble came into my mind
> From unknown causes. I was left alone
> Seeking the visible world, nor knowing why.
> The props of my affections were removed,
> And yet the building stood, as if sustained
> By its own spirit!

This is echoed in *Ode on Intimations of Immortality*:

> The sunshine is a glorious birth;
> But yet I know, where'er I go,
> That there hath passed away a glory from the earth

and

> Whither is fled the visionary gleam?
> Where is it now, the glory and the dream?

However Wordsworth had a mother for long enough to have
developed far into the stage of *extension*, and, like the first stage, this
seems to have gone well. In *The Prelude* (Book v) he is aware of the
danger of idealizing a dead loved one and of the guilt that criticism
of her would be likely to bring. He tries to assess seriously her
development as a mother and the way in which the harmony of
inner and outer worlds was maintained in the *extension* stage.

> Early died
> My honoured Mother, she who was the heart
> And hinge of all our learnings and our loves:
> She left us destitute, and, as we might,
> Trooping together. Little suits it me
> To break upon the sabbath of her rest

* W. H. Auden, 'In Praise of Limestone', from *Collected Shorter Poems*,
Faber and Faber Ltd.

With any thought that looks at others' blame;
Nor would I praise her but in perfect love.
Hence am I checked: but let me boldly say,
In gratitude, and for the sake of truth,
Unheard by her, that she, not falsely taught,
Fetching her goodness rather from times past,
Than shaping novelties for times to come,
Had no presumption, no such jealousy,
Nor did by habit of her thoughts mistrust
Our nature, but had virtual faith that He
Who fills the mother's breast with innocent milk,
Doth also for our nobler part provide . . .

At the age of sixteen, firmly embedded in the *directive* environment of education, Wordsworth is still aware of the power of his inner *cradling* environment and the strength he derives from it.

A *cradling* environment may be prolonged in another way and, provided the environment holds, this can even last a lifetime. It may dominate the individual so that he lives totally within it. The shell of the self may blend with the *cradling* environment. The core of the self is then ignored but, provided the environment holds him, he may live his life normally and peacefully, even if his satisfactions are limited.

As a child Phyllis found that school gave her a strong sense of security. Her parents were Methodists and held strong moral views about the world. They instilled into young Phyllis a fear of the wicked things that happen outside the security of her immediate environment. The excessive rigidity of her parents was to some extent counteracted by the intellectual stimulation which she found at school. She was a good scholar, especially in mathematical and scientific subjects. She won a free place at the girls' grammar school and was soon chosen by her teachers as a likely university candidate. She returned their care and interest by devoting her adolescent years to achieving this ambition. Duly rewarded, she went to university and lived a quiet life for three years and was untroubled by social or sexual temptations. She worked hard and spent her leisure time participating in the activities of the Student Christian Movement. She returned home with a good second-class degree to live with her parents and to teach in her old school. There she remained for the next thirty years, sixteen of them as Second Mistress. She seemed to have no desire to gain experience elsewhere or to apply for a headship. But when her parents died within a short time of each other she began to have regrets. At the same time the cosy world of the girls' grammar school collapsed because the school was merged with others to form a co-educational comprehensive school. This loss of her *cradling* environment was too much for Phyllis and she broke down.

The family firm of the M.'s had flourished since the eighteenth century. Members of it boasted that it had never had a director who was not a member of the family and that it would always find a post for a member of the family. For generations young M.'s grew up in their large country houses and knew few people outside their own clan. Each boy on leaving school went into the firm or one of its branches.

But after the second world war there were changes. Some of the younger M.'s, returning from the war, did not wish to immerse themselves in the family firm. Some of those who were now running the firm found the dynamic and competitive atmosphere of business in the postwar years rather more than they could cope with. The firm declined and eventually, not far from disintegration, was taken over by a former rival. Young M.'s no longer had the assured future they had been brought up to expect as their right. Though still supported by some of the family money, they are basically on their own now and have to make their own way in the world.

A *cradling* environment which merges with the whole self, as happened with Wordsworth, does not fail. It may be lost through change, but it remains as part of the person and continues to succour.

Many people turn their marriages into *cradling* environments. Still more use the family. Within our western framework it is still regarded as acceptable for parents to treat their offspring, whether infants, children or adults, as *parts* of themselves. Moreover there still exist many families and larger groups of people among whom these feelings are so strong that no other possibility is entertained. To such people the whole idea of a state of *separation* is meaningless.

These attitudes are by no means always neurotic. Probably they have survival value under some conditions that can exist in modern life, for example starvation and persecution. Often they are ana-chronistic. But they have deep cultural roots and protect against anxiety which might otherwise be intolerable.

Parents in whom such attitudes seem to stem from cultural more than from neurotic roots usually come from well-definable back-grounds. For example members of Jewish families, particularly mothers and sometimes whole families and communities, not uncommonly try to love without distancing. This sets up a kind of permanent cradling environment within the family. In such a family one can often see some members held totally within the cradle and others struggling to get out, but like big babies, inadequately equipped to deal with the very different world outside. For instance, in British schools, the sons of mothers who breathe every breath with them and whose lives centre on the food offered and its symbolism are at a disadvantage.

In many Jewish families the idea that the child is part of the parent and the family rather than a separate person is regarded as normal, desirable and inevitable. There is something in Jewish culture, at least in the western world today, that makes the child-as-part-of-parent attitude particularly strong. It seems likely that the attitude acts as a cohesive influence, inviting family or people to face a hostile world. 'How else could a child survive,' I have been asked, 'if his mother does not care for him as part of herself?' Such questioners do not understand that, in a physically secure environ-ment, it is possible to care well for a child not as part of his parents, but for himself. The basis of many jokes about the 'Yiddisher momma' is that she has no conception of her children, particularly her sons, other than as parts of herself; and moreover, the jokes often reveal how this stage of affairs is essential to her very existence. Her life consists of living vicariously through her children. It is signifi-cant that western non-Jewish culture tends to produce more jokes about mothers-in-law than about mothers. This is probably because western non-Jewish mothers are more likely to be extension-type mothers and the environment is directive more than cradling. The enclosing mother tries to cradle her son in his adult years. The extension mother tries to direct the lives of her adult children and those whom they marry.

But in a society without gross persecution individual develop-ment, separate yet linked, loving yet maintaining distance, becomes more important.

DIRECTIVE ENVIRONMENTS

A *directive* environment is the counterpart of the second stage of mothering, the stage of *extension*. An *enclosing* environment fits but does not impinge. A *directive* environment moulds and insists, impinges, lacks tolerance, can be aggressive. Its lines of demarcation allow no alternatives. It can be gentle and lead towards freedom or it can be harsh and controlling. A *directive* environment belongs to childhood and is unsuited to infancy. It may also be prolonged, and may dominate the individual so that he lives wholly within it, maybe a shell without core, without real self, but, provided the environment continues to hold, he remains adapted to it.

All societies have their own forms of *directiveness*, some more controlling than others. Any environment with rules is *directive*, no matter whether those rules are laid down specifically or merely understood. We absorb the *directiveness* of our particular society unconsciously. We do this through family and neighbourhood, school and work, tradition and convention. Prison is a *directive* environment and so are religious and church organizations, political regimes and parties, certain clubs and associations and social customs. Structured, demanding, with clear lines of demarcation, a *directive*, like a *cradling*, environment can give shape if not meaning that can last a lifetime. Those who have missed the *cradling* environment of infancy, who have not developed a sense of unity with the world, often substitute a *directive* environment with which they have managed to identify. One might compare it to the way in which riding a bicycle, though not man's natural mode of locomotion, becomes automatic once one has mastered the basic skill.

If there has been weakness in the stage of *extension*, any *directive* environment may be experienced as alien and intolerable. This is what has happened to many hippies and drop-outs. If there has been exceptional emphasis on the stage of *extension*, any *directive* environment may be welcomed and any other kind of environment, either *cradling* or *unsupportive*, is felt to be intolerable. Such people lead orderly lives and seek occupations with clear rules to be kept.

As we saw earlier, H. G. Wells had a typical *extension* type of upbringing. He escaped from its *directive* environment to find his own freedom.

Wells, whose predominantly *extension* type of upbringing has already been discussed, also describes the *directive* environment in which his mother intended him to fit and pass the rest of his life. He tells us about her own background:

It was a world of other ladies'-maids and valets, of house stewards, housekeepers, cooks and butlers, upper servants above the level of maids and footmen, a downstairs world, but living in plentiful good air, well fed and fairly well housed in the attics, basements and interstices of great mansions. It was an old-fashioned world; most of its patterns of behaviour and much of its peculiar idiom, were established in the seventeenth century – its way of talking, its style of wit, was in an unbroken tradition from the *Polite Conversation* of Dean Swift, and it had customs and an etiquette all its own ... By nature and upbringing alike she belonged to that middle-class of dependents who occupied situations, performed strictly defined duties, gave or failed to give satisfaction and had no ideas at all outside that dependence.

... I have no doubt that I should have followed in the footsteps of Frank and Freddy and gone on living at home, under my mother's care, while I went daily to some shop, some draper's shop, to which I was bound apprentice. This would have seemed so natural and necessary that I should not have resisted. I should have served my time and never had an idea of getting away from the shop until it was too late ... And from Messrs. Rodgers and Denyer I got my first impressions of the intensely undesirable life for which she designed me. I had no idea of what I was in for. I went to my fate as I was told, unquestioningly, as my brothers had done before me ...*

Wells felt that he escaped through the chance opportunity that arose in his life for books and physical freedom and he attributes it directly to the environment.

Looking back on this he wrote of the *directive* environment of the lower middle class and points out how it stems from the traditional upper class. A rigid class system produces, within each class, a system of mothering that is predominantly second stage, *extension* mothering, and it shows the advantages and disadvantages of such a system. The system shows how a stable method of personality development is maintained and perpetuated in a manner which supports the society which embraces it.

Traditionally the upper-class system pays little regard to the principle of the supreme importance of the individual but, provided an individual fits into it moderately well, it offers support and

* *Experiment in Autobiography*, Vol. 1.

freedom from anxiety for life. It is not a system of personal exploration and growth but rather one of training for a role in life, to be
part of the system. In the traditional British upper class, delegation
of the mother's role is essential. This is much less common than
formerly but it still exists and it is a good example of a *directive*
environment. It is a system of substitute and intermittent mothering.
The training starts from birth when the child is handed over to the
'monthly nurse' who is usually a trained nurse or midwife and is
supposed to 'know all about young babies'. Monthly nurses move
from 'case' to 'case' to start each baby off on its routine and training.
Their function could have been designed specifically to prevent
the formation of the close bond between mother and child that is
the essence of the first stage of mothering. The monthly nurse helps
to ensure that the mothering the child receives will be predominantly
extension, second stage mothering. As a result the system can form the
child and the child perpetuate the system. The mother who feels
'broody' about her baby has a difficult time developing her intuitive
and imaginative motherly instincts if there is a monthly nurse.
Breastfeeding can be a desperate attempt to make contact with the
baby in a world where rules and traditions take precedence over
feelings. The old traditions are becoming rarer, but they still exist.
At four weeks old the baby comes under the control of his nanny,
who may well be his mother's old nanny. She is a professional substitute mother and, if good at her job, will fit the child into the
system much more efficiently than his mother could ever do. From
the beginning, at least for boys, it is a serious preparation for leaving
home. Boys go to boarding school at eight years old, already
adequately prepared for team spirit, playing the game and not
letting the side down, already able to manage the stiff upper lip and
equipped with the rudiments of good manners, good taste and good
form. Girls leave home later, usually at eleven, and on the whole
for them less emphasis is laid on team qualities and more on good
manners and good taste. Education before the age of eight is usually
provided by governesses or small local schools, either one-sex
preparatory or mixed. At this age the education of both sexes is not
dissimilar. After eight education is in one-sex schools.

At its best the system has turned out excellent administrators and
their wives. It also produces its own difficulties and anxieties not
only for the mother but for her children throughout their lives.
The system makes it difficult or impossible to develop a full or

adequate first stage of mothering. The mother whose baby is organized for her from birth has no opportunity to develop the particular kind of close feelings that are characteristic of the stage of *enclosure*. In most cases the mother is probably unaware even of the possibility of doing so. All except those with the strongest maternal drive are likely to feel content to be relieved of the continuous burden and to be able to return to normal life soon after the baby is born. This does not mean that a mother does not love her baby or that he is doomed. But it does mean that he will grow up without experiencing the earliest type of mothering and his personality will develop accordingly. A typical memory of a child brought up in this manner comes from Graham Greene in *A Sort of Life*:

> I associate my mother with a remoteness, which I did not at all resent, and with a smell of eau-de-cologne. If I could have tasted her I am sure she would have tasted of wheaten biscuits. She paid occasional state visits to the nursery ... My mother's remoteness, her wonderful lack of possessive instinct, was made much easier for her to achieve by the presence of Nanny ... I never remember being afraid of her.

Upper-class mothering is most successful where there is a firm background of privilege rather than merely its residue; where a mother plays a positive, even if traditional, part in the upbringing of her children and does not simply use the system as a means of escape from the realities of motherhood; and where there are family traditions or religious feelings that transcend outward conformity or non-conformity. It is less successful where these conditions do not exist. One is likely then to find a child who has been placed at an emotional distance virtually from birth and learned to exist and perhaps even to flourish as an isolated individual, imbued with certain codes of feeling and behaviour. Although the system is declining, a number of these people remain and are even being produced.

Recently a boy was bullied at a famous public school because he arrived with a title and a cockney accent.

Another went to a school almost as well known and found himself in difficulties because his was the only titled family. He was nicknamed scornfully 'The Hon. John' and suffered much humiliation.

Another young man, the son and heir of a peer, was, like David (on p. 73), unable to pass the examinations necessary to enter the Cambridge college to which his father and ancestors had belonged as if by right. His father was unsympathetic and angry. The fact that he himself had never had to pass an examination did not seem to occur to him. As far as he was concerned, nothing like this had ever happened in the family before. The boy felt humiliated and useless, became more and more depressed and eventually killed himself.

There is no place in our modern society for people who have been brought up in this traditional way and yet who cannot adapt at least minimally to the demands of a more egalitarian society. They find they are no longer protected, are made to feel different and cannot survive psychologically. Their environment can no longer hold them so effectively as in former days.

A problem particularly likely to be encountered by people who have grown up under the traditional British upper-class system of mothering results from inadequacies of the stage of *enclosure*. If they have not experienced a good stage of *enclosure*, which few from this background have, and they are also not firmly part of the Establishment, they are more vulnerable to stress, more dependent on the system within which they are accustomed to live and less adaptable to adverse circumstances. Nowadays the traditional upper-class and upper-middle-class world is much smaller than before. But it is still there for its more successful members. It thrives in high places. It is still the standard in the upper reaches of public life, where it often conflicts with individual feelings and desires. For instance a diplomat's wife is still expected to preside over cocktails rather than put her children to bed, and she may feel unhappy about this and also guilty, knowing that it goes against current beliefs about childrearing.

The system no longer supports its weaker members. It also does not provide them with the necessary equipment or experience that would enable them to fend for themselves. The peer's son who could not pass his A levels is a case in point. Little attention had been paid to his education and even less to his mental state. When it became obvious that getting to Oxbridge was beyond his capacities, no alternatives were suggested though he was a sensitive boy who needed encouragement. Since he had a private income he was able to live without earning, unhappily, and without prospects. His privileged *directive* environment no longer supported him.

A *directive* environment can fail markedly when there is no mother or when the mother virtually leaves the whole upbringing to the system.

An example of this was Sara, whose family was international and unstable. Her mother was more interested in her own life than in her children. Sara spent her childhood shuttling to and from from one country to another in the charge of various relatives and living in enormous houses in fashionable places on both sides of the Atlantic. She had a varied education that did not help her to develop any talents she might have had or to do anything useful for society. By the time she was eighteen she spoke four languages fluently but was more or less illiterate in all of them. At this stage she became disturbed because her parents divorced and her father started to bring to the house a series of mistresses who were about her own age. Sara started to behave badly and her father threw her out of the house, stopped her allowance and told her that he had spent a lot of money on her and she could now earn her own living. She was incapable of anything but unskilled work and the life of pleasure to which she was accustomed made her temperamentally incapable of arriving anywhere on time or persisting at any task which did not please her. She had no idea how to look after herself physically, mentally or financially. She decided to become a model but, despite useful connections, she did not succeed. She drifted towards the hippies as many young girls like her do. One day she disappeared and she reappeared six weeks later exhausted, starved, distraught and pregnant by she knew not whom. During a few months of psychiatric care together with negotiations with her father to induce him to take an interest in her, it became obvious that Sara would never stand on her own feet. Predictably, she has become the mistress of a rich man who tries to control her in body, mind and soul. Every now and again there is a crisis but she always goes back. She is cushioned by wealth and, as in her childhood, she follows the sun from country to country. But her environment does not really support her and she has never had a chance to be anything else. She does not know who she is or what she wants. Sara is a good example of how this kind of upbringing does not support those who do not fit in.

Many upper-class families provide each member with a private income, which may be substantial. This can cushion the effect of inadequacy but it can also have a deleterious effect. Many of these young people do far better if they have to be responsible for themselves.

Typical of these was Miles, who had a small private income. This enabled him to do nothing except lie in bed listening to pop music and drinking whisky until he became an alcoholic. He would certainly have been better off earning his money by regular employment.

Pauline was a rich girl. She tended to become involved with con men and adventurers and never seemed to have developed the ability to distinguish between people who really cared for her as a person and those who were just after her money. One of her difficulties was that she had learned maladaptive patterns of behaviour when dealing with problems. She tended to try to buy everyone off.

Another type of directive environment whose children tend to find it hard to adapt to modern circumstances is that provided by closed religious sects. Moral principles that seem to have little relevance outside, religious beliefs that seem by most people's standards anachronistic or absurd and often also a strong if unconscious denial of the body and its functions, all these can combine to impose a formidable directive environment on a young person that ceases to support because it conflicts so profoundly with the outside world.

Beryl's parents and all their friends belonged to a strict religious sect which involved frequent attendance at religious services and a puritanical code of conduct. The older daughter, thirteen years older than Beryl, had married within the sect but while Beryl was growing up the life of young people in the area changed. Unlike her friends at school Beryl was not allowed out on her own, or in the evening. She was not allowed to be alone with a boy or to associate with boys who were not members of the sect. For some time Beryl accepted this but when she began to rebel and wanted to go out with her friends, her mother became convinced that it was 'all sex and the work of the devil'. Beryl loved her parents and was torn between them and her friends. She made a tenuous friendship with a boy at school but was unable to withstand her parents' attacks and broke it off. At this point she became depressed and aggressive towards her parents, who said they 'couldn't understand what on earth is the matter with the girl – everything we do is for her own good'. As she grew up Beryl became skilful at reassuring her parents while gradually establishing a life of her own. At the time of writing, after a long struggle, she is about to go to a university far from home and she has a stable relationship with a boy whose parents are also members of the sect but who feels, like Beryl, that it is too constricting.

FEELING ALL RIGHT

There are two kinds of people who appear to be mentally healthy. First are those held totally by their environment, by *cradling* or *direction* or a mixture of the two. These are passive and at the mercy of their environment. If the environment fails, they are likely to break down. Second are those who are able to impose themselves on the environment in the sense of the French *s'imposer*. They are not wholly dependent on the environment and they have personal resources on which they can draw. If the environment fails, they survive. They are resilient. They adapt, explore new possibilities and build up a new way of life.

Most stable people manage to balance the two as required and to compensate with one for the deficiencies of the other. Many people who appear to be disturbed and out of tune with their environment are actually healthier than many who appear to fit in. This is particularly true of young people. If they are going to find a way of being their true selves and imposing themselves on the environment, they may have to go through a stormy period. In contrast, those who are relying totally on the environment to *cradle* and *direct* may appear to be calm, conforming and tranquil. This difference is shown in the contrasting cases of David and Elaine.

David had to struggle for his independence against his parents' anxieties. In his efforts to assert and find himself he played truant, took drugs, failed to get up in the morning and had violent rows with his parents. His headmaster believed that he was seriously disturbed. His troubles lasted for several years but eventually he emerged, decided what he really wanted to do, which was forestry, and became qualified in it.

Elaine sat in the corner at school and was careful to keep out of trouble. She worked hard and produced work of consistently high quality. She was well-spoken and well-behaved. Her teachers knew that she had a difficult home background and thought how well she coped with it. But she was developing anorexia nervosa and was finding it increasingly difficult to eat. She also had a number of fears which she kept hidden. She was unable, through fear, to go into a shop, enter a bus or sign her name in public. Only when her weight fell below 70 lbs did her parents and teachers notice that something was wrong with her. Even then her headmistress expressed surprise. 'I've always thought she was such a beautifully adjusted girl,' she said, and Elaine's mother echoed this.

At each stage of mothering and in each type of environment there can be accord or discord between the individual and the environment. Either he seems to fit or he doesn't. Discord involves some kind of rebellion, either inner or outer, and the person can be seen not to fit. This may be the whole person rebelling against what is not right for him or it may be partial, permanent or temporary, productive or sterile. Accord involves an appearance of fitting in. This may mean that the individual is integrated, that his whole self is in a state of dynamic equilibrium with his environment. Or it may mean that he is merely adjusted, in which case part of him, that part which one can call the shell, fits with the environment. The rest, which we can call the core, is elsewhere, probably unconscious and likely to give trouble.

The distinction between integration and adjustment is important. All through the ages rearing children has meant fitting the child into the environment without much regard for the difference between integration and adjustment. In so far as the environment supports, there is little or no need to make the distinction. Language, for instance, and many other habits of life, are largely constant. Whatever else may be difficult and changing, we remain adjusted to the language of our country.

Adjusted means that one's personality is limited or distorted to fit the environment and the environment holds the personality. We adjust to our mother tongue and this limits our potential for speaking other languages that we shall now never learn. For most of us this is not a disadvantage. What we need is not large numbers of languages but a good command of our own. We need to be sure that this is constant and viable however much the world changes and the rest of our environment declines or collapses. But we learn many other patterns in the same way as language. Many of these are increasingly irrelevant, yet they limit our potential for developing others. In particular, they limit choice and flexibility.

All through our lives we tend to try to maintain our accustomed equilibrium by perpetuating our accustomed environment. We do this through our marriages and family lives, work, social activities and our inner worlds of fantasy. And we do it regardless of whether we have been in a state of integration, adjustment or discord. We are likely to reproduce any or all of these according to the pattern of the past.

Everyone needs a *supportive* environment. The more it supports, the fewer personal resources we need, the less developed we need to be as people, the less good mothers we need to have and to be.

The more we understand and the more developed and imaginative we are as people and as mothers, then the more likely we are to be able to get adequate support from what would otherwise be a failing or an *unsupporting* environment.

The last type of environment, the *unsupporting* environment, will be discussed in the next chapter.

7. Insecurity

> Slight, yet very frequent, traumatic experiences are peculiar to the modern world.
>
> Adrian Stokes, *Smooth and Rough*

UNSUPPORTING ENVIRONMENTS

Unsupporting environments are those in which one has to be responsible for oneself to a significant extent. They are the counterparts of the third stage of mothering, the stage of *separation*. An essential part of them is some degree of insecurity.

Feelings of insecurity can come from within, apparently unrelated to the environment. They may also be part of a feeling that the environment is failing. This may stem from the mother directly or from the outside world. The way in which each of us experiences insecurity and also what causes us to feel it depends to a large extent on attitudes related to the three stages of mothering. Except in extreme cases in which everyone would feel insecure, the type of mother we had is also likely to determine the type of situation that makes us feel insecure. Everyone would feel insecure in an earthquake or if a lion unexpectedly leaped into the room, but, if one feels insecure during a thunderstorm or when one's husband or wife enters (or leaves) the room, the chances are that this is related to early experiences with one's mother.

Environments can make us feel insecure and *unsupported* in a number of ways. Physical danger causes fear. Lack of opportunity to develop or to do and be as one wishes or what one feels to be right causes frustration. More subtle forms of psychological failure lead to anxiety, depression, a sense of futility or to attempts to ward off any or all of these. Actual feelings and reactions are highly variable. An *unsupporting* environment can throw us back on ourselves in ways that *cradling* and *directive* environments do not. Unlike them it cannot provide virtually everything that is needed to live within it and it is not possible to live within it almost totally. It demands interaction between itself and the core, not the shell, of ourselves. Although the core is the real self, which makes us authentic, to live by it makes personal demands that require considerable development before they can be met.

The capacity to deal with an *unsupportive* environment and also what constitutes such an environment for a particular individual are strongly influenced by previous experience of *supportive* environments, both *cradling* and *directive*, and so by the way in which we have experienced the three stages of mothering and how we make use of these experiences. In particular, it is connected with the way in which we and our mothers have or have not achieved the third stage, *separation*.

No one can live in an environment that is totally *unsupporting* psychologically. We are all to some extent *cradled* and *directed* by our environment, by our homes and families, our work and way of life, by the language we speak and the customs and mores which we have absorbed, and perhaps also the community in which we live. Probably few of us would survive mentally if we suddenly lost all this and found ourselves alone in a foreign land where we knew no one and did not speak the language, possessed no skill of value in our new surroundings, and where no one stepped forward to support or direct us. Only the most unfortunate of refugees suffer this fate, and even among those more fortunate, who perhaps have relatives with them and can use their skills in work, the rate of breakdown is high. Admission to an institution, perhaps hospital or prison, immediately provides support, albeit unpleasant and frustrating.

Environmental failure likely to beset us is less extreme and more difficult to define. To some extent it affects us all, for total support is unattainable. All our lives from birth onwards we encounter situations in which previous support exists no longer and also situations in which we have perhaps never felt adequately supported. We may continue to develop our capacity to deal with these situations or we may develop it only to a certain extent and then make do with the repertoire developed so far. There may be situations with which we are chronically unable to deal, or for which we develop poor patterns of response. Sometimes we are unable to cope with new situations because we have been too much supported and have never had to develop that resourcefulness that goes with bridging gaps between ourselves and our surroundings, or the self-confidence that comes from having done it. This is one reason why a strong, exclusive *cradling* or *directive* environment may make us incapable when it fails, and why, in mothering, if the stages of *enclosure* and *extension* do not contain the seeds of *separation*, the resulting personality is liable to be limited or unstable.

Sometimes the 'failure' of the environment may be no more than the normal change that occurs with time, such as entering or leaving school or university, having to start or change job or career in middle life, retiring or being widowed. For instance many children with strongly *enclosing* mothers find it difficult to adapt to the more demanding environment of school or the less *supportive* atmosphere of university. Children from *extension*-type families often fit easily into the *directive* educational environment. As a result school comes to provide for them the *cradling* environment that was lacking in their own families and so helps to compensate for the difficulties and deficiencies of their mothers in the stage of *enclosure*. Many people who are ardent 'old pupils' are of this type. Even after they have left, the school continues to symbolize a *cradling* situation.

James stayed on at university as long as he could. He had always been an exemplary pupil and had no difficulty in passing examinations or obtaining postgraduate scholarships and grants. But in his heart he knew he was procrastinating and that despite his academic success he was emotionally ill-equipped to make his way in the world. He toyed with the idea of becoming a don, having seen others in his predicament use this as an escape to a *cradling* environment. He decided against this, went through a period of emotional upheaval and crisis, and eventually settled into the civil service. He will probably always be rather fragile emotionally and able to function well only in a *supporting* environment. On the other hand he is well equipped for finding such an environment.

An elderly engineer had always been protected. All his working life he had been employed in the same large company. He was married to a woman of strong personality who gave him much support. After he retired he became increasingly anxious and depressed. Even his strong, controlling wife could not provide sufficient support. He had always been interested in his body functions; now he became obsessed with them. He had always tended to feel anxious when confronted by new situations; now he was in a state of constant panic about the unforeseen that might occur. His family found him intolerable to live with and this further increased his anxiety.

According to her married children, Mrs H. had always been emotionally unstable and had had much support first from her father and then from her husband. Her husband died suddenly and she floundered. She had no interests. Even her apparent interest in her children and grandchildren was an attempt to gain support from them. In a desperate effort to replace her husband she became involved with a man who was much younger than she. He flattered her and, in her desperation, she believed him. He took £20,000 from her and then departed.

Many married couples collude to maintain a mutually *supportive* environment. This may be predominantly *cradling* or *directive* and is an exaggeration or distortion of the emotional support that married couples normally give each other.

Mrs O., unhappily widowed for five years, married a man whose sole interests were his business and his home comfort. Every morning he drove to the office and Mrs O. spent the day preparing for his return. Every evening they would eat and sit. They had no friends and no social life. Eventually the husband developed a slowly fatal disease. Mrs O. nursed him painstakingly and totally for seven years and meanwhile taught herself to cope with problems of incontinence and mental deterioration. After he died there was nothing that she felt she wanted to do, nothing that she felt she could do and nothing that seemed worth doing. For years she suffered from a severe fluctuating depression that was resistant to all forms of treatment.

These are all examples of what one might call 'normal' changes, with which these particular people were unable to deal. The ability to deal with 'abnormal' change, i.e. of a kind that one might reasonably expect to avoid in one's life, is also determined by similar personal and environmental factors. There is therefore enormous individual variation. In the very situations that most people find insupportable, some find support.

Unexpected changes and impositions for which nearly everyone seems unprepared can have equally varying effects. One has only to study how different people react to, say, war, physical danger, imprisonment, cancer, redundancy or family catastrophe to realize how complicated it is. A man who has been unable to settle to a routine life may become a war hero and distinguish himself in circumstances that ruin others. A woman who has been stable and adequate may be unable to cope after the birth of a handicapped child, but another may find that such a 'catastrophe' gives her life a meaning and purpose that it previously lacked. One middle-aged man may become seriously disturbed at having to find a new job, while another, though perhaps equally disrupted materially, may find the prospect challenging and exciting. Each of the three stages of mothering and how they were experienced are always important in this. The interplay between *cradling* and *directive*, *supportive* and *unsupportive* and how this varies gives a background pattern that imposes itself on self and circumstance.

Some people feel that the environment has never supported. These are usually people who missed a great deal of the *enclosure* stage and who never managed to compensate with the stage of *extension*. In our society they often try to compensate with money, either spending it or making it or both. This is why people with this problem are particularly common among those who have achieved or who were born to positions that many would find enviable. A spending spree or a take-over bid can be an attempt to compensate for essential needs that were not provided by either the mother or the environment.

A thirty-nine-year-old millionaire suffers from 'depression'. 'My trouble is,' he says, only half-joking, 'that I can't decide what I want to be when I grow up.'

He has already made as much money as he will ever need. He needs only to lift the telephone to make more. But to do so seems to him pointless. His life lacks warmth and purpose. He has no interests and no friends. His sense of futility is damaging his marriage. His feelings of worthlessness go back to his childhood. He was the illegitimate child of the sixteen-year-old daughter of a respectable but cold and controlling business man in a small town. He never knew his father. His mother was emotionally under the control of the grandfather and materially dependent on him. His mother seemed more like an older sister. He and she slept in the same room all his childhood and were at the

mercy of his grandfather and his aunts. 'I was raised by com-
mittee', he told me.

I was struck by the similarity of this man's childhood and that of
Jean-Paul Sartre, whose father died young. In his autobiography,
Words, Sartre describes his upbringing in his mother's family
together with the isolated sense of futility and the need to compensate. He tells us: 'I loathe my childhood and all that remains of
it.'

Frederick and his sisters grew up in considerable material
comfort. At the age of ten he was given his own car to drive round
the family farm. But Frederick was always frightened and unhappy
and could bear to be neither alone nor in company. He slept
badly, suffered constantly from overwhelming anxiety that welled
up inside him, and from the age of eighteen he drank too much.
He would lie on his bed all day, sweating from fear. He was sure
that his anxiety dated from his early childhood when he never
knew whether his mother would be at home or away. He adored
his mother without ever knowing her well. He remembered
his childhood as a constant and unsuccessful attempt to come
closer to her. Whatever attempt he made to reach her the result
was always a new bicycle, a new pony, a Mediterranean holiday,
or a party for his friends.

Sometimes an environment specially chosen and adopted turns
out to be disappointingly unsupportive.

Nikos, a Greek Cypriot, had spent his childhood in London.
He quarrelled with his family in England because they said he
had adopted English ways and was interested in English girls.
In the end he 'rebelled' against his London-based family, returned
to Cyprus and married a Greek Cypriot girl from an enclosed,
traditional family. Then he got into difficulties because he found
that his English background made it impossible for him to
conform to what his new family expected. There were tears and
recriminations and he developed what in England would be
called mother-in-law trouble. At one point he was even diagnosed
as schizophrenic. Understanding the way in which he was
trapped between his cultures played an important part in helping
him to come to terms with his life.

Zoë was the daughter of a Greek businessman. She grew up in an enclosed Greek community in Africa. She wanted to become a ballet dancer and after a struggle her father sent her home to Athens to his family. But she found that she could not get the training she needed. It took another five years of fighting with her family before she was allowed to come to study in London during which time the idea of London became a Dick Whittington-like fantasy. When she finally settled down in Soho, aged twenty-one and rather old to train as a dancer, she found the realities very different. She was unprepared for life alone in this cold foreign city. She cried for her mother. She got into financial difficulties. She became pregnant. In the end we sent her back to Greece.

Manuela came from a traditional Spanish family. She rebelled against the formal aspects of Spanish life. She went to university and did well. She had no desire to be a formal Spanish wife in a formal Spanish family. She saw possibilities of escape when she met a young English engineer, who was working briefly in Spain. Against the wishes of her family, they married and came to England. It turned out that the engineer, disliking the increasing independence of English girls and feeling threatened by it, had gone to Spain hoping to find a more docile wife from a traditional and restricted background whom he could dominate and who would bear his children and bring them up according to his wishes. Needless to say the marriage was disastrous.

Each age and each culture *cradles* and *directs* in its own way and has its own ways of failing to support. This is also true of each family and mother within that age and culture.

Certain types of *unsupporting* environment generate *cradling* or *directiveness*. Others throw the individual back on his own resources and so become, for each person, largely a matter of how well the stage of *separation* was achieved.

THE QUESTION OF TODAY

In every society there are *cradling*, *directive* and *unsupportive* influences. A look at our own society, the western world, reveals that much of what is *unsupportive* requires separate, individual solutions and mastery rather than renewed *cradling* and *directiveness*. In other words, to meet these demands *enclosure* and *extension* are not enough. They must have led on to the stage of *separation*.

Law and order

Most of us live in an environment of comparative law and order. This can give both opportunities for *directiveness* and lack of support. A strong totalitarian regime imposes a *directive* environment but we have chosen systems of political and personal freedom. Freedom against a secure background creates for the individual a situation of choice, and for this he must be free within himself.

Our overall achievement of law and order is disturbed at different times and in different ways, including civil disturbance, persecution, international tension and war. Outwardly these disturb in ways that demand and lead to direct attempts to impose a more *cradling* or a more *directive* environment. Persecution is particularly likely to drive the persecuted in on themselves and encourage them to develop a *cradling*, protective environment, in which *enclosing* mothers are likely to play an important part. War tends to involve the whole population in a unified *directive* environment designed to overcome what is threatening and those who are accustomed to strongly *directive* environments are likely to do best and may even flourish. Many war heroes come from strongly *directive* backgrounds. Of course in all these situations individuals react in their own way, but overall the response involves activity directed from outside the individual. But the fear of war and the existence of (as opposed to participation in) sporadic civil unrest are disturbing in a way that involves an individual's personal resources, and therefore depends on the way in which he experienced the third stage of mothering, *separation*.

An able and experienced journalist, sent to Ulster by his newspaper to cover the civil unrest, was trapped in a hotel fire caused by a bomb and was rescued by firemen. During the rescue he behaved impeccably and then sent his report back to his newspaper. But afterwards he froze in panic and, installed temporarily in another hotel, was unable to leave his room. His wife had to fly over to bring him home. The incident precipitated a long period of fears and nightmares. He found it difficult to leave the house, and when he did was sometimes overcome by panic in the street. On one occasion he was marooned in a state of terror in a greengrocer's shop. He had to give up his job on a national newspaper and find a less demanding occupation. He was aware of always having felt insecure. His family environment was strongly directive and geared towards achievement and success. He seemed to have missed out on the stage of *enclosure* and was inadequately prepared to cope with a physically threatening environment.

Those who are preoccupied to an extreme degree with such matters as the breakdown of law and order, pollution and over-population do this in accordance with their personal patterns of *enclosure, extension* and *separation*. This is true regardless of the reality of the threat, though the less realistic the threat the more bizarre the individual's stages of mothering are likely to have been.

A man of twenty-five was convinced that the world was going to rack and ruin. He spent all his spare time busying himself with organizations designed to fight such matters as pollution, overpopulation, poor housing and colour problems. His own personal relationships were tenuous or non-existent. It was not surprising to discover that, as a child, as long as he could remember, he had had a secret fantasy that his mother was about to throw him into a ravine. He seemed to have experienced a poor stage of *enclosure* and very little stage of *extension*. His mother was very much a *separate* mother and in this premature *separation*, existent probably from birth, he had not managed to acquire the strength and resilience that comes from good stages of *enclosure* and *extension*.

A society that functions securely but which is perpetually under the threat of disruption makes demands on individuals that do not exist either in a society that is actually disrupted, for example by war, or in one that is more secure.

Health and food

Another characteristic of our western society compared with most other ages and cultures is good health and adequate food.

Child health has never been so good. Infant mortality and maternal mortality have never been so low. A mother nowadays expects her children to survive and to grow up. If these things do not happen she or her children are regarded as unlucky. Two hundred years ago out of five children born alive, four were dead before their fifth birthdays and it was common practice to give several children in the family the same christian name in an attempt to ensure that at least one of them bearing that name would grow up. A hundred years ago most families still lost one or several children, and motherless families were common both in life and in literature. Today we expect them all to survive and this has important implications for the theme of this book.

In most societies and in most ages nutrition has been poor, disease rife and death common. Such a situation demands a strongly *cradling* environment for the individual so that the child is protected by his *enclosing* mother who feels that he is part of her and gives him the best possible care. It also demands a strongly *directive* environment in which proper food is provided and disease is controlled and prevented. An important part of the *directive* environment consists of education, to help people make the most of the *directiveness* and overcome the dangers of ignorance and fatalism. Early child care manuals and programmes for child health were directed towards this aim, as they still are in developing countries. Under these circumstances ignorance and fatalism can be perpetuated by despair. The child, sick and unlikely to survive, is regarded as *separate*.

[Parents] looked upon it as a matter of fate whether or not their children survived. She would often say to a mother, 'What has happened to the baby?' 'Oh, it has died.' And she would say 'What a pity.' And the reply would be 'What the Lord Allah wishes.' Cicely would say vehemently, 'But the Lord Allah doesn't wish it at all. He gave you a beautiful baby. It died because you are careless. The Lord Allah wants you to use your brain and look after the baby properly.'*

In our society mothers no longer need to devote a large part of their lives to seeing that their children are well fed and healthy. These things occur easily and with the minimum of knowledge and effort. Inappropriate concentration on food and health is a common characteristic of *enclosing* mothers and *extension* mothers.

Many *enclosing* mothers are preoccupied with food and with feeding their children, even their grown-up children. Food comes to symbolize love and refusal of food symbolizes rejection. Food

* Ann Dally, *Cicely: The Story of a Doctor*, p. 103.

becomes part of *enclosure* for its own sake rather than *enclosure* part of caring for the child.

It is common for both *enclosing* and *extension* mothers to become preoccupied with their children's health. They are a trial to every doctor. For them the child's health is not a part of his healthy growing up to be a *separate* person but is a symbol of their love or of their own power and control. *Extension* mothers are often acutely aware of their children's body functions and are fully conversant with such matters as bowel functions, digestion and menstrual periods.

The present good health enjoyed in our society is liberating. But to those unprepared for freedom it can be threatening or else twisted and used.

Social structure

The influence of society and the whole process of fitting into it is *directive*. The stage at which the child is being helped by the mother to fit into society is mostly the stage of *extension*. As we saw in the last chapter, a settled environment demands nothing more, though it may be frustrating.

'All Things Bright and Beautiful' is one of the hymns most frequently sung in British schools. Only during the past twenty years or so has the following verse been deleted from school hymn books:

> The rich man in his castle
> The poor man at his gate,
> God made them high or lowly,
> And order'd their estate.

A settled society is *supportive*. It *cradles*, it *directs*, it forces. It can be frustrating and unpleasant, it can engender physical insecurity, it has many faults, but even for its less privileged members it offers a tradition, and it is predictable.

In a world that changes little, parental influence supports tradition. Tradition supports the distortions and limitations of parental influence. This is a limiting environment but it is also *supportive*.

Cradling and *directive* environments are becoming more difficult to maintain in adult life, for they depend on tradition. Tradition implies continuity, and continuity diminishes as the rate of change accelerates.

During the present century in many parts of the world the life of each generation has been different from that of the previous one. Tradition no longer supports people as it did when changes came more slowly, and when basic beliefs were not questioned as they are today. A big gap appeared between those who were grown up before the first world war and those who were not. The same was true of the second world war. Today those who grew up soon after the last war are conscious of an even greater 'generation gap' between themselves and young people.

Our present society is not settled. It does not support the distortions and limitations of parental influence, but increases them. So much more than before depends on the adequacy of the mother during the three stages.

We live in a society that aims at equality of opportunity. This means a highly competitive society. This makes it *directive* for those who participate and *unsupportive* for those who do not. Hence the increasing incidence of drop-outs whose mothers are liable to blame themselves and be blamed by others. Mothers nowadays try to *direct* their children through the competitiveness of the educational system during the *extension* stage. They may be hoping for conformity, submission or simply that the child will survive intact to reach the stage of being fully himself or able to impose himself on the environment instead of struggling to survive in it.

The ideal of equality of opportunity suits those whose temperament and type of mother enable them to cope with it. For these there is ample opportunity and support. For the rest there is loss of security at the top of the social scale and a new kind of frustration lower down. Both these lead to feelings of insecurity.

Beliefs and customs have probably never changed so fast and this means a loss of environmental support. We have no idea what the future will bring but we have reason to believe that it will be very different from the past and the present. We have no idea how best to prepare for it. In looking at the future we are not *cradled* or *directed* by the past to anything like the same extent as in former days.

Leisure

Probably in our society more people have more leisure than ever before. This is *supporting* as long as the leisure is based on security of work, food, housing and other basic needs. But it is *unsupporting* in the sense that, once these needs have been met, leisure means that people have to do things for themselves, find things in themselves which can be satisfying, and above all decide what to do. In this sense leisure is an *unsupporting* environment that demands independence and a satisfactory stage of *separation*.

The prevailing urban environment also creates difficulties. Not only is it frequently hard, harsh and ugly, but it is increasingly remote from nature and open spaces. Although contact with nature is by no means essential to satisfactory integration, it does make it easier in the sense that it throws less strain on the mother. Among the most *supportive* influences that can surround a mother and support her efforts to raise healthy children are a safe countryside with plenty of space to move about, a number of other caring, *supportive* adults to take an interest in the child and free access to children of comparable ages. Access to these things has been declining for two hundred years. Wordsworth worried about it in 1798:

For a multitude of causes unknown to former times are now acting with a combined force to blunt the discriminating powers of the mind, and unfitting it for all voluntary exertion to reduce it to a state of almost savage torpor. The most effective of these causes are the great national events which are daily taking place, and the increasing accumulation of men in cities, where the uniformity of their occupations produces a craving for extraordinary incident which the rapid communication of intelligence hourly gratifies.*

God

Loss of God is also important. Paul Tillich has written:

The anxiety of doubt and meaninglessness is, as we have seen, the anxiety of our period . . .

The decisive event which underlies the search for meaning and the despair of it in the twentieth century is the loss of God in the nineteenth century. Feuerbach explained God away in terms of the infinite desire of the human heart; Marx explained him away in terms of an ideological attempt to rise above the given reality; Nietzsche as a weakening of the will to live. The result is the pronouncement 'God is dead', and with him the whole system of values and meanings in which one lived. This is felt both as a loss and a liberation. It drives one either to Nihilism or to the courage which takes non-being into itself.†

* Preface to *Lyrical Ballads*, p. 249.
† *The Courage to Be*, pp. 140–1.

Belief in God perpetuates a *directive* environment, often keeps insecurity at bay and makes it less likely that anything further than the *extension* stage of mothering will be required. The decline of traditional Christianity and the widespread loss of belief in a God 'out there' has made it all the more important that, if people are to survive intact psychologically, they need to reach the third stage on a basis of security developed during the first two stages.

The strain on mothers and others

All this throws a great strain on mothers. It seems that not only do they need to be better at their job and more developed than before, but the outside world makes it increasingly difficult for them to achieve this.

The present overwhelming need for mothers is to give their children adequate love and support during the stages of *enclosure* and *extension* and then to help them to be free during the stage of *separation*. But many do not see it like this.

Suddenly, this issue has become important. Many people's problems and difficulties in our society can be seen as aspects of the struggle between trying to relate closely without distancing and trying to distance without true relationship or love, and sometimes, most damaging of all, trying to do both at the same time.

This conflict can be traced through work and play, marriage and family life, education and social welfare, medicine and its practice, and mental health and mental illness. It cuts across old conventional differences between left and right, rich and poor, liberal and reactionary. But it also cuts across new conflicts, even those that have arisen or been influenced by attempts to solve it. For instance there are battles being waged at present about education that is 'child-centred' or 'subject-centred'; about 'permissive' and 'authoritarian' attitudes; about medical practice in which the patient is regarded either as a whole or as a vehicle of disease. These conflicts appear to be about these very questions of relating to people and keeping them at a distance, but what is most confusing is that sometimes they are not at all what they seem. Authoritarian attitudes can be maintained humanely and 'subjects' can be taught with love. A 'child-centred' education and 'permissive' upbringing can mask neglect, intrusiveness and cruelty. A doctor can have a relationship with a patient that is satisfying to both while failing to treat the disease that is killing the patient or failing to treat a treatable disease. A survey of futurology done in the 1920s* discussed the rapidly declining ability of parents to bring up well-adjusted children. So the process is by no means new but for many families the limitations are now extreme.

A mother shut up with her young child in a high-rise flat, in an area made dangerous by traffic, hooliganism, impersonality and lack of access, is unlikely to make the best of any stage of mothering except possibly the first. Nowadays the environment in many ways has more to offer, but it does not support or hold to the same extent or in the same way. Personal relationships are more vulnerable and their development is hazardous. Yet mental health, certainly in so far as it involves coping with the environment, now depends on personal relationships much more than formerly, and these in turn depend largely on early experience. An environment that allows children to flourish and develop their capacity for imaginative activity and good human relations needs to be flexible and imaginative in ways that were not necessary before. Parental influence and parental relationships are for most people the basis of their relationship with the world. Certain types of parental relationship are suited to certain environments and nowadays there seems to be a special need for these relationships to be not so much traditional as flexible, personal, sensitive and imaginative.

We tend to talk glibly of 'good' and 'poor' relationships. 'Good' means loving in a way that values the other more than self and is flexible, sensitive and imaginative. 'Poor' can mean unwanted, careless, insensitive or full of hatred and frustration. In a poor relationship the mother is at a stage of mothering that is inappropriate to the age and development of her child. Either she is rigid and strict, or overprotective and indulgent, or she uses the child as an object to enhance herself and does not distinguish his needs from her own. Such situations can often be held in a *supporting* environment, but when the environment is *unsupporting* they are dangerously damaging.

Good relationships between parents and children are held in exceptionally high esteem at present. The present generation of parents is probably the first to believe passionately that their relationships with their children are all-important. Spock and Bowlby have left their mark, and their views have fallen on fertile

* Discussed in *The Times* (26 August, 1974).

ground. 'Do as I say and not as I do' has fallen into disrepute. Parents whose children run into trouble are blamed by society and feel guilty. Those who find the gaps widening between themselves and their adolescent or adult children may be desperately trying to bridge those gaps. By maintaining contact with their children and trying to follow them along whatever mysterious paths they happen to be pursuing, parents may find themselves setting out on a voyage of adventure and discovery. Through their children they discover that the old values no longer hold and come to work out new ones.

The changes of this century have created a crisis for parents which is now widespread in the western world. It tends to affect not only those who are parents but, increasingly, those who have had parents during the present century. In other words, all of us. Of course there have always been generation gaps. The young have always rebelled against their elders, and parents have criticized, deplored and 'not known what young people are coming to these days'. But the ultimate differences between one generation and the next have never been so great. In the past children mostly grew up to lead lives very much like the lives of their parents and in their turn they fought the same battles with their own children, often within only the first two stages of mothering. Such changes as did occur took place slowly, over several generations. The speed of technological advance has been accelerating for several hundred years but it is only during this century that it has been rapid enough to cause profound changes widely within a single generation, and now even within a few years.

Anyone who has been in close contact with young people over the past fifteen years will be aware of these changes. For instance children in their early and middle teens are very different from what children were even ten years ago.

The changes are of course most marked in large cities like New York and London. Since I live in London and my experience has been largely there, much of what I write may not yet be true of places outside. But it is relevant.

The tensions and burdens of parents are transmitted to their children, affect them, and are passed on in altered form to yet another generation. Most young people today are three or four generations from the first world war. These generations have passed in a changing environment that no longer supports as it did in a world where change was slow.

Yet people still need families, and the support of an accepting social setting. They need variety and change. And they have non-material needs which can be cruelly neglected in this materialistic age. There is also widespread insecurity and unease, due to the loss of belief in 'progress'. It is only in the past few years that the idea of 'freedom broadening slowly down from precedent to precedent' has had to be abandoned by serious people.

Some older people join in rather blindly with demands for a better life through Women's Liberation, through drugs, through divorce or through newer and freer relationships including the modern suburban occupation of 'wife-swapping'. A mixture of boredom and anxiety triggers off a search for novelty that seldom seems to take account of wider human needs or of any essential continuity with the past. The past, if recognized at all, is seen in terms of what is dead and irrelevant rather than in terms of harmony or organic growth. Small wonder then that satisfaction is minimal, rootlessness increased and depression breaks through.

There are more subtle and satisfying ways of dealing with these problems, but they require the courage for constant or repeated reappraisal of moral issues. Liberation can lead to opportunity, to means of more satisfying self-expression. Reshuffles and changes in families due to divorce and remarriage can be seen as attempts to restore the benefits of change for an extended family, the acquisition of new siblings, parents and other forms of step-relations can be exciting and enriching. Religious feelings can find new connections and new expressions outside any religious organization and in ways undreamed of in former days.

But such achievements do not come through the cults of instant satisfaction or avoidance of pain. There is no established or adequate moral code for modern living and we ignore this fact at our peril, either by trying to keep to one that is increasingly irrelevant or by ignoring moral problems altogether. There is no expert to show the way, no guide other than oneself. Each situation that arises is likely to lead to a need for further individual work and this can only be done by the self-development that is the essence of the stage of *separation*. This is something in which there need be no generation gap, and if this exists it is because parents and older people are often less honest, less free and more hypocritical than young people from whom they have much to learn.

What one might call the crisis of parents is at present seen most clearly among the parents of teenagers. They have brought their children through the early years, pehaps without too much difficulty. Knowing the importance of security and close relationships as well as good feeding and healthy living, they were able to provide these. But now they are faced with they know not what. What sort of world will their children live in? It is already very different from that into which they were born. Things happen that they do not understand. They have realized years before that the original hope that the son might follow in father's footsteps was a pipe-dream – and that to pursue it would be to court disaster. They may have been liberal and understanding and tried their best to adapt to the new world. But now the very foundations of their own is challenged – and there are limits to the extent to which they can change. Or they may stick their toes in and give way to the inevitable only with the greatest resistance, inch by inch. Meanwhile the world rushes on and their children may be torn in two.

Recently there has developed what may turn out to be the most dangerous movement of all. Running through Women's Liberation and through a number of campaigns aimed at controlling the world's population is an anti-child feeling masquerading as the common good. 'Babies are pollution,' says one slogan and, 'The world's problem is *your* child.'

Nowadays the children of parents who have little idea of their children as *separate* and ultimately independent beings, perhaps very different from themselves, are less likely than formerly to survive mentally intact, and less likely to thrive in modern western society. The same is true of the children of parents who make the distance so far or so early that a good relationship is never achieved. These attitudes can be protective in some circumstances, but inevitably tend to be non-respecting and non-communicating. They involve both a certain insensitivity and a denial of individuality or closeness which is likely, in our fast-changing society, to lead to unhappiness and psychological handicap.

So it seems that, for many people in the modern world, a reasonable chance of psychological survival means reaching the stage of *separation*, and this is either done the easy way, with their mother, or the hard way, on their own.

All these conflicts can be regarded as attempts to deal with an *unsupporting* environment.

RESPONSES TO INSECURITY

We have seen how feelings of insecurity vary with the three stages and types of mothering and in different environments. Reactions to these feelings are similarly variable.

The child of an *enclosing* mother, accustomed to the *cradling* environment generated by her, is liable to experience the outside world as an impingement, particularly when it makes demands. He reacts accordingly, trying to snuggle deeper into the cradle, shrinking from the intrusion and hoping it will go away. He tries to shut out the outside world and ignore it, to cling to his *cradling* environment and to solve problems by hanging on and being what his mother has made him or told him that he is rather than by taking active measures.

Saul was a gifted journalist, son of a dominating *enclosing* mother who had brought him up to believe that he was beautiful and brilliant with many special talents. All was well as long as Saul's employers shared this view. But when things became difficult and his employers became dissatisfied and demanding, Saul was unable to meet the challenge. He retreated further into himself, failed to cover assignments and to meet deadlines. Eventually he was sacked. His attitude throughout was to deny the gap between himself and the environment, to ignore the pressures, and to cling to his accustomed sensations without attempting to meet the challenge. Ultimately this became an attitude of defeat.

If the *cradling* environment created by mothers such as his is accepted so that it becomes part of ourselves, changes in our surroundings may impair our sense of well-being and this will make us feel insecure.

The child of an *extension*-type mother tends to react to a threatening or *unsupporting* environment in a different way. Here the tendency is to blend with the environment and adjust to it, to deny what cannot be coped with, probably impoverishing the personality by so doing, and to exert rigid control over what can be controlled. Thus the *unsupporting* environment is converted into the falsely *cradling* environment, the self is diminished and developed only at the periphery in an attempt to close the gap between it and the environment. Ultimately this becomes an attitude of submission, to live in a tight little world and try to shut out what does not suit it.

William was a successful young accountant who was doing well in his father's firm. As a boy he had been rather dreamy, had written a great deal of poetry and had wanted to read English Literature at university.

He had been persuaded by his father to study accountancy instead. He was neat, efficient and prosperous but inside there was an unhappy poet, starved and undeveloped and struggling to get out.

More extreme, those whose environments are failing to support and cradle them may indulge in massive denial and flee to some aspect of their environment which gives the appearance of support. In young people this often takes the form of being totally unnoticed by never impinging on anyone or else of doing outstandingly well at school, especially in examinations, or becoming tremendously and successfully involved in extra-curricular activities. This technique is likely to be successful for a limited period because teachers are usually pleased and by their praise and encouragement shore up the failing environment. This can have unfortunate or even tragic results because it delays the facing of the real situation which is the only hope of remedy. Only exceptionally perceptive teachers are able to entertain the idea that a young person who is doing well academically and giving no trouble can be emotionally disturbed.

Charity was having an affair with her stepfather which she was able neither to stop nor to enjoy. She was unable to face the conflict that this involved. Her mother, who knew what was going on, was powerless without support and assistance. One of the difficulties was that Charity denied her conflicts and buried her anxieties in school life. Though not outstandingly clever, she worked feverishly and passed her O levels with excellent grades. She played in the hockey and netball teams and won her colours. She played first violin in the school orchestra. She became a prefect and then head girl. For those who knew what was going on her halo was a transparent defence against anxieties that she could not face. She had created for herself an environment which was now supporting her false self in her intolerable situation. Her schoolteachers were unable to see that anything was wrong. They thought she was the best balanced and most normal girl in the school. But five years later Charity broke down.

The child of a mother whose stages of *enclosure* and *extension* were weak and who is therefore a *separation* mother usually has a kind of built-in insecurity which may have become so much part of him that he is not aware of it as separate from himself. The prematurely *separate* mother tends to ignore the *unsupporting* environment, is unaware of it and presses on regardless. Her failure to enclose and her failure to help the child adjust may lead the child to ignore the gap between himself and the environment. He may go through life with a feeling of being lost, of never having been supported, perhaps with a great bottomless hunger that can never be appeased. Or he may be conscious of intermittent insecurity or lack of support, mostly just insufficient for comfort, sometimes severe and searing. He may even feel supported by lack of support and proud of his refusal to be *cradled* and of his resistance to *directiveness*, in which case he is also likely to be aware of some underlying feelings of insecurity. Ultimately this becomes an attitude of rejection, as Edith Sitwell makes clear to us:

I was subjected, in the schoolroom, to a devoted, loving, peering, inquisitive, interfering, stultifying, middle-class suffocation, on the chance that I would become 'just like everybody else'. . . .
Minds must, in short, be ground down until there is nothing left but flatness.
. . . The middle-class grinders to which I was, as a child, subjected in the schoolroom, and the grinders of upper-class mentality to which I was given over, when a very young woman, have been attempting to subdue me throughout my life. They have never mastered me. The idea that I could be mastered by anyone or anything . . . was simply the effect of wishful thinking.*

Robert's mother was often ill and when not ill she concerned herself more with her social life and friends than with her children. Robert was left very much to his own devices, free, undirected, spoilt, feckless. He got into trouble at school because he disregarded rules, ignored demands made on him and seemed to be unaware of other people's feelings and the effect he had on them. He repudiated responsibility

* *Taken Care Of*, pp. 39–40.

and he did so little work that he failed all subjects in GCE. He was self-indulgent and uncomplaining. Those with whom he was in contact did the complaining. As far as Robert was concerned, as long as he had enough money, good food and drink and plenty of amusement, he was satisfied.

THE BALANCED MOTHER

Those who are fortunate enough to have had mothers sufficiently well-balanced between the three types to provide a secure background, and a firm basis for personal growth and realization, are likely to be undisturbed by the kind of environments that only some people find disturbing, and to deal with situations that they do find disturbing by careful appraisal, making good what is missing, rebellion against what is undesirable, and the use of imaginative curiosity to reach some kind of understanding and compromise. The gap between self and environment is not denied or closed or ignored but bridged.

The ways in which a mother can be 'sufficiently well-balanced' between the three types are vague and difficult to define. It would be easy to slip into the tautology of saying that if a person deals with insecurity by mastery and self-actualization then the mother was good enough and if he doesn't, she wasn't. But this ignores the strength and quality of the individual and also his particular method of dealing with insecurity, which may be constructive or destructive. Some can make up for deficiencies of any stage of mothering, others are unable to deal with even the minor deficiencies that are almost inevitably present since no mother and no environment can be perfect. Some people survive grossly inadequate and distorting experiences at any or all of the three stages of mothering, others seem to be destroyed by much less. Mothers are not the only important influence in learning to deal with a difficult environment.

To sum up, it seems that in our western society at present there is a particular need for the fullest development which a mother can attain both for herself and her children. This has always been needed by some. What is new is the extent to which it is needed today.

Wells could see this. In his autobiography, published in 1934, he wrote:

We are like early amphibians, so to speak, struggling out of the waters that have hitherto covered our kind, into the air, seeking to breathe in new fashion and emancipate ourselves from long accepted and long unquestioned necessities. At last it becomes for us a case of air or nothing. But the new land has not yet definitely emerged from the waters and we swim distressfully in an element we wish to abandon.*

We have now mapped the terrain of mothers and can turn to specific aspects of their influence.

* H. G. Wells, *Experiment in Autobiography*, Vol. i.

8 Mothers and Sex

He that does not love a woman sucked a sow.

Proverb

Oh, thou hast been the cause of this anguish, my
mother!

Thomas Haynes Bayly

One of the most important aspects of mothers' influence is in the sex lives of their adolescent and adult children.

Mothers are by far the strongest influence in most people's sexual lives. This is even more true of men than of women.

Many men marry women who are like their mothers. Some marry women who are apparently markedly unlike their mothers. Of these some turn out to be unexpectedly similar to the mothers they thought they were avoiding.

Angus disliked his mother and was convinced that his neurotic troubles stemmed from her. She was unsympathetic, hard, controlling, ambitious and fat. He married a slim and pretty little girl who told him how much she loved him and made him feel he was a big boy who made all the decisions. After ten years of unhappy married life he realized that his wife was unsympathetic, hard, controlling and ambitious. She had also grown fat.

But the influence of mothers on their children's sexual relationships goes deeper than looks and apparent character. It begins with the earliest contacts between mother and child. Freud perceived it as stemming from the infant sucking at the breast:

Sucking at the mother's breast is the starting point of the whole of sexual life, the unmatched prototype of every later sexual satisfaction, to which phantasy often enough recurs in times of need. This sucking involves making the mother's breast the first object of the sexual instinct. I can give you no idea of the important bearing of this first object upon the choice of every later object, of the profound effects it has in its transformations and substitutions in even the remotest regions of our sexual life . . .*

The influence is much wider and deeper than sucking at the breast or bottle. As Freud recognized, the breast is symbolic. Infants become dependent on whatever satisfies their needs. This is the basis of love. If the situation is satisfactory it shows later in the capacity to love in recognizable form. If it is not satisfactory it shows later as incapacity to love in recognizable form. Since infants' needs are usually satisfied by mothers, it is mothers who most influence the growth of the capacity to love. This was the basis of John Bowlby's important book *Maternal Care and Mental Health*, published in 1951.

'Love' develops from the original dependence of the child and from the satisfaction of needs in this dependent situation. The child is at the mercy of whoever or whatever satisfied his needs.

If 'love' is the aggregate of feelings which develop from the satisfaction of infant needs and from lack of this satisfaction it may and often does turn out to be different from what we usually think of as love.

Each of the three stages of mothering plays its part in the development of the capacity to love and the form it takes, and also the capacity to perform sexually.

SEX AND THE STAGE OF ENCLOSURE

The basis of what we think of as a close, loving sexual relationship is the mother–infant relationship, the stage of *enclosure*. Freud wrote:

when children fall asleep after being sated at the breast, they show an expression of blissful satisfaction which will be repeated later in life after the experience of a sexual orgasm. This would be too little on which to base an inference. But we observe how an infant will repeat the action of taking in nourishment without making a demand for further food; here, then, he is not actuated by hunger. We describe this as sensual sucking, and the fact that in doing this he falls asleep once more with a blissful expression shows us that the act of sensual sucking has in itself alone brought him satisfaction.†

In the most satisfactory mother–infant relationships the satisfaction of needs by the provision of food and comfort, both physical

* *Introductory Lectures on Psychoanalysis*, lecture 20.
† ibid.

and mental, are associated with feelings of security and of closeness to the other person. The stage of *enclosure* is a period in which the development of *rapport* and communication is based essentially on physical contact. It forms the basis of future sexual gratification.

> I will go back to the great sweet mother,
> Mother and lover of men, the sea,
> I will go down to her, I and no other,
> Close with her, kiss her and mix her with me.*

In his autobiography *Cider with Rosie* Laurie Lee describes his own stage of *enclosure*, prolonged somewhat by the family circumstances.

I was still young enough then to be sleeping with my Mother, which to me seemed life's whole purpose. We slept together in the first-floor bed-room on a flock-filled mattress in a bed of brass rods and curtains. Alone, at that time, of all the family, I was her chosen dream companion, chosen from all for her extra love; my right, so it seemed to me.

So in the ample night and the thickness of her hair I consumed my fattened sleep, drowsed and nuzzling to her warmth of flesh, blessed by her bed and safety. From the width of the house and the separation of the day, we two then lay joined alone. That darkness to me was like the fruit of sloes, heavy and ripe to the touch. It was a darkness of bliss and simple langour, when all edges seemed rounded, apt and fitting; and the presence for whom one had moaned and hungered was found not to have fled after all.

He also describes the slightly ominous feelings that heralded the end of this blissful state.

The sharing of her bed at that three-year-old time I expected to last for ever. I had never known, or could not recall, any night spent away from her. But I was growing fast; I was no longer the baby; brother Tony lay in wait in his cot. When I heard the first whispers of moving me to the boys' room, I simply couldn't believe it. Surely my Mother would never agree? How could she face night without me?

Lawrence describes the same *enclosure* feelings, though Mrs Morel, as we have seen, was unwilling to pass on to other stages:

Paul loved to sleep with his mother. Sleep is still most perfect, in spite of hygienists, when it is shared with a beloved. The warmth, the security and peace of soul, the utter comfort from the touch of the other, knits the sleep, so that it takes the body and soul completely in its healing. Paul lay

* Swinburne, *The Triumph of Time.*

against her and slept, and got better; whilst she, always a bad sleeper, fell later on into a profound sleep that seemed to give her faith.*

These were the feelings from which Freud forged the Oedipus complex.

The myth of King Oedipus, who killed his father and took his mother to wife, reveals, with little modification, the infantile wish, which is later opposed and repudiated by the *barrier against incest*. Shakespeare's *Hamlet* is equally rooted in the soil of the incest-complex, but under a better disguise.†

Elsewhere Freud writes: 'The Oedipus complex can, moreover, be developed to a greater or less strength, it can even be reversed: but it is a regular and very important factor in the child's mental life.'‡

If the mother is strongly of the *enclosing* type, she is likely to encourage the Oedipus complex, particularly when she regards her relationship with her son as the most important in her life and more important than her relationship with her husband.

'And I've never – you know, Paul – I've never had a husband – not really –'
He stroked his mother's hair, and his mouth was on her throat.§

She sits on the edge of the bed in her padded bra and her girdle, rolling on her stockings and chattering away. Who is Mommy's good little boy? Who is the best little boy a Mommy ever had? Who does Mommy love more than anything in the whole wide world? I am absolutely punchy with delight, and meanwhile follow in their tight, slow, agonizingly delicious journey up her legs the transparent stockings that give her flesh a hue of stirring dimensions. I sidle close enough to smell the bath powder on her throat – also to appreciate better the elastic intricacies of the dangling straps to which the stockings will presently be hooked (undoubtedly with a flourish of trumpets). I smell the oil with which she has polished the four gleaming posts of the mahogany bedstead, where she sleeps with a man who lives with us at night and on Sunday afternoons. My father they say he is. On my fingertips, even though she has washed each one of those little piggies with a warm wet cloth, I smell my lunch, my tuna fish salad. Ah, it might be cunt I'm sniffing.‖

Such mothers make it difficult for their sons to break away and make their own lives. Paul Morel, now out in the world, is earning

* D. H. Lawrence, *Sons and Lovers*, p. 68.
† *Five Lectures on Psychoanalysis*, IV.
‡ *Introductory Lectures*, lecture 13.
§ *Sons and Lovers*, p. 213.
‖ Philip Roth, *Portnoy's Complaint*, p. 48.

his own living, comes home every night to his mother: 'His life-story, like the Arabian Nights, was told night after night to his mother. It was almost as if it were her own life.'*

The sons of *enclosing* mothers have particular difficulty in sexual relationships and sexual performance. Morel and Portnoy, in different cultures and settings, both feel the immense pull of their powerful mothers and are weakened by it in their capacity to build up relationships with women. For such a boy mother remains his physical world. He may be unable to escape from her or he is filled with guilt about sex because the idea of doing it with his mother is incest and the idea of doing it with anyone else is infidelity. Such feelings are usually regarded as unacceptable in conscious thoughts and so are repressed. But the effect is apparent. A common result is a kind of negative homosexuality or bisexuality.

Michael, the only son of a mother who was widowed early, spent his childhood in close *rapport* with her. When he went to university she moved to the same town to look after him, and they stayed together thereafter. Michael, who was a doctor, had a wide circle of friends, a few rather weak sexual relationships with women and one or two, equally effete, with men. His mother was by far the most powerful influence in his life. As she grew old, he cared for her assiduously and she always maintained that no one could wish for a better son. After she died, Michael had several more mild affairs with men and finally settled down with a quiet, gentle, passive woman who looked after him, was not a threat to him and made only minimal sexual demands on him.

Paul Morel's mother fought actively against his girlfriend, Miriam, and won.

And in the same way she waited for him. In him was established her life now. After all, the life beyond offered very little to Mrs Morel. She saw that our chance for *doing* is here, and doing counted with her. Paul was going to prove that she had been right; he was going to make a man whom nothing should shift off his feet: he was going to alter the face of the earth in some way which mattered. Wherever he went she felt her soul went with him. Whatever he did she felt her soul stood by him, ready, as it were, to hand him the tools. She could not bear it when he was with Miriam. William was dead. She would fight to keep Paul.

And he came back to her. And in his soul was a feeling of the satisfaction

---

* *Sons and Lovers*, p. 113.

of self-sacrifice because he was faithful to her. She loved him first; he loved her first . . .*

Yet he fights against his mother too and the conflict is typical of the conflict of many struggling people.

Sometimes the sexual difficulties of the son of an *enclosing* mother are more concerned with his need to be admired and his confidence that this will happen.

> What could be more like Mother or a fitter background
> For her son, the flirtatious male who lounges
> Against a rock in the sunlight, never doubting
> That for all his faults he is loved; whose works are but
> Extensions of his power to charm? . . .†

In other fields, too, the connection between the early mother–child tie and later sexual behaviour is well known.

Thus there is good evidence that in primates as well as in other orders and classes of animal the properties of attachment behaviour and of sexual behaviour are distinct; nor is there reason to suppose that man is any exception. Nevertheless, distinct though the two systems are, there is good evidence also that they are apt to impinge on each other and to influence the development of each other. This occurs in other species as well as in man.

Attachment behaviour is made up of a number of component patterns and the same is true of sexual behaviour. Some components are shared. They are thus seen as elements in both sorts of behaviour, though usually more typically in one than in the other. For example, movements seen typically during courtship in some species of duck are seen also in newly hatched ducklings, in which case the movements are directed towards whatever object elicits their following response (Fabricius, 1962). In man, clinging and kissing are examples of patterns common to both types of behaviour . . .

. . . In man, overlaps between attachment behaviour, parental behaviour, and sexual behaviour are commonplace. For example, it is not uncommon for one individual to treat a sexual partner as though the partner were a parent, and the partner may reciprocate by adopting a parental attitude in return. A possible, indeed probable, explanation of the behaviour of the partner who takes the juvenile role is that, in that partner, not only has attachment behaviour persisted into adult life, which is usual, but it has,

* D. H. Lawrence, *Sons and Lovers*, p. 222.
    † W. H. Auden, 'In Praise of Limestone', from *Collected Shorter Poems;* Faber and Faber Ltd.

for some reason, continued to be almost as readily elicited as it is in a young child, which is not usual.*

If the stage of *enclosure* was difficult or distorted or absent, physical intimacy in later life is likely to be difficult to achieve and sexual relations tend to take other forms. For instance there may be a dislike of physical contact or a mechanical attitude to sex, regarding it as something which has to be done with technical skill, a kind of function and discharge of tension for which the participation of someone, usually of the opposite sex, is required. Or there may be perversions and these may be related in detail to actual past experiences with the mother. The fact that such attitudes to sex are widespread in our society is probably an indication of the great prevalence of disorders of the first stage of mothering.

SEX AND THE STAGE OF EXTENSION

The stage of *extension*, when the child is symbolically an *extension* rather than a *part* of the mother, normally gives the growing child the confidence to be himself, supported in the background but nevertheless courageous and exploratory, learning to deal with new situations, and learning to make new relationships. If he has experienced an adequate stage of *enclosure* the stage of *extension* is the period during which he begins to learn to assess the world and its different relationships. This is the period when a little girl makes a relationship, usually strongly sexual, with her father, which is so important in her sexual development that one might regard it as essential to a normal second stage of mothering. It is important for the little girl not only that she has a father but that he is capable of making this relationship with her, and that her mother is sufficiently secure and mature to allow it without being jealous, envious or competitive. The way in which her mother tolerates this relationship between father and daughter and the way her father reacts to this is likely to colour the girl's future relationships with other women. Also a father may allow himself to be controlled by his small daughter's seductiveness. There are many adult women who use sexual stimulation and withdrawal as a means of controlling their husbands, and often their sons too.

The peculiarities of mothering characteristic of the traditional

* John Bowlby, *Attachment*, pp. 233–4.

British upper class are often associated with sexual peculiarities. Jonathan Gathorne-Hardy, in his book on the British nanny, suggests that the nanny system has led to an idealization of the remoteness of the mother, and worshipping her from afar as an object pure and perfect and not to be defiled by 'dirty' ideas. This, he suggests, may account for the pattern of behaviour which has certainly in the past been common among upper-class men, of marrying a 'pure' wife who can be idealized, while exercising more robust sexual appetites on lower-class women. According to Gathorne-Hardy, the rise and fall of the British nanny coincided with the period when gentlewomen were not supposed to enjoy sex.

Many people who have had *enclosing* mothers are aware that in that early relationship lies the basis of later sexual relationships. Freudian psychology makes sense to such people and psychoanalytic insight into the maternal origins of sexual relationships comes easily to them. In contrast, those who have been raised by mothers of the *extension* type do not usually have this awareness and do not acquire this type of insight easily.

H. G. Wells, who had a strongly *extension*-type mother, describes this difference, and, in an impressive passage, attributes it to racial differences.

I do not wish to call in question the accounts the masters of psycho-analysis give us of the awakening of sexual consciousness in the children they have studied. But I believe that the children who furnished material for the first psycho-analysts were the children of people racially different, and different in their conceptions of permissible caresses and endearments from my family. What they say may be true of Austrian Jews and Levantines and yet not true of English or Irish. I cannot remember and I cannot trace any continuity between my infantile physical reactions and my personal sexual life. I believe that all the infantile sensuality of suckling and so forth on which so much stress is laid, was never carried on into the permanent mental fabric, was completely washed out in forgetfulness; never coagulated into subconscious memories; it was as though it had never been. I cannot detect any mother fixation, any Oedipus complex or any of that stuff in my make up. My mother's kisses were significant acts, expressions not caresses. As a small boy I found no more sexual significance about my always decent and seemly mother than I did about the chairs and sofa in our parlour.

It is quite possible that while there is a direct continuity of the sexual subconsciousness from parent to child in the southern and eastern Europeans, due to a sustained habit of caresses and intimacy, the psycho–sexual processes of the northern and western Europeans and Americans arise *de novo* in each generation after a complete break with and forgetfulness of the mother–babe reaction, and so are fundamentally different in their form and sequence. At any rate I am convinced that my own sexual life began in a naïve direct admiration for the lovely bodies, as they seemed, of those political divinities of Tenniel's in *Punch*, and that my first inklings of desire were roused by them and by the plaster casts of Greek statuary that adorned the Crystal Palace. I do not think there was any sub-conscious contribution from preceding events to that response; my mind was inherently ready for it. My mother had instilled in me the impropriety of not wearing clothes, so that my first attraction towards Venus was shamefaced and furtive, but the dear woman never suspected the stimulating influence of Britannia, Erin, Columbia and the rest of them upon my awakening susceptibilities.*

The child of an *enclosing* mother will have a totally different approach to sexuality from the child of an *extension* mother, a *separate* mother, or a mother balanced between the three stages. When the attractions of each are apparent it may be difficult to choose.

For several years Marian had two boyfriends, both of whom apparently wanted to marry her. She described them as follows: 'One of them is a lovely Jewish mother's boy, so soft and cosy and understanding. I get a lovely warm feeling when I'm with him. But he never really seems to do anything. He's just a lovely person to be with. Also he has lots of sexual hang-ups which I find rather trying. The other boyfriend is typically English, all stiff and polite. He was brought up by a cold mother and a cold nanny. He always had to do everything himself. He's so competent and reliable, but he's not cuddly.' Eventually she married the Englishman, not unhappily, but she still went through periods of yearning for the 'lovely Jewish mother's boy'.

SEX AND THE STAGE OF SEPARATION

If the first two stages have been experienced satisfactorily the child and the mother enter the third stage, *separation*. This is the stage during which actual sexual attachments and relationships are first likely to be formed. If the stage is not yet achieved there are likely to be difficulties due to this. Many of the storms and vicissitudes of adolescence are due to the coincidental struggles to establish the

---

* H. G. Wells, *Experiment in Autobiography*, Vol. 1, pp. 79–80.

stage of *separation* together with the pain and difficulties of learning about sexual experiences and relationships.

A young person who has not yet fully reached the stage of *separation* is unlikely to be capable of a relationship in which each regards the other as a *separate* person in his own right. One is only capable of this in so far as one has reached the third stage. A good example of courting based largely on the persistence of the early stages of mothering is that of Freud, described by his biographer Ernest Jones. Freud's pursuit of his fiancée Martha Bernays, his insecurity, his misinterpretation of reality and his inordinate and continual jealousy would have put off many girls.

Jones writes: 'Freud was throughout unnecessarily concerned with her health, and would often say that she had only two duties in life, to keep well and to love him.'* This could be a description of a typical *enclosing* mother and her child. Further:

Their relationship must be quite perfect; the slightest blur was not to be tolerated. At times it seemed as if his goal was fusion rather than union ... He learned all the tortures of which jealousy is supreme ... The suffering was so great that it would cost him nothing to drop his pen and sink into eternal sleep ... He was tortured by periodic attacks of doubt about Martha's love for him and craved for repeated reassurances of it ... inappropriate and unreasonable − ... [He demanded] complete identification with himself, his opinions, his feelings and his intentions.

Remnants of the earlier stages form a normal part of the stage of *separation* just as the beginnings of the later stages form an essential part of normal early stages.

If a young person has reached the stage of *separation* prematurely, the development of sexual or potentially sexual relationships will evoke other feelings and memories. There may already be too great a distance between self and others for close relationships, either physical and mental, to be possible. There may be a fantasy life that is self-absorbing and admits to no other participant. Copulation, if it occurs at all, is then symbolically no more than masturbation, which may indeed take precedence.

Charles came from a traditional upper-class background. He had never felt that he was in contact with his mother or with anyone else. He had been a loner for as long as he could remember and, married uneasily for the past two years, became impotent

* Ernest Jones, *Life and Work of Sigmund Freud*, chapter 7.

with his wife. Whenever the preliminaries of sexual intercourse began Charles developed an overwhelming urge to masturbate and he would leave the bed and go to the bathroom for this purpose.

A marriage or love affair always tend to elicit feelings that were experienced earlier in life. Thus some people who experience the stage of *separation* prematurely, when they fall in love, regress psychologically to the time when they suffered acutely from lack of contact with the mother. The loved person then tends to symbolize a substitute mother and is used as such. This is true of both men and women. Women also often seek father-substitutes in the men they love or marry.

Many people who have missed important parts of the early stages of mothering and compensate for this by mental activity develop a fantasy of a *Doppelgänger* or twin soul with whom they identify. One might say that they go through life looking for an identical twin of the opposite sex. This is the basis of many unsatisfactory marriages and of some satisfactory ones. When someone makes comments such as 'We're so alike', 'We have so much in common', 'We know exactly how the other feels', there is likely to be an element of this fantasy in the relationship.

Aberrant development of the relationship between mother and child can lead to a variety of other differences and difficulties. Since infants become dependent on whatever satisfies their needs and this forms the framework of the way in which in later life they will feel and express their love, it follows that loving and being loved in this sense covers a wide variety of situations, some of them far from the usual idea of love, and each of them can dominate a person's relationship with others for the rest of his life.

Loving or being loved in this sense may become associated with such feelings and situations as uneasiness and unrest; conflict, competition, rivalry; humiliation; feelings of rejection and fear or perhaps real danger of abandonment; generalized or specific anxiety; hating or being hated; feeling angry, frustrated, resentful or not understood; being controlled, violated or beaten; controlling, violating or punishing; manipulation and playing one person off against another; feeling empty, meaningless, futile.

Any of these feelings, or a combination of them, if they are associated in the unconscious mind with infantile dependence and the satisfaction of infant needs, will tend to be translated into sexual terms as the person grows up. They can often be traced or inferred in cases of sexual difficulty or perversion.

All her life Kathleen had suffered on occasions from a form of anxiety that seemed to be triggered off by situations of emotional importance. She felt it during her early days of sexual intercourse with the man she later married. She felt it on the day she agreed to marry him, again on the wedding day and thereafter whenever they disagreed seriously or he seemed to her to have been insensitive. Her first memory of this anxiety was of when she was about three years old and her mother had dressed her in knickers whose elastic was too tight. Her mother was a clumsy, pushy, insensitive woman who never took much trouble over what she did. I feel sure that she handled her babies in an awkward insensitive way. In fact it would be difficult to imagine her holding her babies with any sensitivity. It was not difficult to imagine the disjunctive relationship she would have had with any child. It did not surprise me that Kathleen frequently felt the same anxiety in connection with her own small daughter.

George and his wife had both been beaten and humiliated by their parents during childhood. Their marriage was based on violence and humiliation. George largely took over the role of aggressor while his wife remained as a kind of victim. An important part of their sexual relationship consisted of tying each other up and George used to beat his wife before intercourse. She encouraged him to do this. Sometimes, unknown to her, he went to a prostitute and persuaded her to beat him. After this he felt better and was then usually able to make love to his wife without the aid of string and whips.

A young man thought of his mother every time he tried to make love to his wife, and was impotent.

Another associated feelings of sex and security with physical violence.

Another felt that sex was basically competitive and always wanted two women present for it.

Another felt that the girl he loved was blaming him for not being what he wasn't, taller, handsomer, richer. He interpreted every remark she made as criticism of himself. When she apologized for being late he took that as a criticism of himself for being early. When they passed a tall man in the street he felt she was hostile to his average height. When a Rolls Royce passed he thought she resented the fact that he didn't own it. In bed he was impotent, always thinking she was blaming him. All this was derived clearly from his paranoid mother.

Mary was unable to sustain any love affair because she always developed an overwhelming terror that her loved one would reject her or leave her, so she became impossibly demanding and hysterical until what she feared most would happen. Her own mother had left her father on several occasions during her early life, abandoning her children apparently without conscience. In this vicious circle Mary's adult experience confirmed her childhood association of close relationship and satisfaction of needs with the feeling of being abandoned. This is a typical example of how people set up the situations of their infancy and then relive them.

Helen was an elderly virgin who had once been a successful actress. According to her own account, her life had been one long history of talented men falling in love with her. In every case, just as she was coming round to the idea of love or marriage, some disaster would occur. The man would disappear, die or turn out to be married. One of them turned out not only to be married but actually to be in the process of getting divorced and marrying someone else. In each case Helen added one more tragedy and loss to her life of tragedy and loss and she lived in a fantasy world of lost loves which neatly balanced her feeling of desertion first by her mother, who never really developed rapport with her, and then by her father, who died when she was fifteen.

Bridget was one of those not uncommon people who yearn to train in a profession in which 'relationship' is important. She herself had had a cold mother, no close relationships with anyone and was still a virgin at the age of thirty-five. She felt that she would be able to form close relationships with patients in the safe and structured setting of psychotherapy. She trained and practised as a psychotherapist and talked much about 'relationship', but I had the feeling that she never related to anybody. I believe that in her mind the feeling we have called love meant a combination of isolation, superior–inferior stratification, and control.

THE DIRECT INFLUENCE OF MOTHERS ON THEIR CHILDREN'S SEXUAL LIVES

Apart from feelings of identification which mothers induce in their children and the feelings that are developed in association with early contact and the provision of necessities, mothers also influence their children's sex lives in other ways. First, they have considerable influence on the way in which children find a sexual identity and the extent to which they are secure in this. Each parent tends to give to a child of the same sex a feeling of identification and also acts as a model against which the young person can match and compare himself. The parent of the opposite sex provides a model of the person to be loved, ideally not so much in personal characteristics as in range of possibilities, and this includes opposites. Sometimes the process becomes more complicated.

For instance a man whose mother was a bully married a quiet, obliging girl whom he proceeded to bully in the way his mother had bullied him.

Even more complicated was the sexual identity of Ronald. He was adopted by a married couple who were both practising homosexuals. Their house was constantly filled with eccentric people of indeterminate sex who performed strange activities in different parts of the house. It was not surprising that Ronald, an only child, seemed to have no idea who or what he was, was unable to form any relationships other than the most banal and superficial, and was a confirmed alcoholic by the age of twenty.

There can also be confusion about generation. There are certain mothers so seductive in manner and behaviour towards their young sons that they greatly confuse their search for self, damage their development and make future satisfactory relationships unlikely or hazardous. Some take delight in titillation, displaying themselves in scant clothing or seductive underwear, finding excuses for the boy to try on their clothes or touch their breasts.

One mother of this type brought her son up to pretend that they were brother and sister. He was never allowed to call her mother in public. In private she told him that because they pretended to be brother and sister in public this meant that they could sleep in the same bed. It is not surprising that at the age of eighteen the boy was in an acute stage of confusion, tension and depression. He felt that he had no identity, no background and no mother. He was terrified of girls, of sex, of work, of examinations. For the past two years he had escaped into himself, smoking a good deal of cannabis and experimenting with other drugs. Lately he had been trying heroin.

Such seductive mothers have a threatening influence on their sons and seem to diminish their masculinity. They are known as 'castrating mothers'. They manage to give their sons the impression that they are not and never will be truly men. Some of these mothers are basically hostile to everything masculine. The result is often a life devoted to endless reassurance on this point, perhaps by some kind of repetitive Don Juan behaviour, boasting, or by more bizarre means such as are found in men who have a compulsion to take frequent photographs of their penises. Such a compulsion may dominate the whole way of life. For instance, for obvious reasons, a dark room will have to be set up at home or a job will have to be found with access to one. Much time and effort will have to be devoted to concealing these habits, particularly if there is also a compulsion to file all the photographic prints cross-referenced according to date, mood, sexual activity and so on. Also in such a case discovery, perhaps by boss, wife or child, is likely to have dramatic consequences.

A mother of this type is also likely to wreck her daughter's development, often by being envious, competitive or crushing.

Some mothers control through guilt, through sex or through guilt about sex.

Such was the mother of William. He was impotent with his wife and had homosexual problems. He described his mother as 'frightened to death of life', and gave a vivid account of how she ruled her husband and her three sons from the living-room sofa, where she spent most of her days lying down between visits to hospital for investigation of symptoms. Her sofa was placed so that everyone had to pass it all the time. When the children walked past her she would grab them each in turn and make them describe exactly what they had been doing. 'It became safer not to do anything,' said William, 'because I always knew I would have to tell.' William also found his mother 'very seductive' and she used various devices to make him touch her breasts. Several times she persuaded him to dress up in her bra. On one of the rare occasions when she rose from her sick bed she took him shopping. He was about twelve years old. In a department store he became excited and had an erection. His mother laughed and pointed and said, 'What's that?' He felt humiliated about this for months afterwards and it still came into his mind as an upsetting memory. Sometimes he thought of it while trying to make love to his wife.

Mothers often have a direct influence on their children's early love affairs and this can be crucial, especially when feelings are raw or difficult and sexual identity is fragile. A mother who laughs at the wrong moment, or who is otherwise insensitive, rigid, prejudiced, controlling or intrusive at a crucial stage, can do much damage.

Jean's mother terrified her teenage daughter by telling her that she could always tell when virgins had been kissed. Jean thought this had something to do with getting pregnant.

Mrs B. assured me that her daughter Meg discussed all her problems with her and that she herself was an enlightened parent. Meg herself had told me only a few minutes before of these beliefs held by her mother and said that the first was untrue and the second only true in comparison with the only other people she knew who all, like her parents, belonged to a religious sect of exceptional closeness and strictness. Meg's problem was that she had formed an attachment to a boy ouside the sect. The sect strictly forbade all physical contact before marriage, and Mrs B. spent much time making sure that the rules were kept. One day she returned home to find the young people unexpectedly alone in the house. She thought the bed looked rumpled and made so many scenes about it during the following weeks that eventually Meg, dazed and confused, broke off her relationship with the boy and relapsed into an adolescent depression. Her mother had no idea what had brought this on and assured me that Meg had no worries, but absolutely no worries, so it must have come 'from heaven'. A few months later Meg formed an attachment to a boy who had also been brought up within the sect and who was also finding it difficult to adjust the beliefs and principles of his parents to the realities of the modern world.

Much of the way in which a mother influences her children's sexual lives depends on her own early experiences and in particular the way in which her own mother, and her father too, behaved towards her. Mothers who are unsure of their own sexual identity or sexual capacity and who lack the capacity to trust are of course less likely to be able to help their children than are mothers who are secure in these matters. The feelings tend to be passed from generation to generation.

'If you want to have sex, you've got to trust the core of your heart, the other creature.'* Trust, perhaps more than all other attributes, is passed from mother to child.

* D. H. Lawrence, *Sex and Trust*.

9 Hostility

If there was one thing he hated more than another it was the way she had of waking him in the morning ... It was her way of establishing her grievance for the day.

Katharine Mansfield, *Bliss*

Daily observations can show us how frequently the emotional relations between parents and their grown-up children fall behind the ideal set up by society, how much hostility is ready to hand and would be expressed if it were not held back by admixtures of filial piety and affectionate impulses.

Freud, *Introductory Lectures*, lecture 13

So long as the good and the bad are separated, children can tolerate violence, death and other things which might be expected to disturb them. But to discover that the person one believed was on one's side is actually malign is to enter so unpredictable and unsafe a sphere of experience that children become alarmed; just as an adult might if he discovered that the injections which his doctor was giving him were poisonous rather than therapeutic.

Anthony Storr, *Human Aggression*, p. 62

The worse sin towards our fellow creatures is not to hate them, but to be indifferent to them; that's the essence of inhumanity.

George Bernard Shaw, *The Devil's Disciple*

Gott ist raffiniert, aber boshaft ist er nicht.
(God is subtle but he is not malicious.)

Albert Einstein

Il faut haïr tout ce que j'aime.
(I must hate everything I love.)
Louis Aragon, *Richard II quarante*

If society is in danger, it is not because of man's aggressiveness, but because of the repression of personal aggressiveness in individuals
D. W. Winnicott, *Collected Papers*

Only in recent years has society accepted the existence of hostility between parents and children, particularly hostility of children towards their parents. Traditionally, the only permissible manifestation of hostility in the parent–child relationship has been that of parents for the purpose of training the child, or of dealing with annoying behaviour. Thus William Blake:

> Thou, mother of my mortal part
> With cruelty didst mould my heart,
> And with false self-deceiving fears
> Didst bind my nostrils, eyes and ears.

and Lewis Carroll:

> Speak roughly to your little boy
> And beat him when he sneezes,
> He only does it to annoy
> Because he knows it teases.

Since Freud it has been socially permissible to believe not only that it is normal for children to feel hostile towards their parents, but also that all children have such feelings and that most hostility in adults stems from hostility against the parents induced in childhood. At the same time traditionally permissible hostility of parents towards children ceased to be so acceptable, and verses such as those above could have been quoted at any time during the past forty years as examples of how not to bring up children.

During the past fifty years, while children's normal hostile feelings, along with their normal sexual feelings, have come to be accepted and better understood, parents have been expected to be accepting and understanding. Mothers in particular have also been idealized to a remarkable degree. In the middle classes, where theories of childrearing originate and whence they spread, a series of attitudes have ruled in none of which was concession made to individual variation in mothers, to their personal difficulties or to any antagonism or hostility that they might have towards their children. Occasional anger or distaste might be permitted, but not other forms of hostility unless heavily disguised. In the 1920s and 1930s Truby King urged control from birth at a time in which many articulate middle-class people wanted only one or two children. In the 1950s Bowlby warned of the dangers of separating mother and child, Spock preached common sense and Winnicott bolstered up self-confidence. It was the beginning of the era of 'demand feeding', 'attachment' and 'separation-anxiety'. Families seemed to be larger. Everyone seemed to have or to want children. Though lip-service was paid to mothers who had interests or intellects, hardly a word was written or whispered to encourage them to pursue these, at least until their children went to school. Every middle-class mother knew her duty and great pressure was brought on her to feel guilty if she did not perform it in the accepted way. Anxious mothers wrote to magazines inquiring whether it was psychologically 'safe' to leave a baby asleep with grandma while mother went shopping, or whether a few nights away would cause 'permanent damage'.

There was also tremendous pressure on women to get married and have children, whether they were really suited for motherhood or not. The era of semi-respectable spinsterdom which had been caused by the existence of some three million 'surplus' women after the casualties of the first world war was over. The second world war did not cause nearly so many casualties and there were now nearly enough men to go round. Women who let it be known that they weren't interested were likely to encounter hostility and opprobrium. The greater the idealization of motherhood, the greater were the pressures to become involved in it, however unsuited you were to it and however happily you might be involved with other matters.

During that time and later hardly anyone spoke of the falsity and denial that lay under the idealization. No one spoke of the cost at which Bowlby's commands (issued not by him but by those who chose to misinterpret him) were obeyed, and few noticed how often they were kept to the letter but in a manner that obscured the enormous numbers of lonely children who were emotionally without care or understanding. Some of the worst cases of this that I saw personally during this time were the children of psychoanalysts and other 'experts' who were busy propagating their gospel.

Mrs D., a psychotherapist, spent much time working for the cause of persuading mothers not to separate from their children under any circumstance. She did this from home, so that she could practise what she preached and not be separated from her own children. She only went out to give lectures and attend seminars in the evenings when her husband was home. What was obvious in entering her house was the lack of contact between her and her children. Physically she was never absent from them but in every other way she was hardly present. Wrapped up in her own thoughts about the dangers of separation she was markedly separate from her own children. She seemed like a modern Mrs Jellyby, the lady in *Bleak House* who was so preoccupied with charitable activities for the benefit of the natives of distant Borioboola-Gha that she neglected her own family. I was not surprised to discover later that Mrs D. suffered from a kind of neurotic anxiety which made her unable to touch people, even her own children. Since these were adopted it seems likely that her fear of physical contact may have been very extensive indeed.

It is not uncommon for a mother to feel physical distaste for a child. 'My baby reminds me of a skinned rabbit,' said one. Another felt that she might have been more attracted to her baby if he had been furry. Only recently has it been possible to say such things openly with comparative ease.

Until recently it was not acceptable to express overt hostility to young children, to admit to having strong negative feelings towards them or even to be conscious that, however much they were loved, they could also be an enormous and at times almost intolerable burden. Cruelty to children was something that always seemed to happen somewhere else. The existence of 'battered babies' was not even discovered until the late 1940s and it was another two decades before they were freely discussed, even in professional circles. More recently they have been headline news but in a way that seems unrelated to ourselves or to the people next door. Similarly, the work of the National Society for the Prevention of Cruelty to Children was not a subject for polite conversation and its reports always seemed to deal with cases so bizarre (for example a child made to stand to attention in a back garden for hours at a time, and another who was kept by his mother in a chicken house as though he too was a chicken) that normally devoted mothers felt nothing in common with them and the effect, if any, was more likely to be one of smugness.

Virtually nothing was written for lay people about unwanted children or about the practical problems of unmarried mothers or one-parent families. Virtually every mother's manual and magazine article assumed that the baby in question was wanted, loved and had two loving and relatively well-off parents.

Looking back on it now one can see what a strain this imposed on many mothers and, to a lesser extent, on fathers too. For instance, the idealization of childrearing meant that much of the difficult side got left out. The emphasis laid on the importance of parents, particularly mothers, caused (and still causes) an enormous amount of guilt in parents when things go wrong. This actually makes things worse because it increases the idealization and therefore perpetuates the denial of the darker side, hostility, and so increases the vicious circle.

Another source of discrepancy during this period came from the fact that in a way it was also a peak period for women's education. More girls than ever before were staying at school beyond the statutory leaving age and more were going to university. Most of these then got married and soon after finishing a high-powered course training her mind and opening her eyes to infinite possibilities in the world, a young woman tended to find herself tied to a baby and reading books on child care, struggling to do everything right and forcing herself to be different from what she had grown up and been trained to be. The result was a good deal of suppressed unhappiness and depression whose accompanying hostility could only find outlets through surreptitious channels.

For many people it was also a period of decreasing marital stability. With the decline of Christianity, the increase of worldly opportunities, particularly for women, the increasing sexual freedom and greater interest in human relationships, more people were refusing to accept their lot and were turning towards new arrangements, new solutions and often the divorce court. The illegitimacy rate was also rising. Thus an increasing number of mothers found themselves paying lip-service to the conventional attitude of happy childrearing in the midst of a loving family when they were actually locked inside impossible marriages or else on their own, unloved and unsupported.

The backlash was inevitable. As we have seen, it started in the United States with Women's Lib. Though not in itself hostile to babies, many of the movement's members were and are. Later the attack on babies came from other sides too. For instance, there was suddenly an interest in 'battered babies' (a subject hitherto un-mentionable in the popular press despite extensive documentation). Another sign of the times was a popular car sticker which said 'World Pollution is Your Baby'. Hostility to babies was suddenly creeping up on all sides. There was also increasing awareness of the generation gap, and of the fact that many young people were not growing up in the way their parents had and were not going to step into their shoes or be content with the same kind of lives.

An interesting development recently has been Dr Spock's much-publicized 'recantation'. This was not really a recantation at all because he has only actually said that he now feels that some of his ideas may have been too 'permissive'. Yet this has been taken in some quarters as though it was a total reversal of everything that Spock has ever said or taught. Another interesting aspect of the matter is that Spock has been 'recanting' in this same mild way for years, and in the same magazine. So why did the British press, who ignored it before, suddenly in 1974 choose to make it news head-lines? The answer to this must be that by then it was a common feeling (common enough to sell newspapers) that there is something amiss with the accepted views of childrearing that have been spread during the past twenty-five years or so. And one result of all this is that hostility to children comes more into the open.

Nowadays it is becoming fashionable to say that you don't want children, though the idea provokes anxiety in some who have children. It is now common knowledge that too many unwanted babies are born and that they turn into unhappy adults and produce more unhappy children. We all know too that many young mothers of even the most wanted children suffer from severe depression. As yet we can only guess the effect this has on the children. It is now acceptable to say in even the most starry-eyed women's magazine that having children is not a must for everyone and that bringing them up requires hard work, persistence and self-denial along with talent and inclination.

Of course during all those years of idealization there must have been an enormous amount of suppressed hostility. During the Truby King era and earlier parents could easily unload their hostile feelings by being excessively insistent on matters such as cleanliness and toilet-training. Psychoanalytic influences ceased to make this outlet respectable, but during the past few years unhappy hostile parents have been able to take it out of their offspring by other means, for example extreme attachment (amounting to extreme control) by subterfuges such as pushing into achievement (early reading, 'creative activity', or language development).

Now it is becoming even more difficult. In the old days hostile feelings were at least 'held' with a supporting environment which helped whatever love was there to emerge. Nowadays if you are unhappy with your baby or young children you are more likely to encounter the attitude that you have only yourself to blame for having them at all and so society is providing less of this kind of support.

The word hostility covers all forms of unfriendly and antagonistic feelings. A certain amount of it is part of being a mother or a child. As in all close relationships hostility can be normal, helpful, destructive or pathological. It may comprise distaste, anger, hate, jealousy, envy, malice, attack, abuse or a combination of these.

Distaste between mothers and children usually concerns only part of themselves or their activities. Thus a mother may find distasteful such things as her baby's crying or his dirty napkins, her toddler eating woodlice in the garden, her older child's table manners or behaviour, or her adolescent's appearance, unwashed smell or choice of friends. Having these feelings does not mean that she does not love the child. The child too may feel distaste for certain things the mother is, says or does. He may feel annoyed when she does not understand, discontented at what she imposes on him or embarrassed at some of the things she says and does. This does not mean that he does not love her.

Anger is a short-lived emotion which is readily experienced towards those we love. It is provoked by frustration, and also by anxiety. For instance, a mother may feel frustrated because her child dawdles and then angry if, as a result, they miss the train. Or she may be desperately anxious because her child is lost but the minute he is restored to her she has an outburst of anger towards him. Many situations which cause distaste can also easily spill over into anger. For instance a mother may feel distaste at the careless and clumsy way in which her child comes into the room but if, in so doing, he breaks a vase, she is likely to become angry.

Distaste and anger are aspects of hostility which are normal and inevitable. Provided they are conscious, accepted and expressed, even if only privately to oneself, no harm is likely to be done. But some people are unable to express them or even consciously to feel them. Therefore they are unable to accept them or to come to terms with them. The hostility then remains, tends to be inwardly destructive and is liable to take other forms.

> I was angry with my friend
> I told my wrath, my wrath did end.
> I was angry with my foe:
> I told it not, my wrath did grow.*

Hate is more enduring than distaste or anger. According to McDougall (1908) anger is a simple, primary emotion, whereas hate is a sentiment, i.e. 'an organized system of emotional dispositions centred about the idea of some object'. Freud (1915) wrote that hate is the response of threats to the ego or self. In his later writings he viewed it as a manifestation of the death instinct. For the purpose of this book hate is regarded as an enduring, composite emotion which is by no means always conscious and sometimes never so. In many people it floats in and out of consciousness, triggered by circumstances, intimately associated with love and, like love, directed against the whole person, not merely an aspect of character or behaviour. It is misleading to think of hate as the opposite of love. It is only the opposite as the reverse of a coin is really part of it. The true opposite of love is indifference, which is not part of hostility, though some forms of hostility can feign indifference when they remain unaccepted and unconscious. Thus hate is part of every loving relationship, though not necessarily a prominent part. Provided it is conscious and accepted, not too powerful for too much of the time, and balanced by love, it is unlikely to harm.

Peter's mother always had too much to do and was always late. He disliked having to wait for her whenever they made a

* William Blake, 'The Poisoned Tree'.

rendezvous. One might say that he had a distaste for this characteristic of his mother, though he knew he loved her very much. But on occasions he felt more than this. One day she was so late arriving at his school concert that not only did she embarrass him because everyone stared at her and some of the boys laughed, but she even missed his own part in the concert. That day he knew he hated as well as loved her.

Mary's baby yelled and yelled. Neither she nor her husband had had more than two hours' consecutive sleep since he was born. They were beginning to quarrel more than before, largely from fatigue. Mary felt the baby coming between herself and her husband, and preventing her from being at her best and doing what she wanted. She felt she hated him.

Mrs P.'s son Tom didn't turn out as his parents would have wished. They had a clean, tidy home and Mr P. had a clean, tidy, job. Tom was dirty, forgetful, indifferent to middle-class values, with virtually no interests in common with his parents. Mrs P. felt disappointed and threatened. There were times when she hated Tom.

Hate is part of love and also derived from the way in which we were treated in our early years. Introspective people can often trace the way in which they hate to feelings they had during childhood. Some situations are particularly likely to bring out feelings of hate. Every mother has sensitive areas which may be activated. Every mother can feel frustrated, some more than others. Some mothers, however much they desire and love their children, have other needs which the existence of children makes it difficult or impossible to satisfy. Sometimes there is something in the child himself which makes him particularly easy to hate. This may be behaviour which the mother finds particularly difficult to tolerate, perhaps because it touches on old wounds or reminds her of her own faults. It may be some disappointment caused by the child, perhaps because he is abnormal or handicapped, or simply because he has failed to live up to the mother's expectations. Sometimes there are conditions in the environment which encourage a mother's hate, perhaps poverty or poor housing, or social pressures which a mother either feels unable to keep up with or else regrets that she has.

Sonya never really wanted children. She was happy in her job in a travel agency and living with her husband in a small apartment in the West End of London. But in the 1960s social pressures to have babies were considerable. Childlessness was regarded as socially reprehensible. By the time Sonya and her husband were in their early thirties nearly all their friends had moved out with their young families to the suburbs and the chief topic of conversation on social occasions was babies and children. They decided to give way to the pressures and start a family. Sonya produced one normal and one handicapped child and hated both at least as much as she loved them. Within a very few years she noticed that the climate of opinion was changing and it was now respectable to be childless. 'I wish to God I had remained that way,' she said, looking at the long years ahead.

Another form of hostility essentially associated with love is jealousy. Unlike hatred it involves three parties, one of whom loves another and a third who arouses anxiety in the first about his security in the loved one's affections. Typically, jealousy is evoked as part of the Oedipal triangle. For instance the mother and daughter are jealous of each other concerning the father's affections or the father and son are jealous for the attention of the mother. But jealousy in a family does not always go with this pattern of the sexes.

Stanley looked forward to becoming a father but after the baby, a daughter, was born he found that he felt strongly jealous of the attention which she required from his wife.

Kate's relationship with her husband turned sour after the birth of two sons. In compensation he turned increasingly to the children for love and general emotional satisfaction. Kate became increasingly jealous of the boys without being in any way capable of repairing the relationship with her husband.

Envy is a form of hostility that is sometimes confused with jealousy but is in fact quite different. Envy is the hostile contemplation of another's advantage. In contrast to jealousy it involves only two people, the envier and the envied. According to McDougall (1931) envy 'is a binary compound of negative self-feeling and of anger'. According to Freud 'penis envy' occupies a central position in the psychology of women. This idea has been fiercely attacked in recent years, with good reason, but it is still true to say that envy of men is important in the psychology of some women. Melanie Klein went much further in developing theories about envy and went so far as to postulate innate envy of the mother's breast and its 'creativity'. Nowadays the feelings she describes are more likely to be attributed to faults in the early relationship between mother and child rather than to any innate processes. For practical purposes we can ignore these theories and concentrate on envy as the grudging contemplation of another's good fortune. Mothers can envy their children their youth, their freedom, their opportunities. They may envy other mothers who seem to have more rewarding children, or childless women who have no maternal responsibilities. Children can envy their parents in a number of ways. It seems, however, that envy only develops as a result of deprivation. Though common, it is not part of normal hostile feelings as are anger and hate.

Malice is an active wish to injure or destroy. It may result from any of the forms of hostility mentioned so far and it may itself take many forms. It may consist of a temporary, or even momentary, desire to hit out, either physically or mentally. When we are angry or suddenly filled with hate, this is a normal reaction, conscious and easily understood. But often it is much less straightforward. Since it is frequently unacceptable to have malicious thoughts, particularly against those closest to us, we do not always acknowledge them in a straightforward way, and frequently we cannot even allow ourselves to be conscious of them. This is particularly true when the malicious thoughts are strong or bizarre, or in people who have difficulty in acknowledging or expressing their hostile feelings.

Straightforward strong malicious feelings can be distressing. Mothers are not infrequently distressed by sudden desires to injure or torture their babies, and they are not necessarily bad or unsuccessful mothers. Other mothers have similar thoughts but are unable to acknowledge them as their own. The hostile ideas seem to come out of the blue and from elsewhere. Such mothers usually feel a great need to reassure others that they love their babies, that such thoughts are 'utterly alien' to them and so on. Another way of dealing with unacceptable malice is by underplaying it. For instance one might acknowledge that sometimes one feels somewhat hostile towards someone without realizing the real extent of that hostility.

This was the method used by Sally against her devious mother from whom she was unable to separate. She would acknowledge, smiling, that she sometimes felt angry with her mother, but meanwhile the full extent of her feelings went unrecognized and was wrecking her development.

Often the malice does not come into consciousness at all. It is repressed, denied, displaced, or changed into something else. There may be idealization, in which there is an inability to see the other person as a real, whole person with faults as well as virtues. This usually goes with a poor judgement of external reality. Or the malice may be projected from one's own children on to other people's children or on to their school. Malice towards one's mother may be converted into a hatred of political oppression or pollution or of other mothers. An example of this was an ardent voluntary worker in the cause of birth control. She had an intense desire to stop other people having babies and this stemmed from profound malicious feelings towards her own mother.

Sometimes the malicious feelings are turned into what appears to be their opposite, for instance an intense preoccupation with one's child's or one's mother's welfare. Excessive solicitude contains a powerful element of malice.

In the presence of hate and envy, especially when it is concealed, there is a tendency for malice to be activated by normal distaste and anger.

The forms of hostility discussed so far concern feelings and are therefore in essence passive. Any of them may be converted into active forms of hostility which are attack and, if damage is done, abuse. Some people convert their feelings into action easily, but luckily only a few do this to an extreme degree. There was a recent newspaper report about a man who cut off his mother's head. His explanation was that 'she got on my nerves'. Such an action is extremely rare even among madmen. But many people convert their feelings easily into some form of action, perhaps lashing out either physically or mentally. Others find it less easy or have greater control, and some find it impossible. Yet others tend to do it indirectly.

Mothers who easily convert their hostility into action include some of the best and also some of the most damaging. If the relationship is sound the child gradually learns, like the mother, to express hostility without the fear of losing love. But when it is unrestrained or inappropriate the mother's expression of hostility can damage the child. Most parents who batter their children and damage them are people who cannot express hostility without physical violence, usually because that was the way in which their own parents behaved, and the previous generation before them. Among all conditions for which children are admitted to hospital only cancer is more likely to be fatal than 'battered child syndrome'.

Psychological battering, though more difficult to detect, is probably much commoner than physical battering, and just as likely to be permanently damaging in its effects. Not much is known about it as yet, though many case histories appear in different parts of this book.

Sometimes there is a combination of the two.

Betty's mother, a strongly *extension*-type of mother, wanted her children to be a credit to her. When Betty failed the eleven plus examination her mother was angry and shouted that she had let her down. Betty became upset and pulled out all her eyelashes. This made her mother even angrier. She couldn't bear Betty to detract from her good looks in any way. She felt that it detracted from her own. She hit her.

People who have difficulty in expressing normal hostility usually develop various secret methods of dealing with it. They are 'secret' because they are usually hidden from those who use them, though often not from others.

When hostility is unconscious or unexpressed, it usually leaks out. In this leakage, hostility is expressed, not openly, but only by words or deeds under the guise of something else.

A common form of leakage of hostility is simply over-reaction to a situation in which a certain amount of reaction would be justified or desirable. For instance a mother whose child has failed to wash his face when asked to do so may seize him angrily and scrub his face herself, roughly and painfully. She may at the same time remember being flung across the room in her childhood by her own angry mother. Similarly a child who is mildly frustrated by a parent or teacher may react violently. Being crotchety or 'getting out of bed the wrong side' usually means that some pent-up hostility is being discharged through a series of minor irritations.

Mothers can also vent their hostility by under-reacting to situations in which participation or activity would be more appropriate. For example a mother who is unconsciously hostile to her child may be unduly careless of his safety in traffic, crowds or other dangerous situations. She may fail to educate him about such dangers as electricity, cliffs and strange dogs, or in matters of social behaviour, so that he makes a fool of himself. One mother, while dressing and behaving impeccably herself on social occasions, managed to imbue her daughters with a sense of guilt if they did so themselves. Thus the mother retained her own sense of superiority and kept them in their place.

Another form of leakage of hostility is by over-control. This often masquerades as just the opposite of hostility, genuine concern. I met a mother the other day who would only allow her talented daughter to go to university provided she studied law, a subject in which she had no interest. This is a typical manifestation of hidden hostility. Then there are mothers who insist that if their children go out to play, they mustn't get their clothes dirty, and those who, apparently with the best intentions, make their children wear peculiar clothes or hairstyles, guaranteed to cause them to be teased at school. There are mothers who won't let their children join in with others because, they say, it is dangerous or unseemly or not what they expect a child of theirs to do. There are mothers who insist on knowing what their children are doing every minute of the day. There are thousands of ways of leaking hostility under the guise of loving interest and care. The child may get his own back by leaking his own hostility by refusing to give his mother any information about himself, however trivial. Or he may deliberately set out to make his mother anxious by, say, failing to return at the appointed hour or to telephone as promised, or by making out that the company he keeps is far more irresponsible and unsavoury than is in fact the case. In such cases the child is probably aware of his feelings of hostility, more so than is his mother.

Hostility can also be leaked by false reaction, for example by the faint praise that is really damnation. A mother managed to put her son off going to art school by repeating *ad nauseam* such remarks as 'Yes, darling, that's a lovely drawing, but I don't *really* think you've got much talent, do you?' She wasn't really interested in whether or not he had talent, she simply wanted him to become a chartered accountant. There is also a kind of hostile pseudo-praise that causes embarrassment. Some mothers react to their children's drawings as though they were at least equal to Picasso's.

Another type of leaking hostility can be seen in various forms of so-called 'mistakes', clumsiness or error, which may be physical, verbal or behavioural. The mother 'forgets' to attend the school sports or to keep some promise she has made. The child 'forgets' his mother's birthday or the errand she asked him to do on his way home from school. She loses his book and it happens to be the one she doesn't approve of. He borrows a hundred things from her and fails to return ninety-nine of them. 'I'm terribly sorry' they say to each other unless they have an out-and-out row. Society has its own way of accepting such 'errors' and permits hostility to be expressed in this way. This can be a real safety valve.

So-called 'slips of the tongue' are also permitted. We tend to ignore what is often their true significance. A mother says to her child 'It's time you were dead', when she means 'in bed', and then adds quickly, 'I'm sorry dear. I was thinking about that poor little bird we found with a broken leg.' She may well get away with it.

Last, a common type of leakage of hostility can be seen in certain types of lack of reciprocity. There may be an apparent unawareness of the other person, perhaps talking too loudly or too softly or boring the other almost to tears, going on and on about something, ignoring the other's tiredness, sensitivities, preoccupation elsewhere. Hostility can be leaked by withholding information, or by insistence on inappropriate truthfulness, or by wrong timing in almost anything. Or a mother may expect her grown-up son to be as interested in the details of home life as he was when he was small. A grown-up son or daughter may make the same demands on an ageing mother that they made when they were incapable of doing things for themselves. Thus a longed-for visit can turn into a nightmare for the old lady, especially if the long-awaited son or daughter brings along a spouse and a row of children who settle down and expect to be provided for.

Of course all these unmutual activities also engender hostility as well as being manifestations of it. In this way vicious circles are formed and perpetuated.

Hostile activity can be anything from occasional and momentary to continuous and dominating the whole relationship. Sometimes even the most overwhelming hostility seems to take only one form, for example a mother may be unable to bear children to be friends with each other, or she may have an excessive preoccupation with her own or her children's health which can be a form of hostility. Or she may instil insidiously into her child a drive to failure that will affect everything he does for the rest of his life.

The most malevolent mothers not only activate their hostility. They also impinge and violate.

The quantity of hostility between mother and child and the form it takes varies at different stages of mothering and according to whether the mother is predominantly an *enclosure* mother, an *extension* mother or a *separation* mother. At the stage of *enclosure* hostility develops in the mother because of dirt, crying, mess, discontent, being disturbed, being tied and general lack of *rapport*. These things engender hostility particularly when the stage of *enclosure* is difficult and in mothers who cannot achieve it. Hostility during the first stage can lead to rejection and even catastrophe. Prolongation of the first stage leads to its own form of hostility, the so-called 'smothering' love that is basically hostile. There is probably an element of this in all *enclosing* mothers.

The second stage of mothering, *extension*, engenders hostility involving particularly shame, disgrace, failure, competitiveness and problems of control. In mothers who are predominantly *extension* mothers this may be extreme, especially in so far as they feel that the child has let them down. Unrealistic expectations may further increase the hostility on both sides. Conversely a relative lack of *extension* feelings may lead to hostility due to annoyance and feelings of being impinged upon.

Hostility at the stage of *separation* may be part of a battleground in which both mother and child fight each other and themselves. A sense of loss is part of this stage and a sense of loss creates hostility. Also, old feelings and old hostilities are reactivated and trigger situations in which opportunities for doing this abound. Moreover, if the mother is incapable of achieving the stage of *separation*, she may develop enormous hostility to her child's bid for independence. Alternatively, if *separation* comes too easily, to the point of being neglect, there may be the hostility of rejection, perhaps even to the extent of turning the disappointing young person out of the house.

A certain amount of hostility in both mother and child is probably necessary if both are to develop to the stage of *separation*. Hostility is an integral part of finding independence.

10 Rebellion

There is a generation that curseth their father, and doth not bless their mother.

Proverbs 30:11

Your mother shall be sore confounded; she that bore you shall be ashamed.

Jeremiah 50:12

There are times when parenthood seems nothing but feeding the mouth that bites you.

Peter de Vries

The best remedy for disturbances is to let them run their course, for so they quiet down.

Baltasar Gracián

In our society rebellion is part of normal growing up. Children begin by loving uncritically so that whatever their parents are or do actually becomes the substance of the child's love. As children grow up they begin to judge. Rebellion is part of the process by which young people find themselves, work out their adult relationships with their parents and decide who they want to be. The process has come to be known as the crisis of identity. In the terms of this book, the young person's crisis is a need to answer the question, 'Am I a part of my background, an *extension* of it, or am I a *separate* being?' Rebellion takes the form of feelings, protest and struggle.

The feelings involved in childhood and adolescent rebellion are most often anger, anxiety, doubt, guilt and curiosity. These are often combined with a desire to mix with contemporaries. Protest takes the form of saying or doing what is uncongenial to the parents or against their principles. This often involves appearance, cleanliness or lack of it, political views and sexual behaviour. When it comes to open struggle, the battleground can be any area of conflict or disagreement that the child or parent can find.

The type of rebellion varies with the type of mother or background. Feelings of rebellion against an *enclosing* mother are predominantly those of guilt and anxiety. The protest is often hidden from both sides and the struggle reveals itself unexpectedly and is often almost like a struggle for air. Along with the desire for freedom and individuality goes an incompatible desire to be *enclosed*.

George was in his late thirties but was still struggling with his adolescent rebellion against his *enclosing* mother. One day he had a dream that showed clearly the conflict between wanting to be free and wanting to be dependent. He dreamed that at last he had grown up sufficiently to leave school and that to celebrate this event he had ordered a new suit. When the suit arrived he tried it on and found that he had ordered it to be made with short trousers.

He had been born and raised in England, but his parents were Greek. A common ambition among Greek mothers is to have a son who is a shipowner. At the age of thirty-eight George found himself in a position to buy a ship and thus satisfy his mother's ambition. However, not yet having come to terms with his rebellious feelings against his mother, he turned them against the ship. She was a small cargo vessel and he had difficulty in remembering to organize her voyages and her cargoes. If he remembered to do this he would 'forget' the insurance or some other essential matter. One day she suffered slight damage abroad and George decided that at the moment when she was in a particular port he would telephone a colleague there who could examine the damage and make necessary arrangements at little cost. He then 'completely forgot' about it until next day, by which time the ship had left. George had to make an expensive personal visit during which time he lost a big contract through not being in his office. Soon after this he decided that his ambivalent feelings about his ship/mother were so strong that he had better sell before he went bankrupt.

In rebellion against *extension* mothers, the feelings are usually of guilt from a recognizable conscience, together with protest about conformity. The struggle is more overtly concerned with becoming free. The most dramatic rebellious struggles are with *extension* mothers. This is true when the mother regards her child either as a personal *extension* of herself or as an *extension* of the system or community of which she and the whole family is part. *Extension* mothers are the so-called schizophrenogenic mothers described by Bateson and by Laing and his followers.

Mandy, aged twenty-one, was engaged in a conflict with her mother which, to her, was a life and death struggle. Her parents were respectable business people in a country town within reach of London. Mandy was determined to make a career as a model in London and in this she was being quite successful, though her father still paid the rent of her small apartment. But her mother had other ideas. In her view Mandy should live at home and be a visible credit to her in the local community. She should work in a local boutique, join the Young Farmers and the Young Conservatives, learn to drive a car and think about getting married. Mandy had no inclination to do any of these things and every weekend there were rows between her and her mother. Yet she continued to go home every weekend, as if for a further beating. She made no attempt to break free and was dependent on her weekend visits home not only emotionally but also for practical reasons. She had never learned to wash or iron her own clothes (doubtless this was a form of collusion between herself and her mother to keep them tied together), and, although she had lived alone in London for four years, she had never visited a launderette and was too frightened to try. She therefore went home ostensibly so that her mother could deal with her laundry and the mother gained the greatest possible emotional advantage from it. If she brought little laundry, her mother, alarmed, would upbraid her for her dirty habits and emphasize that these would interfere with her career. If she brought a quantity of washing, her mother, now secure, would complain loudly and describe to everyone within earshot how her entire weekend would be spent dealing with Mandy's clothes so that she could go on following that ridiculous career in London, etc., etc. Eventually Mandy, unable to solve her problems of *separation*, took to drink.

Rebellion against *separate* mothers sounds like a contradiction in terms. How can one struggle for freedom against someone who wants one to be free? Possible answers are that there are likely to be remnants of earlier stages, that, however potentially *separate* a mother is, if she cares about her child there will be limits to her tolerance and to her belief in what is good for her child, what will not harm him in the future and so on. Moreover it also seems that, regardless of their circumstances, young people need to rebel before they find themselves and in a way the better-equipped parents are for this, the more difficult it is for the young person. As one of them put it, 'The trouble is that there's absolutely nothing wrong with my parents. I've got nothing to complain of. That's what makes me so angry.'

So it may be fortunate that for most mothers a period of personal struggle usually accompanies the period of rebellion in their offspring. In a way it is part of her own struggle for self-awareness. Often it finishes her own adolescent problems or else it reactivates them and opens old wounds.

When is rebellion finished and when is it successful? W. H. Auden gives an answer:

> A young man has discovered his true identity when he becomes able to call his thoughts and his actions his own. If he is an exceptional young man, these thoughts and actions will be exceptional also, publicly recognizable as new and revolutionary. So Freud became Freud when he hit on the idea of the Oedipus complex, Darwin Darwin when he perceived that higher species must have evolved from lower, Luther Luther when he heard in St. Paul's phrase *The Just shall live by Faith* the authentic voice of God.*

Not everyone can reach these heights but everyone has the potentiality to be himself or herself, a unique individual being. 'Had I to carve an inscription on my tombstone,' wrote Sören Kierkegaard 'I would ask for none other than "The Individual".'

Is rebellion necessary for everyone? The answer must be no because when the environment holds and supports totally rebellion is not only impossible but also superfluous.

Ruth is a charming girl who always smiles and has never rebelled. Her mother is an *enclosing* mother who is herself controlled by a grandmother of the *extension* type. She has a quiet, loving father, a quiet, loving husband, many relatives in different countries and a family firm to support her and her close relations. At present there is no need for her to rebel and attempting to find herself would be likely to be quickly thwarted by the powerful older women in the family and so would be not only painful but also probably

* *Forewords and Afterwords*, p. 86, Faber and Faber Ltd.

fruitless. Let us hope for Ruth's sake that nothing ever happens to disrupt her *enclosing, supporting* environment.

But in our modern world it is increasingly difficult for the environment to hold and support sufficiently to avert an identity crisis and to obviate the need for identity. Freud recognized this, though he showed no awareness of the nature of the stage of *separation*. He wrote: 'A culture which leaves unsatisfied and drives to rebelliousness so large a number of its members neither has a prospect of continued existence nor deserves it.'*

But we now have such a culture in which nearly all of our young people, if they are to survive psychologically, need to rebel and to find themselves. For this reason it has become important to look carefully at people in whom rebellion does not seem to have occurred and to find out why. Maybe, as in the case of Ruth, circumstances did not demand it. But sometimes rebellion fails to occur when really it needs to occur and sometimes it appears not to have happened when it has really been going on in hidden ways, which can be strange and even bizarre. Moreover sometimes it may merely appear to have happened as a cover-up for conformity. And sometimes rebellion takes a form so destructive or self-destructive that one doubts whether freedom, identity or individuality will ever be achieved.

When rebellion has not occurred, and clearly should have done, often one or other of the first two stages was too powerful.

Hannah was a teacher who was twenty-five years old and looked sixteen. She had a powerful *enclosing* mother and was the eldest of four children, each more obviously neurotic than the last. The youngest was crippled by asthma and extreme dependence on his mother. Though Hannah seemed to be the most normal of the family, she remained childish in appearance and behaviour and though pretty had never had a serious boyfriend. She spent all her spare time and holidays working for a religious youth organization.

John's mother had hoped that he would do her credit by becoming the outstanding musician that she believed his talent deserved. He didn't. He lived at home, had little social life, and taught music at a local school. This was so far below his musical potential that one might regard it as a form of rebellion.

* *The Future of an Illusion.*

Sometimes rebellion fails to occur because the first stage of mothering failed and the second stage controls but does not hold or support sufficiently to make *separation*, individuality and independence superfluous. In other words, you cannot become independent if you are always looking for the love your mother was unable to give you, especially if she is now using you as an instrument.

Vera's mother showed no interest in her children when they were small. After her marriage broke up she realized that she would be better off financially if she retained control of Vera and her brother, which she proceeded to do. At fifteen Vera, though adequate at school, was emotionally flat, withdrawn and indifferent to everything that normally interests girls of her age. Although she gave the impression of being a lively, intelligent person underneath, yet there was no sign of life, rebellion, or desire to find herself or to understand what was happening to her. It sounded as though her brother was much the same.

Rebellion is the healthy reaction of a young person in a failing or inadequate environment. But there are other ways of trying to solve the problem. We have seen how possible alternatives include limitation of development, failure to expand into the outside world, and restriction of feeling and personality. Sometimes there is excessive conformity to parental beliefs and principles, as though the young person is desperately trying to shore up the inadequate environment by his own support of it. Sometimes there is some kind of breakdown, physical or mental. There may be food refusal, excessive concentration on school or university work, secret collusion with a mother's anxieties or neuroses, or symptoms such as misery, depression, anxiety or feelings of worthlessness. Some of these can be forms of rebellion but without direction, not leading to maturity or an increased sense of identity.

Excessive conformity is a common form of rebellion. For instance a young person whose parents are intellectually ambitious for him may carry this to extremes and study to an excessive degree and to the exclusion of all else. Or the child of tidy parents may rebel by becoming so excessively tidy that all waking moments are spent tidying up and the household is controlled by it. A child whose parents like him to be independent may rebel in acts of delinquency. There may be an almost conscious twisting of the parents' desires or precepts.

A young woman whose father angrily called her a whore because she stayed out till midnight soon afterwards became a whore.

A young man whose mother had always encouraged him to be talented and elegant rather than to do or achieve anything rebelled by failure to do or achieve.

Another form of self-destructive rebellion is to pretend that normal rebellion is taking place.

Antony's parents were convinced, and secretly delighted, when he showed what they thought were the signs of adolescent rebellion. He became hairy and ragged, attended political meetings different from theirs, and hitch-hiked across Europe with a girl-friend. But there was no rebellion in Antony. He had always tried to please his parents and he sensed that this was the way to do so. Underneath, like everyone else who does not find themselves, he lived in the shell not the core of himself. Not surprisingly, he had feelings of unreality and despair and was aware that he was alienated from his true self.

Where there is rebellion there is need for appraisal, for finding out, for understanding, and usually for compromise. There may be reasons why this cannot or should not be achieved but the need is there just the same. The effort and endurance required to become free is small compared with that required to remain free. Both require imaginative curiosity.

11 Finding Out

> Where is your sword
> Discrimination?
> Draw it and slash
> Delusion to pieces.
>
> > Bhagavad-Gita

> Who was her mother?
>
> > Thomas Hood, *The Bridge of Sighs*

> Be not curious in unnecessary matters; for more things
> are shewed unto thee than men understand.
>
> > Ecclesiastes 3:23

> Curiosity killed the cat.
>
> > Nanny saying

> Satisfaction brought it back.
>
> > Reply

'He who would understand himself needs first to understand his mother.' I began this book with this statement. The time has now come to examine it.

In chapter 6 we saw that to feel all right one must either be almost totally identified and blended with one's environment, or else bridge the gap and achieve a sense of self. We also saw why it is increasingly difficult in our modern world to blend with the environment and therefore why achieving a sense of self is particularly important. This is the basis of the so-called 'identity crisis' about which so much has been written.

The so-called problems of identity are essentially concerned with those things that give inner stability and continuity to human life. Erikson, in his book *Identity*, takes his definition from William James, and I follow him in this. James uses the word character for what we now call identity.

A man's character is discernible in the mental or moral attitude in which, when it came upon him, he felt himself most deeply and intensely active and alive. At such moments there is a voice inside which speaks and says: 'This is the real me!'

Such experience always includes

an element of active tension, of holding my own, as it were, and trusting outward things to perform their part so as to make it a full harmony, but without any guaranty that they will. Make it a guaranty . . . and the attitude immediately becomes to my consciousness stagnant and stingless. Take away the guaranty, and I feel (provided I am ueberhaupt in vigorous condition) a sort of deep enthusiastic bliss, of bitter willingness to do and suffer anything . . . and which, although it is a mere mood or emotion to which I can give no form in words, authenticates itself to me as the deepest principle of all active and theoretic determination which I possess . . .*

This gives a picture of what a sense of identity is. When we say that someone lacks it or is unsure of it, we mean that he is uncertain about his feelings, desires and beliefs. He may not know the sort of person he is or the sort of person he wants to be. He is probably conscious of a gap between himself and the environment. He may try to ignore the gap or to close it but to find himself he must bridge it.

He may try to do this by looking for a role in life, and this does not necessarily require delving into the past or studying his surroundings in a new way. But the so-called 'search for identity' may involve a search for increased self-awareness. In this case he need achieve not total understanding, for this is impossible, but rather compromise with the past, which usually means to a large extent his mother. For this he needs a mixture of curiosity, imagination and courage.

Curiosity is an important means by which an infant and child learns about the world, finds his place, and achieves mastery of it. Exploration and experimentation are essential to normal youth. Many adults retain curiosity all their lives and many find it one of the most important things in life. Feelings of curiosity usually go with feeling all right. Feeling not all right is usually associated with lack of or loss of curiosity. Sometimes feelings of curiosity can be twisted to ward off feelings of not being all right.

* Henry James (ed.), *The Letters of William James*, Vol. 1, p. 199.

People vary enormously in the amount of innate curiosity they possess. Even in a nursery for new-born babies we can distinguish infants who are either more alert and responsive to the environment than average, or less so. Some people seem to retain enormous curiosity all their lives and others lack it to a remarkable degree. It is hard to believe that such differences are always due to environmental influences.

Mothers influence their children's curiosity at every stage. They may encourage, ignore, smother or destroy it. The mother who leaves too small a gap between herself and her child, who does not appreciate distance, tends to smother or destroy his curiosity. This is true even when she appears to herself or to others to be encouraging his curiosity actively.

Some *enclosing* mothers drive the child's curiosity into himself, so that it is no longer a means of exploring the outside world though he may retain it in regard to the workings of his own body, mind and feelings. Other *enclosing* mothers keep so close to their children that there is no room for curiosity. They provide everything that is provided and prevent anything else from impinging. Curiosity is smothered, maybe for good. Often it becomes associated with guilt, particularly when the smothered curiosity concerns sex, as it so often does, spreading outwards from there.

Freud believed that curiosity stemmed from 'primal scene fantasies' about the parents' sexual intercourse. He worked out his theories at a time when there was much frustration and taboo about sex, and in a community whose neuroses centred primarily on sex. As a result much psychoanalytic writing seems to suggest that literal 'primal scene fantasies' are the basis of neurotic confusions. But, looking at our world today, we have already seen that it seems more convenient and constructive to see the concept of 'primal scene fantasies' as symbolic of an individual's conscious and un-conscious reactions to everything that goes on when he is not there and which he does not understand. Of these actual 'primal scene fantasies' about parents are only a part. Lack of curiosity can become a powerful defence against threat.

Extension mothers may be so busy imposing a system that, again there is no place for curiosity, which may even appear to be disloyal. Curiosity about beliefs and accepted attitudes leads to questioning, the last thing the *extension* mother wants, unless the questions are to her liking, promote her system and enhance her control.

Curiosity is part of a normal stage of *separation*, and this is part of the price paid for its loss. There is also likely to be boredom, and the tendency both to be exploited and to develop physical symptoms.

Separate mothers are likely to impair curiosity in their children by the apathy and rootlessness that they induce. The child whose mother was too *separate* may see no point in being curious.

Easy as it seems to be to stifle, curiosity abounds in many forms. The simplest and straightest comes directly from the natural curiosity of the child which continues in the adult. 'Know Thyself' has come down through the millennia, along with *Homo sum, humani nil a me alienum puto* (I am a man and I regard nothing human as foreign to me).* 'There is a will to live,' wrote Camus 'without rejecting anything of life which is the virtue I honour most in the world.' D. H. Lawrence describes its importance in another way;

There are two classes of men:
those that look into the eyes of the gods, and these are few,
and those that look into the eyes of the few other men
to see the gleam of the gods there, reflected in the human eye.
All other class is artificial.
There is, however, the vast third homogeneous amorphous class of anarchy
the robots, those who deny the gleam.

One can feel an urgent need to understand. In its simplest form this can be simply a desire to record what happened. In another poem, Lawrence links the quarrels of his parents with the storm outside:

Outside the house an ash-tree hung its terrible whips.
And at night when the wind rose, the lash of the tree
Shrieked and slashed the wind, as a ship's
Weird rigging in a storm shrieks hideously.
Within the house two voices arose, a slender lash
Whistling she-delirious rage, and the dreadful sound
Of a male thong booming and bruising, until it had drowned
The other voice in a silence of blood, 'neath the noise of the ash.

A sudden urge to understand is often a response to crisis or unhappiness, acute or chronic. An unhappy young woman who had been adopted in infancy conned an adoption society and stole documents in order to trace her original mother. This kind of urgency is often a desire to make up for what was missing at each or

* Terence.

any stage of mothering. John Stuart Mill and Matthew Arnold, both tormented by the imposition of a directive environment and lack of cradling, turned to the poetry of Wordsworth, who understood the enclosure stage so well. They turned to him for solace, as a modern young intellectual might turn to psychoanalysis or transcendental meditation. Another writer who felt overwhelmed by the effects of an extension-type mother and needed to work it out was H. G. Wells. 'I have a sense of crisis,' he writes in the introduction to his auto-biography, 'that the time has come to reorganize my peace', and

> I need freedom of mind. I want peace for work. I am distressed by immediate circumstances. My thoughts and work are encumbered by claims and vexations and I cannot see any hope of release from them . . . I am in a phase of fatigue . . . I find it difficult to assemble my forces to confront this problem which paralyses the proper use of myself.

So, he tells us, 'I am putting even the preference of other work aside in an attempt to deal with this situation. I am writing a report about it – to myself.' Later in this report he tells us, 'I am trying to restore my mother's mental picture of the world, as she saw it awaiting her, thirty years and more before I was born.'

Rather similar reasons for self-examination were given by another writer of very different era and background: St Augustine, whose strongly enclosing mother has been described earlier, also came to a crisis in middle life which led to his writing his autobiography or Confessions. His biographer describes the situation in which Augustine found himself* in AD 397 at the age of forty-three, now a bishop in Africa, cut off from his 'spiritual' friends in Europe and forced to adjust to a new existence. The ideals on which he had hoped to build his life had been set aside. The first optimism of conversion had dis-appeared. He realized that he must base his future on a different view of himself, and part of this was to understand the quite un-expected emotions that he had felt on the death of his mother, Monica, 'the sudden numbing of all feeling, the febrile talking, the unnatural self-control, the crushing shame'. In the act of exploration that was the writing of the Confessions Augustine distils a new feeling, and a new understanding of his mother.

Monica, the idealized figure that had haunted Augustine's youth like an oracle of God, is subtly transformed, by Augustine's analysis of his present feelings on remembering her death into an ordinary human being, an

---

* Peter Brown, *Augustine of Hippo*, pp. 161ff.

object of concern, a sinner like himself, equally in need of mercy . . . In this attempt to find himself, every single fibre in Augustine's middle age grew together with every other.*

Sometimes the unhappiness that stirs the curiosity is slower. An example is the American poet Conrad Aiken. As a boy of eleven he was in the house when his father shot dead first his wife, the boy's mother, and then himself. The young Conrad heard the shots, found the bodies of his parents, kept his younger brothers and sister away, went to the police, and spent the rest of his life trying to come to terms with what had happened.†

Sometimes the unhappiness is forced at an early age. The thirteen-year-old Anne Frank, hiding with her family from the Germans in the attic of an Amsterdam office building, was prematurely forced into the kind of introspection that is a search for relief.

Sometimes the curiosity is hidden, in which case it tends to cause trouble.

Katherine was an intelligent eight year old who had been adopted in infancy and brought up in Canada. She was getting on badly at school and was teased because of her accent and her unusual ways. Her headmistress was convinced that Katherine's unusual background was the cause of her difficulties at school. Her mother assured me that there had never been any problem about the adoption. Katherine had been brought up knowing that she was adopted and had always seemed to accept it without further inquiry.

However, during the first few minutes of conversation, Katherine revealed her intense anxiety about her origins and her desire to know more. She had never liked to ask, feeling that it would some-how be awkward for her parents. I advised her parents to tell her, at the first opportunity, everything they knew about her biological parents, however vague or trivial the information might seem. They did this willingly and, although they did not know very much, they managed to produce a few details of the kind that a child would long to know. Her 'first' mother had been a nurse, her father a medical student. They couldn't marry or keep their baby because they hadn't finished their studies. The adoptive parents didn't know whether the 'first' parents had eventually married.

* *Augustine of Hippo*, pp. 164–5.
† Conrad Aiken, *Ushant.*

They could probably find out if Katherine really wanted to know. She did. That was about all, but it was enough. At our next meeting Katherine told me how relieved she was to know these things. She returned to school happy and adjusted, and gave no further trouble.

Feelings of anxiety, guilt, depression, hostility or plain unhappiness are often associated with hidden curiosity. Ignorance, forgotten memories and painful inconsistencies seem to shut themselves up inside people and can only be maintained in that state at considerable cost to the person in emotion and psychic energy which can deplete and damage present living. Topsy in *Uncle Tom's Cabin* is an example of this:

'Who was your mother?' 'Never had none!' said the child, with another grin. 'Never had any mother?' 'What do you mean? Where were you born?' 'Never was born!' persisted Topsy ...
'Do you know who made you?' 'Nobody, as I knows on,' said the child ... 'I 'spect I grow'd.' ...
'Cause I's wicked – I is. I's mighty wicked, any how. I can't help it.'

The kind of curiosity I have been discussing is seldom a straight-forward fact-finding operation. It is usually rather imaginative, strongly influenced by pain and pleasure, and imperfect both in fact feeling.

Our very life depends on everything's
Recurring till we answer from within.
The thousandth time may prove the charm.*

Under conditions in which it is difficult to survive psychologically, imagination can protect and can facilitate intact survival. Where it is difficult to raise children without neglect and violation which leaves them damaged and vulnerable, imagination, both in parent and child, protects.

By imagination I mean the ability to feel and perceive outside oneself and the ability to see and appraise oneself from outside. This involves vicarious as well as direct experience, and also awareness of inner reality and the ability to relate to material reality. Both the awareness and the ability vary according to age, experience and individual circumstances. Imagination involves the ability to conceive representations of what is not actually present. Its development

* Robert Frost.

depends on the expansion of consciousness and the formation of connections, both internal and external.

So the kind of curiosity discussed here is related to literal truth to only a small extent. Much more important is its concern to balance the inner fantasies with outside existence. A literal outlook is often limiting and therefore self-defeating.

So the 'primal scene fantasies', discussed earlier, are not a search for literal knowledge of what goes on or went on in one's absence. They are an attempt to reconcile and balance inner with outer. Sometimes this can only be done by denial of the literal truth or by stimulation of a fantasy because therein lies the balance. One finds this where someone obstinately insists in the truth of something that is blatantly untrue. Benjamin Disraeli told untruths about his ancestry. So did Henrik Ibsen, who used to assert that he had not a drop of Norwegian blood when in fact thirteen of his sixteen great-great-grandparents were Norwegian. A rumour that he was not his alleged father's son reached him in childhood, haunted him all his life, and recurs in different forms in many of his plays. Although a strong piece of evidence against his illegitimacy was his resemblance to his legal father, Ibsen chose to believe the rumour. It fitted his inner life, just as most of us choose facts or fables about our past, or our ancestors, because they best fit our ideas or desires about ourselves and so help to bridge the gap between inner and outer. Many of us feel proud that one of our ancestors was, say, a highwayman, a prince or the mistress of someone important.

In this way curiosity becomes imaginative and imagination becomes the highest form of mental activity with which to bridge the gap. Sometimes the pursuit of knowledge about ourselves, our origins, our mothers, may not serve us well.

> I, being poor, have only my dreams;
> I have spread my dreams under your feet;
> Tread softly, because you tread on my dreams.*

Oedipus, when he finally discovered the truth, or could no longer deny it, found that it was more than he could bear. He put out his own eyes. 'Blessed are those who forget,' wrote Nietzsche, 'for they thus surmount even their mistakes.' Forgetfulness can also be a kind of freedom.

So there is no proof of true reality and imagination reigns.

* W. B. Yeats, *He Wishes for the Cloths of Heaven.*

Memory is inaccurate. Different participants have different memories of the events they shared, and memories of the same events differ from time to time. Augustine knew that he would never fully understand and never know what he was really like.

For there is in me a lamentable darkness in which my latent possibilities are hidden from myself, so that my mind, questioning itself upon its own hidden powers, feels that it cannot rightly judge its own report.*

Nevertheless, the search and the attempt to understand, painful as it can be, is liberating, an achievement of the final stage of growing up. What people are aiming at in trying to understand themselves and their mothers is a relief from inner tension and a compromise between inner and outer lives that is likely to be liberating and can at best be a source of acute pleasure.

* Confessions.

12 Circles

The way out is through the door. Why is it that no one
will use this method?

Confucius

Confidence is a plant of slow growth.

William Pitt, Earl of Chatham, 1766

Mothers in western civilization are increasingly held in a Catch 22
situation. The better equipped they are to be good mothers the more
difficult they find it to put this into practice.

Our modern world has produced a complicated conflict for
mothers. Since being a mother is a vital part of being a woman, it is
also a conflict for women in general. Although the conflict has
always been latent, it has only recently become widespread and an
essential part of being a mother. This means that it can now be
denied or ignored only with peril.

The conflict is in the mother herself. It concerns the incompati-
bility and difficulty of reconciling herself as a mother with the rest
of herself as a person. This tends to create tension in the self, which
is one of the most important problems that women have to face
today. The health and lives of future generations depend on how
mothers face this at the present time.

Bearing and rearing children is part of most women's destiny. In
general, motherhood is an essential part of a woman's development.
Most women need it. Without it they become deprived. How it
happens and develops is of the greatest importance to both mothers
and children throughout their lives. The world is geared for women
to become mothers. Only exceptional women are able to be free,
fulfilled and fully involved in life without becoming mothers. But
the world is now changing rapidly.

In an enclosing or traditional environment there is little change from
one generation to another. The environment supports both mother
and child. There is no need for children to develop other than as

parts of their mothers and no need for mothers to develop beyond the stage of *enclosure.*

In a *directive* environment the system prevails. The child is an *extension* of his parents and, like them, part of the system. The system is *supportive.* The mother's role is to support the system, to fit her children into it and to maintain it. There is no need for mothers to develop beyond the stage of *extension.* But they usually have to provide the *enclosing* environment necessary to the stage of *enclosure* and this requires more than simply being part of a system. Failure in this is an important cause of difficulty in *directive* environments.

It is much more difficult for mothers to be successful in an *unsupporting* environment, as ours has largely become. Here the mother herself usually has to provide both the *enclosing* and the *directive* environments that her child needs at different stages of development. It is increasingly difficult for her to do this adequately unless she herself has developed beyond both stages.

Our modern world is less structured and less supportive than formerly. Increasingly the mother has to provide the necessary environment that her child needs for healthy development. She needs to go through the stages of *enclosure* and *extension* with her child and to reach with him the stage of *separation.* To do this she must either have reached it herself first or she must have retained a capacity to mature herself as her child grows and changes.

Yet to develop sufficiently to carry her child through the stages of *enclosure* and *extension* to the stage of *separation* she needs to develop in a manner that makes it more difficult for her to provide for him during the early stages.

Our society is changing with an acceleration that is probably unprecedented except for brief periods of war and natural catastrophe. Traditional patterns of childrearing are becoming increasingly difficult to follow and often seem to be no longer relevant because of new knowledge or changing social conditions, or both. Motherhood is even becoming optional in a way it never was before. Safe contraceptives, consciousness and conscience concerning world population and the tragedies of unwanted children, and also the existence of positive and enjoyable alternative ways of life all make becoming a mother something of a serious decision instead of an automatic step in life. As a result, for women who want to do it well, which means most women, it becomes a question of self-confidence in a way it never was before. Many women's confidence is sapped by the very existence of the choice. Yet lack of self-confidence hampers them as mothers and tends to create in them the very inadequacy that they fear.

Our modern world offers women opportunities unknown to them in past ages. They can have education, professional training, economic freedom, leisure in all its varieties, and almost any kind of relationship either in marriage or outside it. Amid this *embarras de richesses* motherhood is a positive choice. It may be made as an escape by those who are unable to enjoy the other things in life and who hope to find peace and security in their own children. These are often mothers who are incapable of reaching the stage of *separation* and remain forever in an earlier stage. Luckily the decision to have children is most often made by women who have considerable capacity to enjoy other aspects of life and make use of opportunities. They tend to find that the exigencies of motherhood prevent their taking advantage of what modern life offers them. Yet unless they benefit or have benefited from these opportunities they are unlikely to reach the stage of *separation* without which it is impossible, in our society today, to be an adequate mother.

Motherhood is part of women's destiny but it is only part. Few women find total fulfilment in it for more than short periods of time. If they do, then, as we have seen, they are likely to be inadequate not only as people but also as mothers, and emotionally dependent on their children. Mothers who are stuck at the stage of *enclosure* or *extension* are likely to cause their children difficulty in the modern world.

Though motherhood is an essential part of most women's lives it is actually likely to impede the development of the other parts which are also essential. This is a big problem for women in the modern world and it has profound significance for their children. Nearly all mothers want to be good mothers and try hard to be so. But in the early stages good mothering is likely to be incompatible with other important aspects of a woman's life, so that almost inevitably they or else the children are neglected. The stage of *separation* is essential to good mothering and so is necessary to both mother and child. It cannot be reached if the mother has not developed in other ways. Thus there is likely to be conflict between the mother and the rest of herself as a person.

Thus the eternal conflict and the particular conflict of women in the modern world is that good mothering tends to prevent that personal development and liberation without which it is impossible to be a good mother. Success, fulfilment and liberation lie in the compromise that results from facing and dealing with this conflict.

There are three main tendencies in the way in which mothers react to this conflict. First is the tendency to master it. This involves development of both logical and intuitive powers and the capacity to work out personal and individual forms of compromise. It leads towards survival, health and the development of the person as a whole. It requires confidence and it also increases confidence.

Second is the tendency to deny the conflict. This leads towards the destruction of mother and children in whole or in part. The mother may sacrifice her children for the sake of herself or she may appear to sacrifice herself for the sake of her children. The latter is often really the former. The tendency to master and the tendency to deny conflict are both important aspects of modern life which would require much more space for discussion than is available here.

Lastly the mother may lack the confidence even to deny the conflict. She appears not to be able to cope and to be benefiting neither herself nor her children.

The solution, in so far as there is a solution, usually lies in some kind of personal compromise and the confidence to achieve it. Yet here is another riddle. The confidence to compromise also requires the ability to compromise. Without this there can be no confidence. Yet the ability to compromise also depends on having the confidence to do so.

Here then lie some of the roots of the present crisis of confidence that afflicts so many mothers. But the future is not gloomy. It may be true that more mothers than ever before are lacking in confidence. It is also true that more mothers than ever before are acquiring it. The overwhelming need in our society is to achieve the stage of *separation*, and this is a challenge. Mothers are tending to rise to the challenge and to develop as people much more than did their mothers and grandmothers. Society, while making this difficult for them, also provides the opportunities. To make use of these opportunities sometimes requires originality, often requires individuality and always requires intuition and confidence. Confidence comes through reaching the stage of *separation* after adequate stages of *enclosure* and *extension*. Mothers who have confidence breed confidence and this is based on allowing freedom both to the individual personality and to intuition tempered by logic and experience.

Bibliography and Selected Background Reading

Aiken, Conrad, *Ushant*, W. H. Allen 1963

Auden, W. H., *Forewords and Afterwords*, Faber 1973

Bateson, Gregory, *Steps to an Ecology of Mind*, Paladin 1973

Bernstein, Basil, *Class, Codes and Control*, Vol. I, Routledge & Kegan Paul 1971

Bronfenbrenner, Urie, *Two Worlds of Childhood: USA and USSR*, Allen & Unwin 1971

Bowlby, John, *Maternal Care and Mental Health*, WHO Monograph 1951

Bowlby, John, *Attachment and Loss*, Vol. I Attachment, Vol. II Anxiety and Anger, Hogarth Press 1969 and 1973

Brown, Heter, *Angustine of Hippo*, Faber 1967

Buber, Martin, *Between Man and Man* (1947), Fontana Library 1961

Buber, Martin, *Distance and Relation in Psychiatry*, Vol. 20, 1957

Buber, Martin, *I and Thou*, Charles Scribner's Sons 1970

Camus, Albert, *The Myth of Sysiphus*, Alfred A. Knopf NY and Hamish Hamilton, London 1955

Churchill, Winston, *My Early Life*, (1930), Macmillan 1944

Cooper, David, *The Death of the Family*, Allen Lane 1971

Dally, Ann, *Cicely. The Story of a Doctor*, Gollancz 1968

Dally, Peter, *The Fantasy Factor*, Weidenfeld and Nicolson 1975

Drabble, Margaret, *Wordsworth*, Evans 1966

Erikson, Erik H., *Childhood and Society*, Penguin Books 1965

Erikson, Erik H., *Identity*, Faber 1968

Fairbairn, W. Ronald D., *Psychoanalytic Studies of the Personality*, Tavistock Publications 1952

Frank, Anne, *The Diary of Anne Frank*, Pan Books 1955

Freud, Anna, *The Ego and Mechanisms of Defence*, Hogarth Press 1937

Freud, Sigmund, *Introductory Lectures in Psychoanalysis* (1916), Pelican Books 1974

Freud, Sigmund, *On Narcissism* (1914), Standard Edition, Vol. 14, Hogarth Press 1957

Freud, Sigmund, *The Future of an Illusion* (1928), Hogarth Press and Institute of Psychoanalysis 1962

Freud, Sigmund, *Civilization and its Discontents* (1930), Standard Edition, Vol. 21, Hogarth Press 1961

Freud, Sigmund, *New Introductory Lectures in Psychoanalysis* (1933), Pelican Books 1973

Gathorne-Hardy, Jonathan, *The Rise and Fall of the British Nanny*, Hodder & Stoughton 1972

Gorky, Maxim, *Childhood* (1913), translated by Margaret Wettlin and Jessie Coulson, Oxford University World Paperbacks 1961

Hardy, Thomas, *Jude the Obscure* (1895), Macmillan Papermac 1966

Helfer, Roy E. and Kempe, C. Henry, *The Battered Child*, University of Chicago Press 1968

Hoban, Russell, *The Mouse and his Child*, Faber 1969

James, Henry, *The Letters of William James*, Boston, The Atlantic Monthly Press 1920

Jones, Ernest, *The Life and Work of Sigmund Freud*, Pelican Books 1964

Klein, Melanie, *Contributions to Psychoanalysis*, Hogarth Press and Institute of Psychoanalysis 1948

Klein, Melanie, *Envy and Gratitude*, Tavistock Publications 1957

Klein, Melanie, and others, *Developments in Psychoanalysis*, Hogarth Press and Institute of Psychoanalysis 1952

Laing, R. D., *The Divided Self* (1960), Pelican Books 1965

Lawrence, D. H., *Sons and Lovers*, Secker 1932

Lawrence, D. H., *Collected Poems*, Vols. I and II, Heron Books 1964

Lee, Laurie, *Cider with Rosie* (1959), Penguin Books 1962

Lomas, Peter (Ed.), *The Predicament of the Family*, Hogarth Press and Institute of Psychoanalysis 1967

Lomas, Peter, *True and False Experience*, Allen Lane 1973

Lorenz, Konrad, *On Aggression*, Methuen 1966

Lynd, Helen Merrell, *On Shame and the Search for Identity*, Routledge & Kegan Paul 1958

McDougall, W., *An Introduction to Social Psychology* (1908), 22nd Edition, Methuen 1931

Meyer, Michael, *Ibsen* (1967), Penguin Books, 1971

Newson, John and Elizabeth, *Infant Care in an Urban Community*, George Allen & Unwin 1963

Newson, John and Elizabeth, *Four Years Old in an Urban Community*, George Allen & Unwin 1968

Oxford English Dictionary, Oxford University Press. Concise Edition 1971

Pringle, Mia Kellmer, *The Needs of Children*, Hutchinson 1974

Renvoize, Jean, *Children in Danger*, Routledge & Kegan Paul 1974
Roth, Philip, *Portnoy's Complaint*, Corgi Books 1971
Rycroft, Charles, *A Critical Dictionary of Psychoanalysis*, Nelson 1968
Rycroft, Charles, *Imagination and Reality*, Hogarth Press and Institute of Psychoanalysis 1968
Rycroft, Charles, *Anxiety and Neurosis*, Allen Lane 1968
St Augustine, *Confessions*, Everyman's Library 1949
Sartre, Jean-Paul, *Being and Nothingness* (1943), University Paperback 1969
Sartre, Jean-Paul, *Words* (1964), Penguin Books 1967
Segal, Hanna, *Introduction to the Work of Melanie Klein* (1964), Hogarth Press and Institute of Psychoanalysis 1973
Sitwell, Edith, *Taken Care Of*, Hutchinson 1965
Spock, Benjamin, *Baby and Child Care*, The Bodley Head 1958
Spock, Benjamin, *Bringing Up Children in a Difficult Time*, The Bodley Head 1974
Storr, Antony, *The Integrity of the Personality* (1960), Pelican Books 1963
Storr, Antony, *Human Aggression*, Allen Lane 1968
Stowe, Harriet Beecher, *Uncle Tom's Cabin*, 1852
Tillich, Paul, *The Courage to Be* (1952), Fontana Library 1962
Trasler, Gordon, and others, *The Formative Years*, BBC 1968
Wells, H. G., *Experiment in Autobiography*, Jonathan Cape 1934
Winnicott, D. W., *Collected Papers*, Tavistock Publications 1958
Wordsworth, William, *Lyrical Ballads*, Wordsworth and Coleridge, (1798–1805). University Paperback, 1968
Wordsworth, William, *The Prelude* (1805–6 and 1850), Penguin Edition 1971

Index